SPIDER ✷ GWEN
GREATER POWER

JASON LATOUR
WRITER

ROBBI RODRIGUEZ (#1-4 & 6)
& CHRIS VISIONS (#5)
ARTISTS

RICO RENZI
COLOR ARTIST

VC'S CLAYTON COWLES
LETTERER

ROBBI RODRIGUEZ
COVER ART

DEVIN LEWIS
ASSISTANT EDITOR

NICK LOWE
EDITOR

JENNIFER GRUNWALD
COLLECTION EDITOR

JEFF YOUNGQUIST
SENIOR EDITOR, SPECIAL PROJECTS

AXEL ALONSO
EDITOR IN CHIEF

SARAH BRUNSTAD
ASSISTANT EDITOR

DAVID GABRIEL
SVP PRINT, SALES & MARKETING

JOE QUESADA
CHIEF CREATIVE OFFICER

ALEX STARBUCK
ASSOCIATE MANAGING EDITOR

JAY BOWEN
BOOK DESIGNER

DAN BUCKLEY
PUBLISHER

MARK D. BEAZLEY
EDITOR, SPECIAL PROJECTS

ALAN FINE
EXECUTIVE PRODUCER

SPIDER-GWEN VOL. 1: GREATER POWER. Contains material originally published in magazine form as SPIDER-GWEN #1-6. First printing 2016. ISBN# 978-0-7851-9959-5. Published by MARVEL WORLDWIDE, INC., a subsidiary of MARVEL ENTERTAINMENT, LLC. OFFICE OF PUBLICATION: 135 West 50th Street, New York, NY 10020. Copyright © 2016 MARVEL No similarity between any of the names, characters, persons, and/or institutions in this magazine with those of any living or dead person or institution is intended, and any such similarity which may exist is purely coincidental. **Printed in Canada.** ALAN FINE, President, Marvel Entertainment; DAN BUCKLEY, President, TV, Publishing & Brand Management; JOE QUESADA, Chief Creative Officer; TOM BREVOORT, SVP of Publishing; DAVID BOGART, SVP of Business Affairs & Operations, Publishing & Partnership; C.B. CEBULSKI, VP of Brand Management & Development, Asia; DAVID GABRIEL, SVP of Sales & Marketing, Publishing; JEFF YOUNGQUIST, VP of Production & Special Prpjects; DAN CARR, Executive Director of Publishing Technology; ALEX MORALES, Director of Publishing Operations; SUSAN CRESPI, Production Manager; STAN LEE, Chairman Emeritus. For information regarding advertising in Marvel Comics or on Marvel.com, please contact Vit DeBellis, Integrated Sales Manager, at vdebellis@marvel.com. For Marvel subscription inquiries, please call 888-511-5480. Manufactured between 3/18/2016 and 4/25/2016 by SOLISCO PRINTERS, SCOTT, QC, CANADA.

10 9 8 7 6 5 4 3 2 1

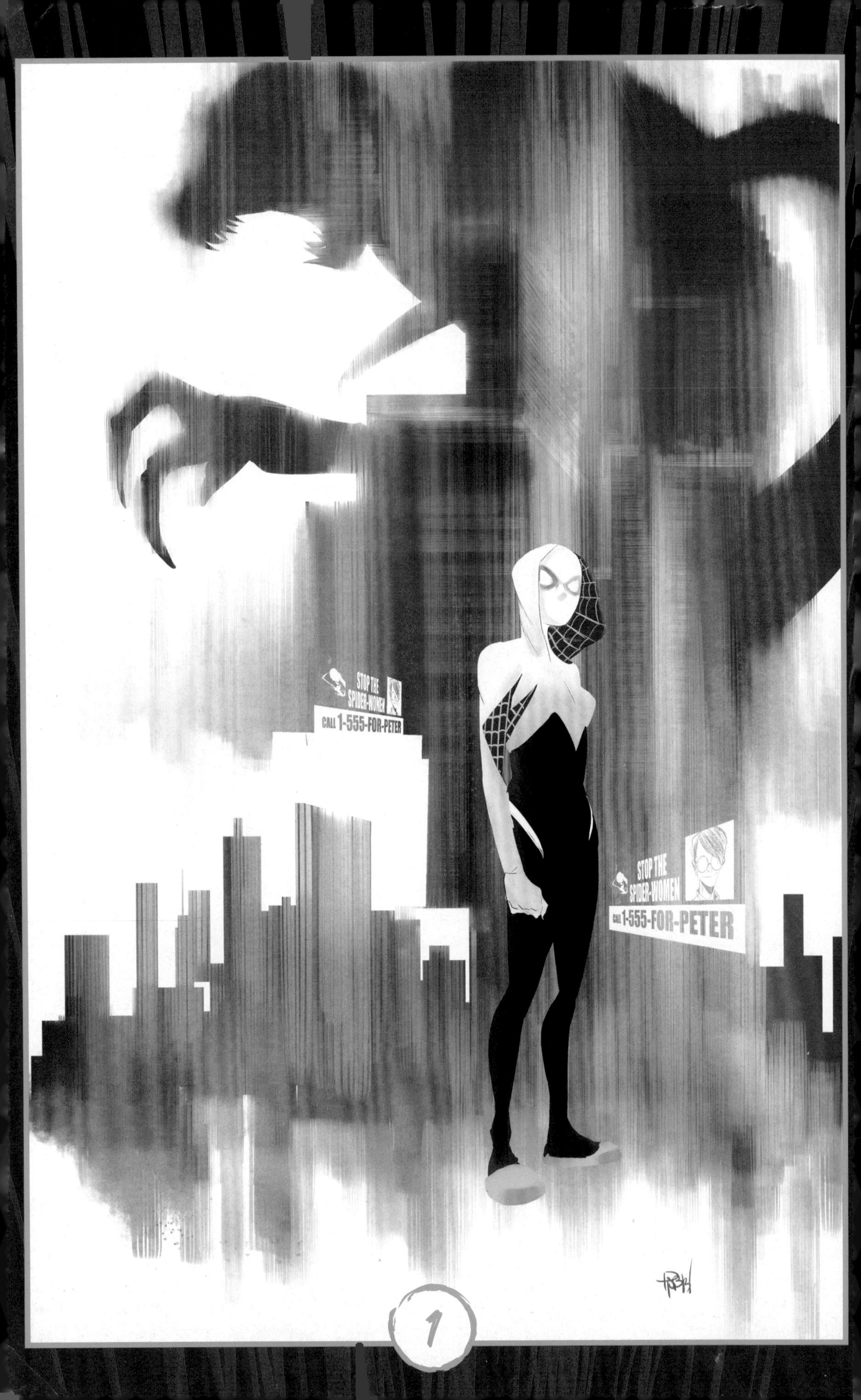
STOP THE SPIDER-WOMEN
CALL 1-555-FOR-PETER
STOP THE SPIDER-WOMEN
CALL 1-555-FOR-PETER
1

AS A TEENAGER, GWEN STACY WENT TO A DEMONSTRATION ON RADIOACTIVITY AND WAS BITTEN BY A MUTATED SPIDER. THE BITE TRANSFORMED HER, GRANTING HER AMAZING POWERS: A PRECOGNITIVE AWARENESS OF DANGER, ADHESIVE FINGERTIPS AND TOES, AND THE PROPORTIONAL SPEED AND STRENGTH OF A SPIDER. TO THE RESIDENTS OF NEW YORK, SHE IS THE DANGEROUS VIGILANTE CALLED SPIDER-WOMAN, BUT YOU KNOW HER AS...

SPIDER-GWEN

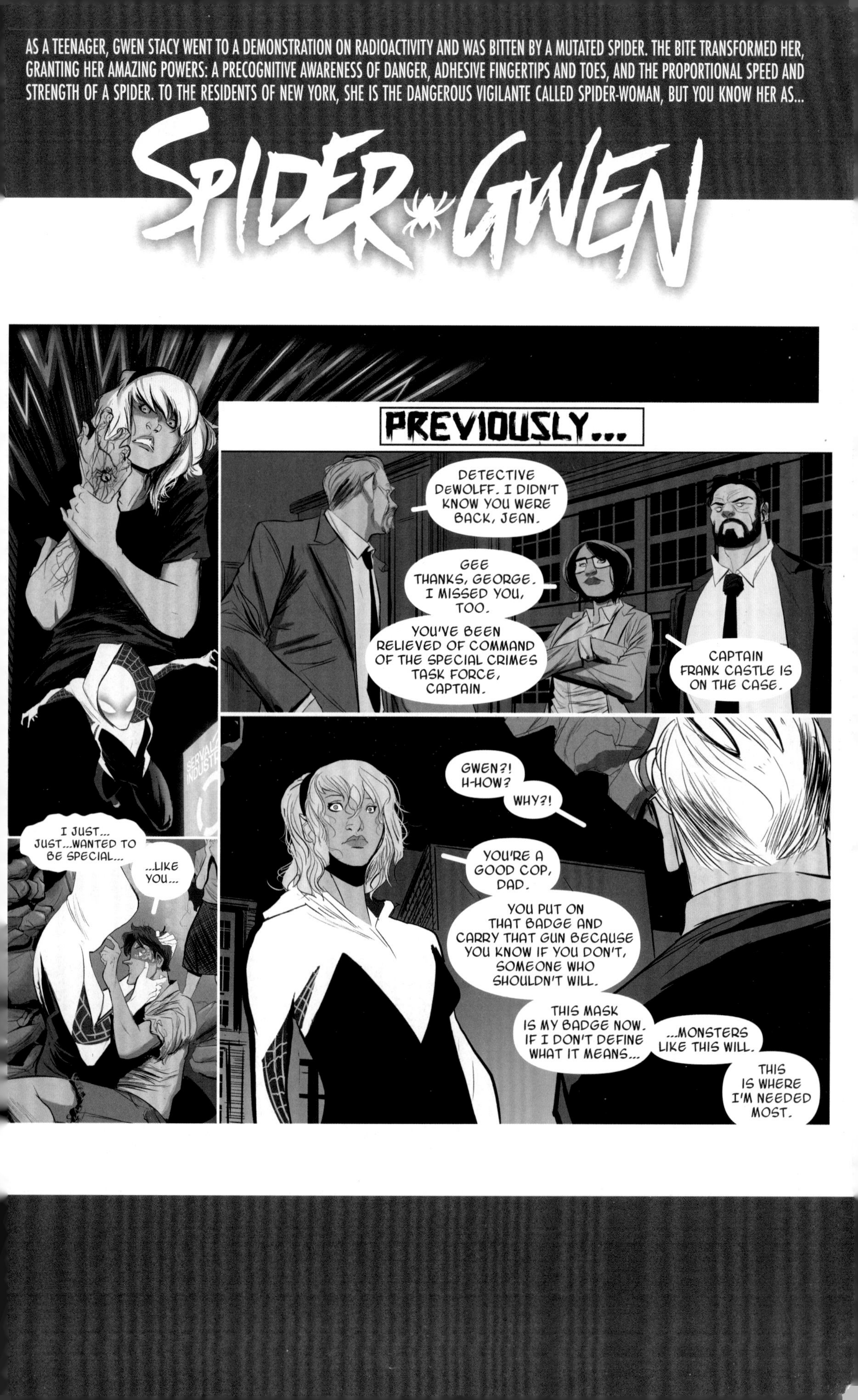
PREVIOUSLY...
DETECTIVE DEWOLFF. I DIDN'T KNOW YOU WERE BACK, JEAN.
GEE THANKS, GEORGE. I MISSED YOU, TOO.
YOU'VE BEEN RELIEVED OF COMMAND OF THE SPECIAL CRIMES TASK FORCE, CAPTAIN.
CAPTAIN FRANK CASTLE IS ON THE CASE.
I JUST... JUST...WANTED TO BE SPECIAL...
...LIKE YOU...
GWEN?! H-HOW?
WHY?!
YOU'RE A GOOD COP, DAD.
YOU PUT ON THAT BADGE AND CARRY THAT GUN BECAUSE YOU KNOW IF YOU DON'T, SOMEONE WHO SHOULDN'T WILL.
THIS MASK IS MY BADGE NOW. IF I DON'T DEFINE WHAT IT MEANS...
...MONSTERS LIKE THIS WILL.
THIS IS WHERE I'M NEEDED MOST.

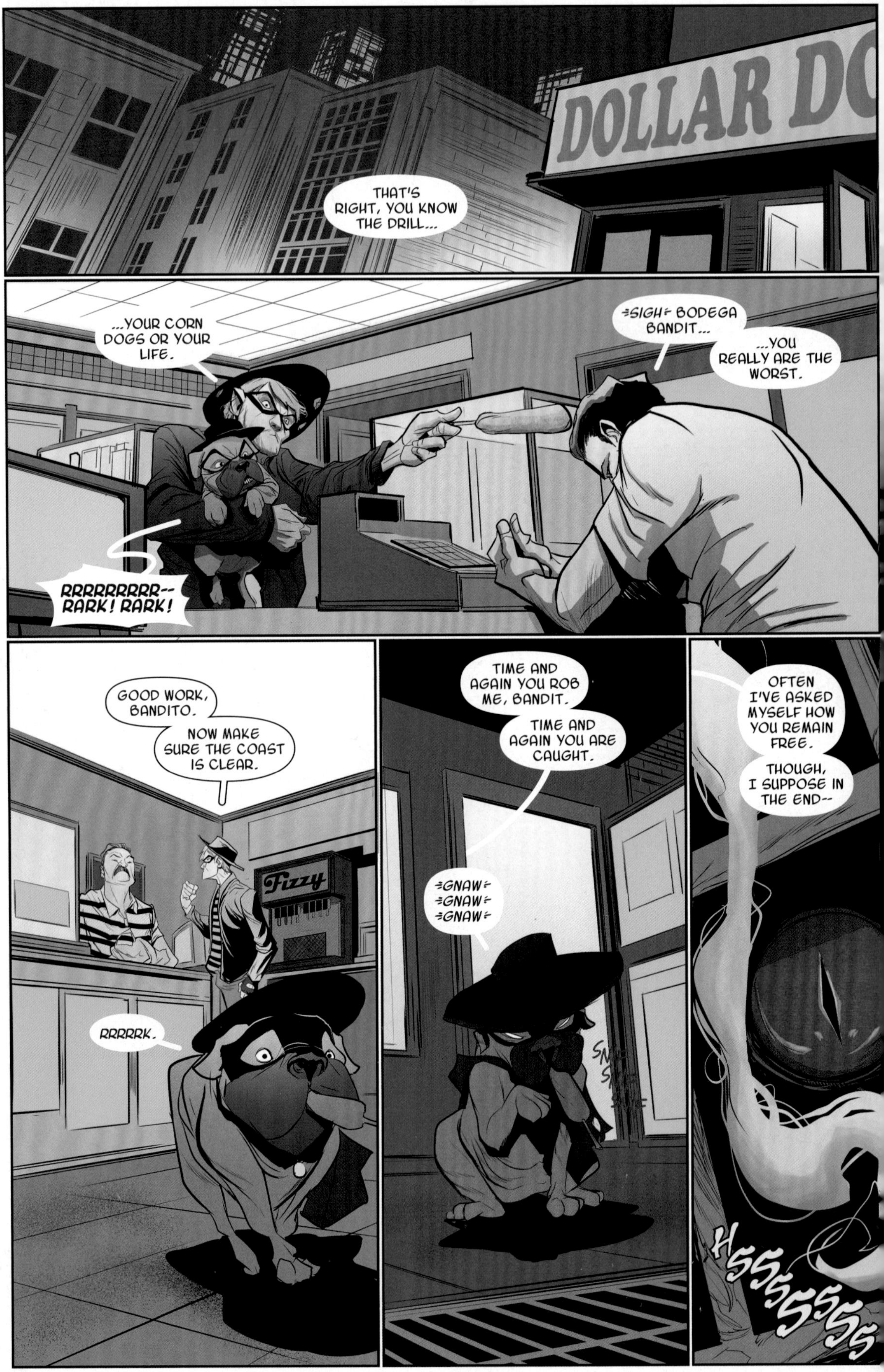
DOLLAR DO
THAT'S RIGHT, YOU KNOW THE DRILL...
...YOUR CORN DOGS OR YOUR LIFE.
=SIGH= BODEGA BANDIT...
...YOU REALLY ARE THE WORST.
RRRRRRRRR-- RARK! RARK!
GOOD WORK, BANDITO.
NOW MAKE SURE THE COAST IS CLEAR.
Fizzy
RRRRRK.
TIME AND AGAIN YOU ROB ME, BANDIT.
TIME AND AGAIN YOU ARE CAUGHT.
=GNAW= =GNAW= =GNAW=
OFTEN I'VE ASKED MYSELF HOW YOU REMAIN FREE.
THOUGH, I SUPPOSE IN THE END--
HSSSSSSS

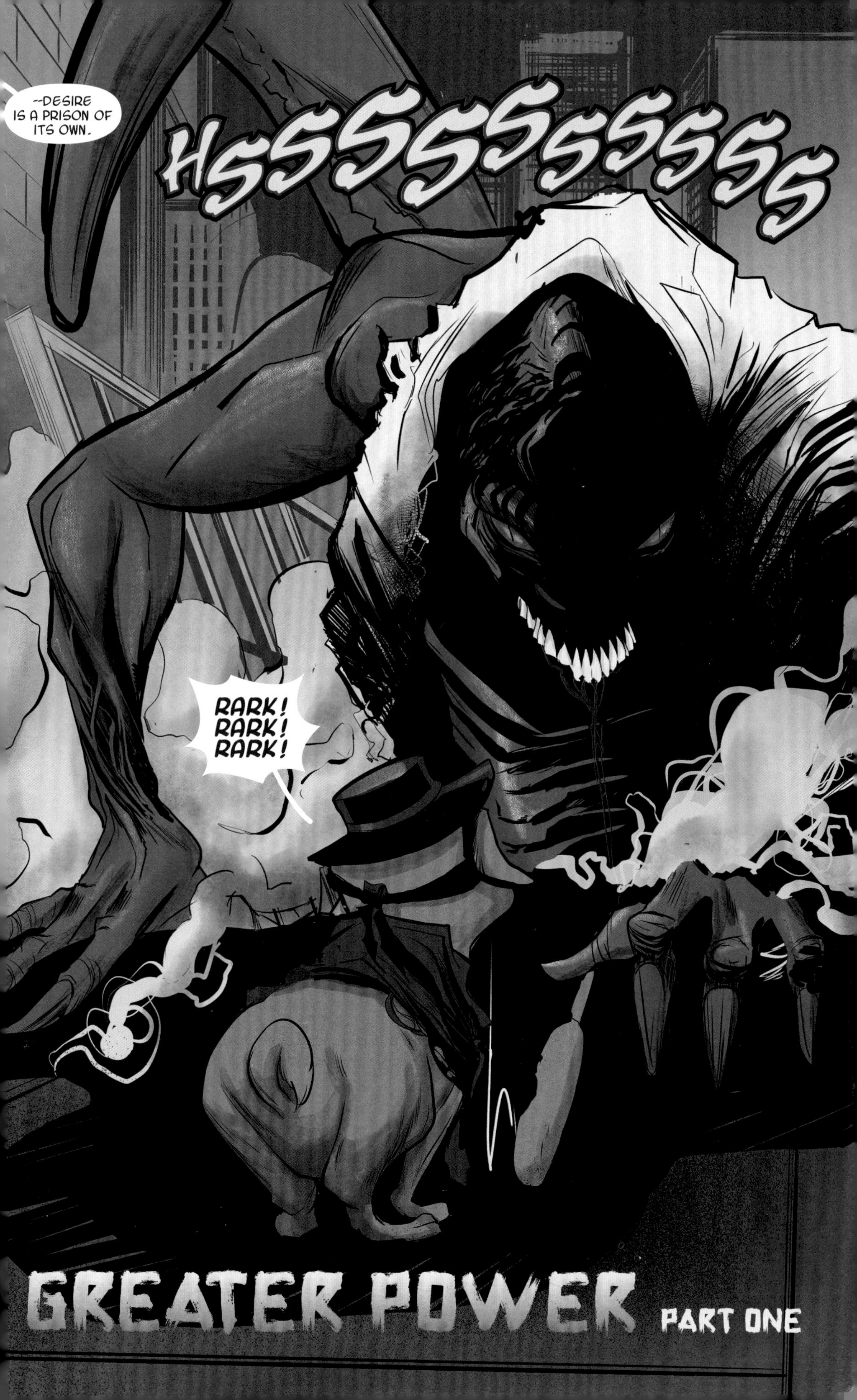
--DESIRE IS A PRISON OF ITS OWN.
HSSSSSSSSSSS
RARK! RARK! RARK!
GREATER POWER PART ONE

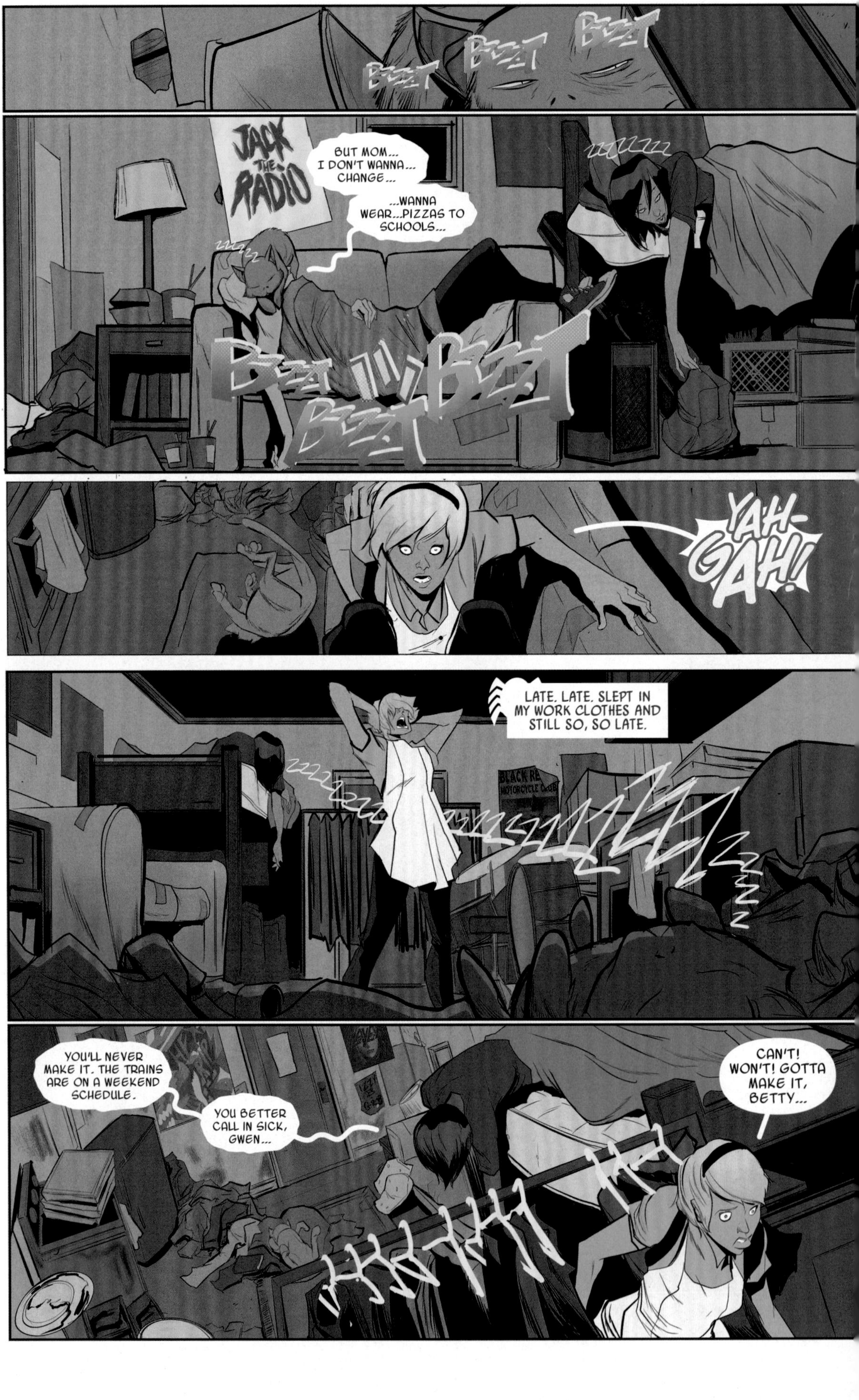

BZZT BZZT BZZT
JACK THE RADIO
BUT MOM... I DON'T WANNA... CHANGE...
...WANNA WEAR...PIZZAS TO SCHOOLS...
BZZT BZZT BZZT
YAH-GAH!
LATE. LATE. SLEPT IN MY WORK CLOTHES AND STILL SO, SO LATE.
MOTORCYCLE CLUB
YOU'LL NEVER MAKE IT. THE TRAINS ARE ON A WEEKEND SCHEDULE.
YOU BETTER CALL IN SICK, GWEN...
CAN'T! WON'T! GOTTA MAKE IT, BETTY...

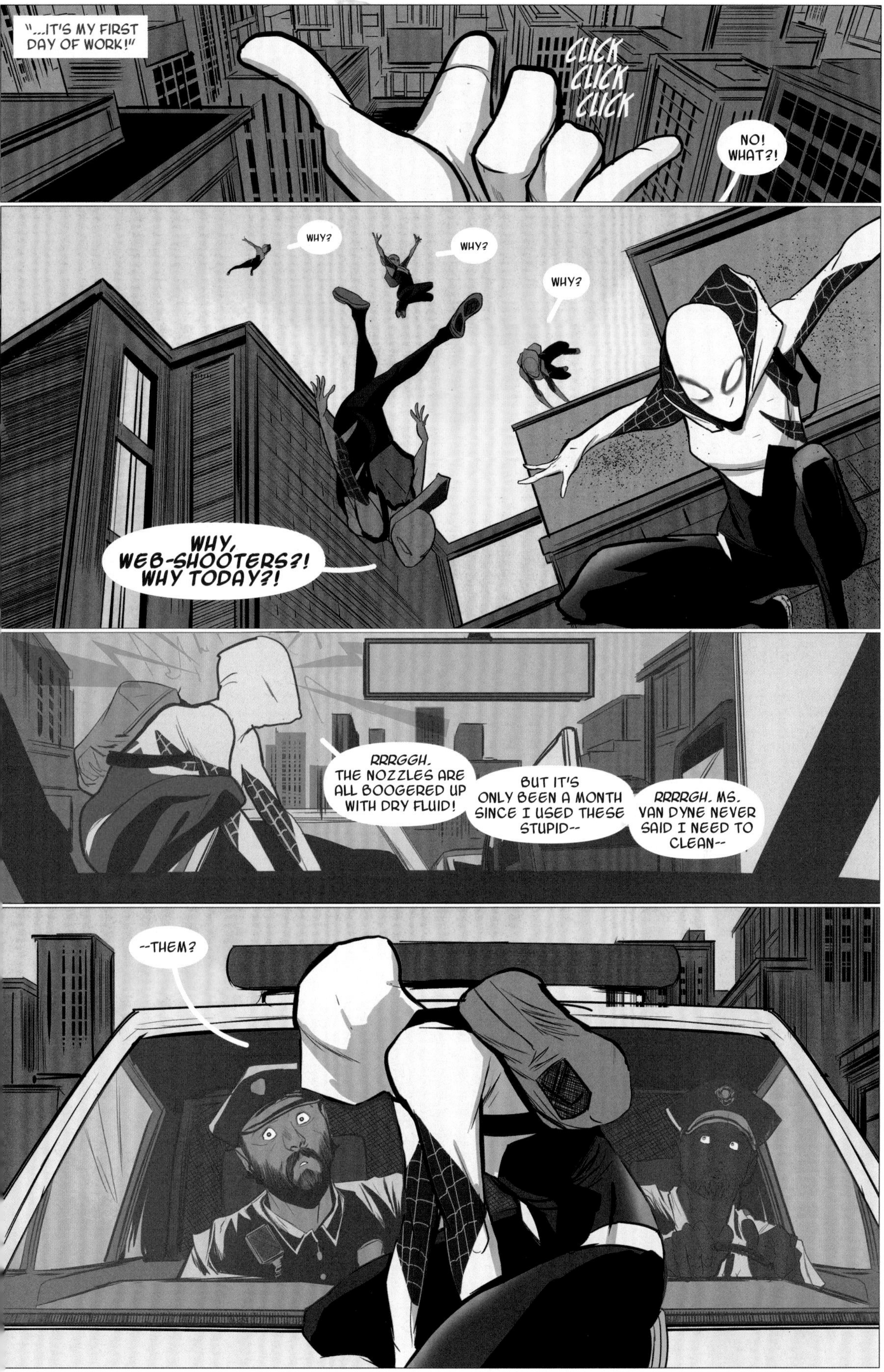

"...IT'S MY FIRST DAY OF WORK!"
CLICK CLICK CLICK
NO! WHAT?!
WHY?
WHY?
WHY?
WHY, WEB-SHOOTERS?! WHY TODAY?!
RRRGGH. THE NOZZLES ARE ALL BOOGERED UP WITH DRY FLUID!
BUT IT'S ONLY BEEN A MONTH SINCE I USED THESE STUPID--
RRRRGH. MS. VAN DYNE NEVER SAID I NEED TO CLEAN--
--THEM?

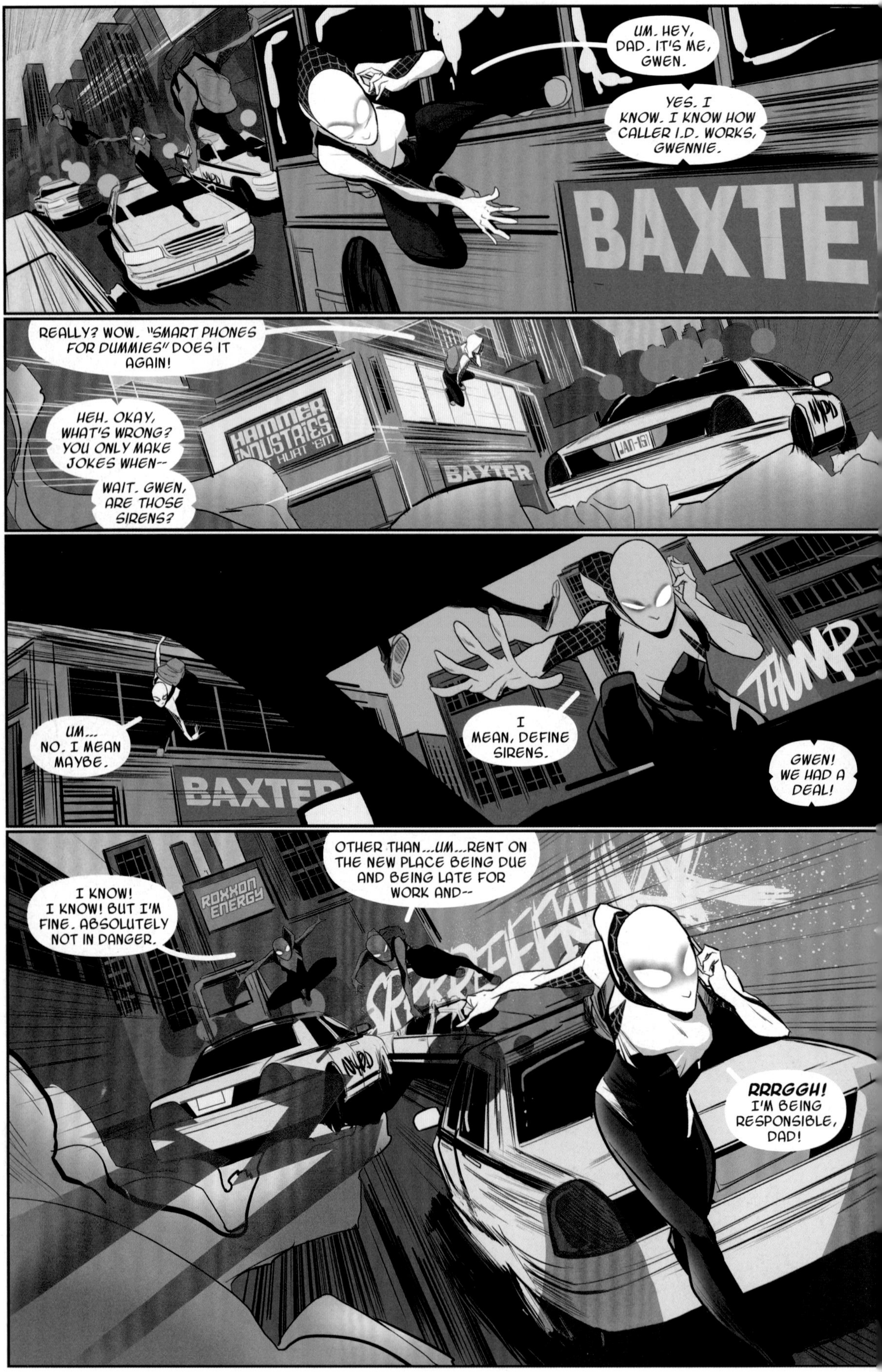
UM. HEY, DAD. IT'S ME, GWEN.
YES. I KNOW. I KNOW HOW CALLER I.D. WORKS, GWENNIE.
BAXTER
REALLY? WOW. "SMART PHONES FOR DUMMIES" DOES IT AGAIN!
HAMMER INDUSTRIES
HEH. OKAY, WHAT'S WRONG? YOU ONLY MAKE JOKES WHEN--
BAXTER
WAIT. GWEN, ARE THOSE SIRENS?
UM... NO. I MEAN MAYBE.
BAXTER
I MEAN, DEFINE SIRENS.
THUMP
GWEN! WE HAD A DEAL!
ROXXON ENERGY
I KNOW! I KNOW! BUT I'M FINE. ABSOLUTELY NOT IN DANGER.
OTHER THAN...UM...RENT ON THE NEW PLACE BEING DUE AND BEING LATE FOR WORK AND--
RRRGGH! I'M BEING RESPONSIBLE, DAD!

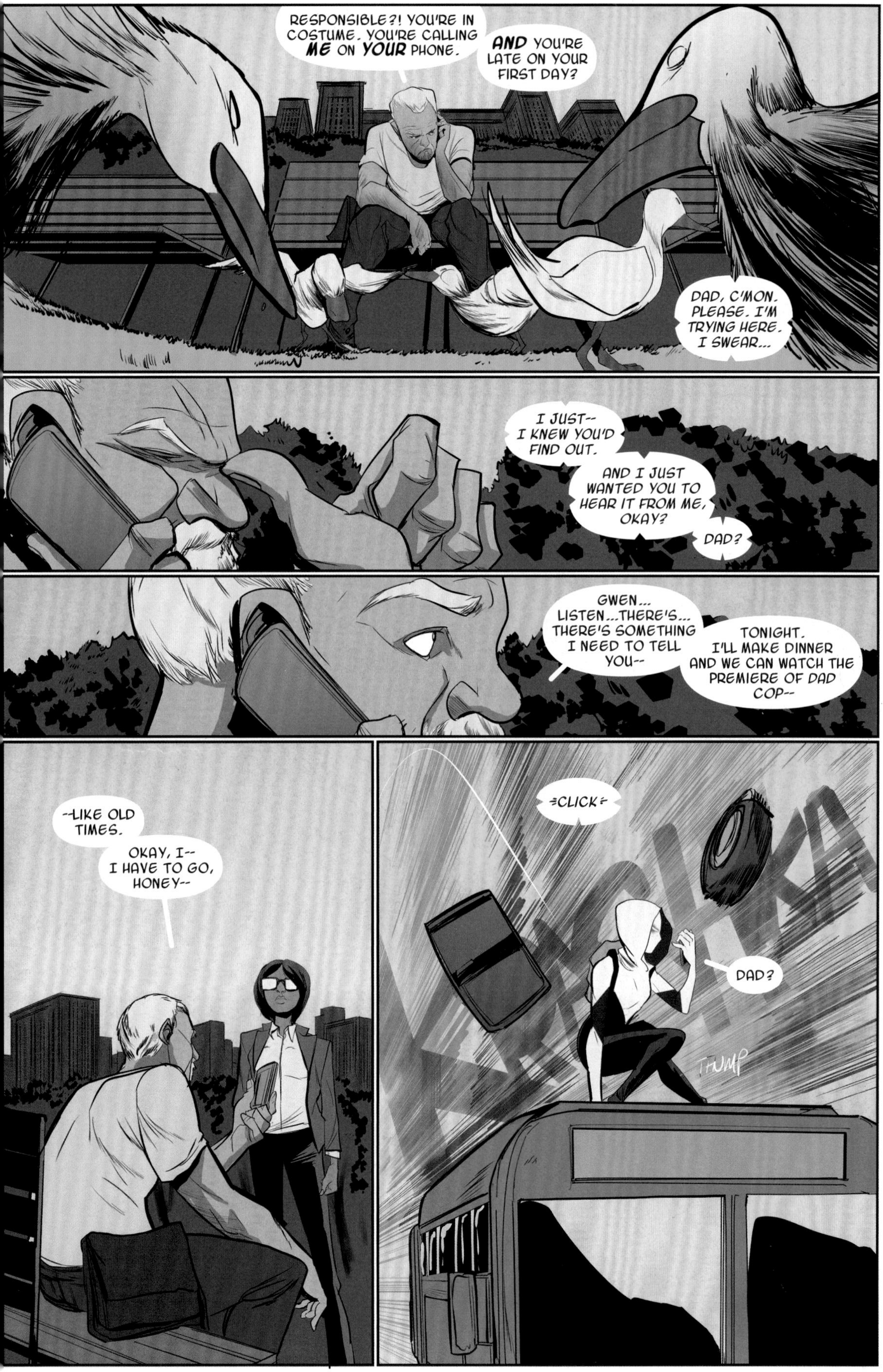
RESPONSIBLE?! YOU'RE IN COSTUME. YOU'RE CALLING ME ON YOUR PHONE.
AND YOU'RE LATE ON YOUR FIRST DAY?
DAD, C'MON. PLEASE. I'M TRYING HERE. I SWEAR...
I JUST-- I KNEW YOU'D FIND OUT.
AND I JUST WANTED YOU TO HEAR IT FROM ME, OKAY?
DAD?
GWEN... LISTEN...THERE'S... THERE'S SOMETHING I NEED TO TELL YOU--
TONIGHT. I'LL MAKE DINNER AND WE CAN WATCH THE PREMIERE OF DAD COP--
--LIKE OLD TIMES.
OKAY, I-- I HAVE TO GO, HONEY--
=CLICK=
DAD?
THUMP

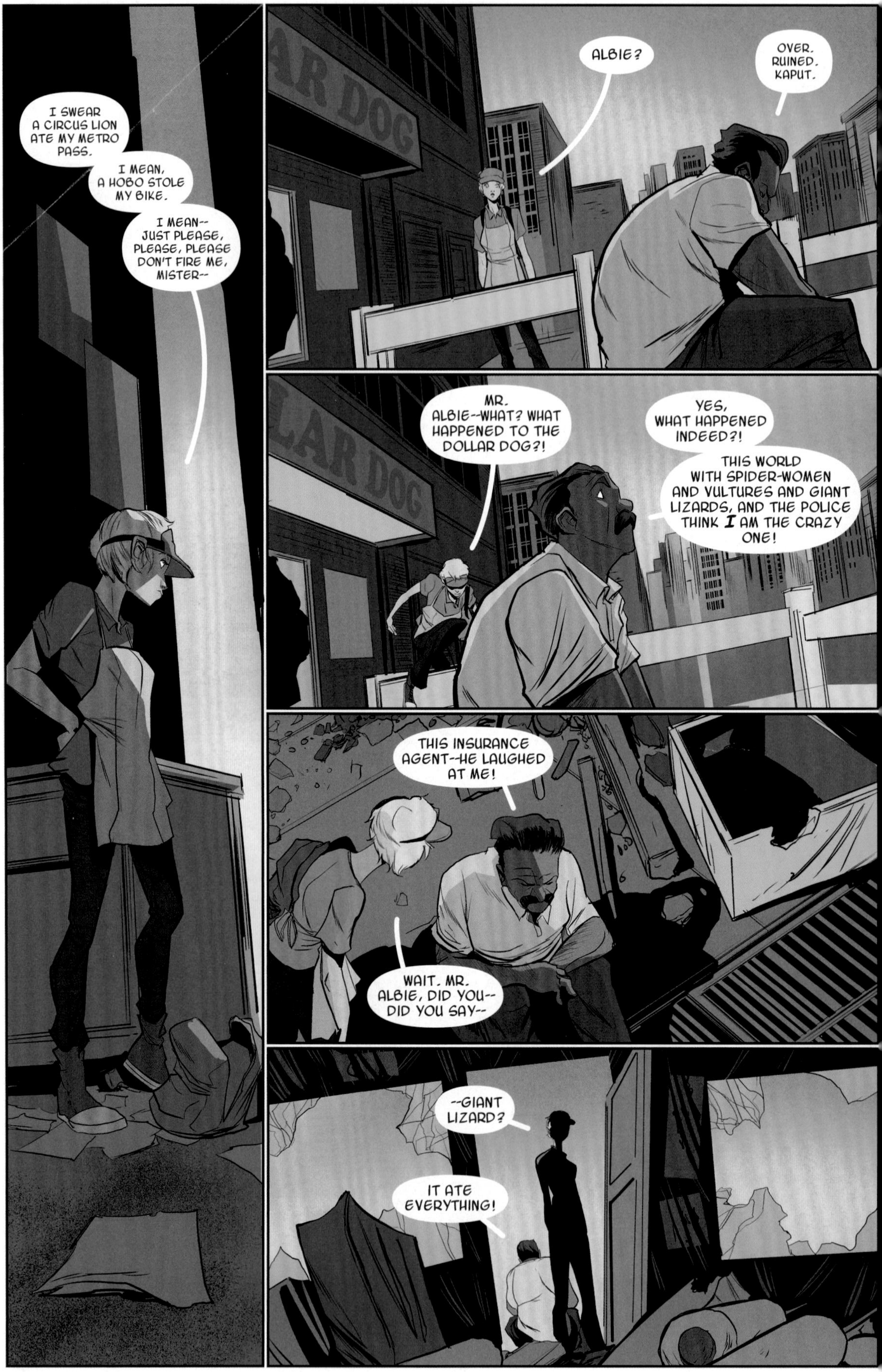
I SWEAR A CIRCUS LION ATE MY METRO PASS.
I MEAN, A HOBO STOLE MY BIKE.
I MEAN-- JUST PLEASE, PLEASE, PLEASE DON'T FIRE ME, MISTER--
ALBIE?
OVER. RUINED. KAPUT.
MR. ALBIE--WHAT? WHAT HAPPENED TO THE DOLLAR DOG?!
YES, WHAT HAPPENED INDEED?!
THIS WORLD WITH SPIDER-WOMEN AND VULTURES AND GIANT LIZARDS, AND THE POLICE THINK *I* AM THE CRAZY ONE!
THIS INSURANCE AGENT--HE LAUGHED AT ME!
WAIT. MR. ALBIE, DID YOU-- DID YOU SAY--
--GIANT LIZARD?
IT ATE EVERYTHING!

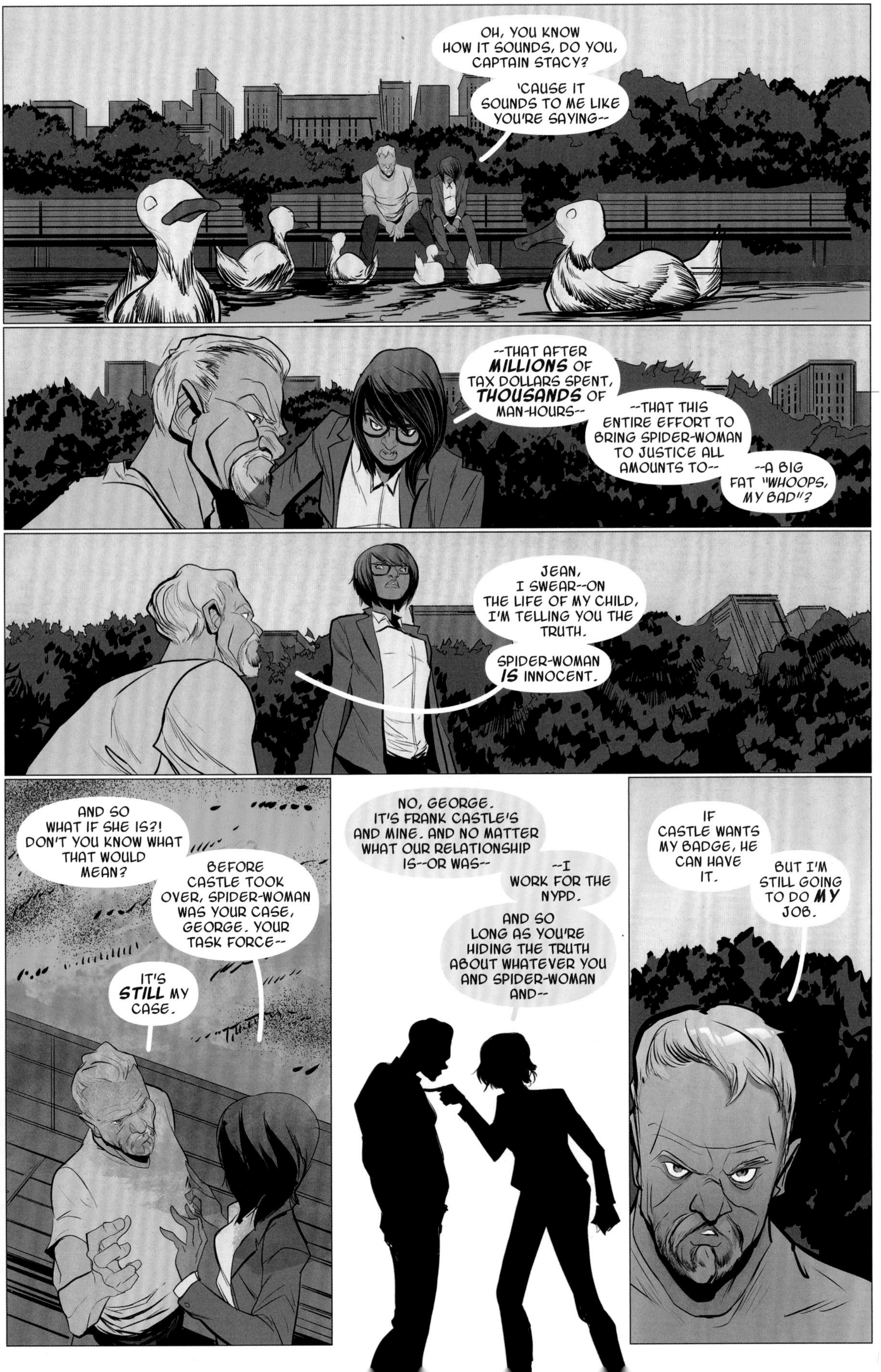
OH, YOU KNOW HOW IT SOUNDS, DO YOU, CAPTAIN STACY?
'CAUSE IT SOUNDS TO ME LIKE YOU'RE SAYING--
--THAT AFTER MILLIONS OF TAX DOLLARS SPENT, THOUSANDS OF MAN-HOURS--
--THAT THIS ENTIRE EFFORT TO BRING SPIDER-WOMAN TO JUSTICE ALL AMOUNTS TO--
--A BIG FAT "WHOOPS, MY BAD"?
JEAN, I SWEAR--ON THE LIFE OF MY CHILD, I'M TELLING YOU THE TRUTH.
SPIDER-WOMAN IS INNOCENT.
AND SO WHAT IF SHE IS?! DON'T YOU KNOW WHAT THAT WOULD MEAN?
BEFORE CASTLE TOOK OVER, SPIDER-WOMAN WAS YOUR CASE, GEORGE. YOUR TASK FORCE--
IT'S STILL MY CASE.
NO, GEORGE. IT'S FRANK CASTLE'S AND MINE. AND NO MATTER WHAT OUR RELATIONSHIP IS--OR WAS--
--I WORK FOR THE NYPD.
AND SO LONG AS YOU'RE HIDING THE TRUTH ABOUT WHATEVER YOU AND SPIDER-WOMAN AND--
IF CASTLE WANTS MY BADGE, HE CAN HAVE IT.
BUT I'M STILL GOING TO DO MY JOB.

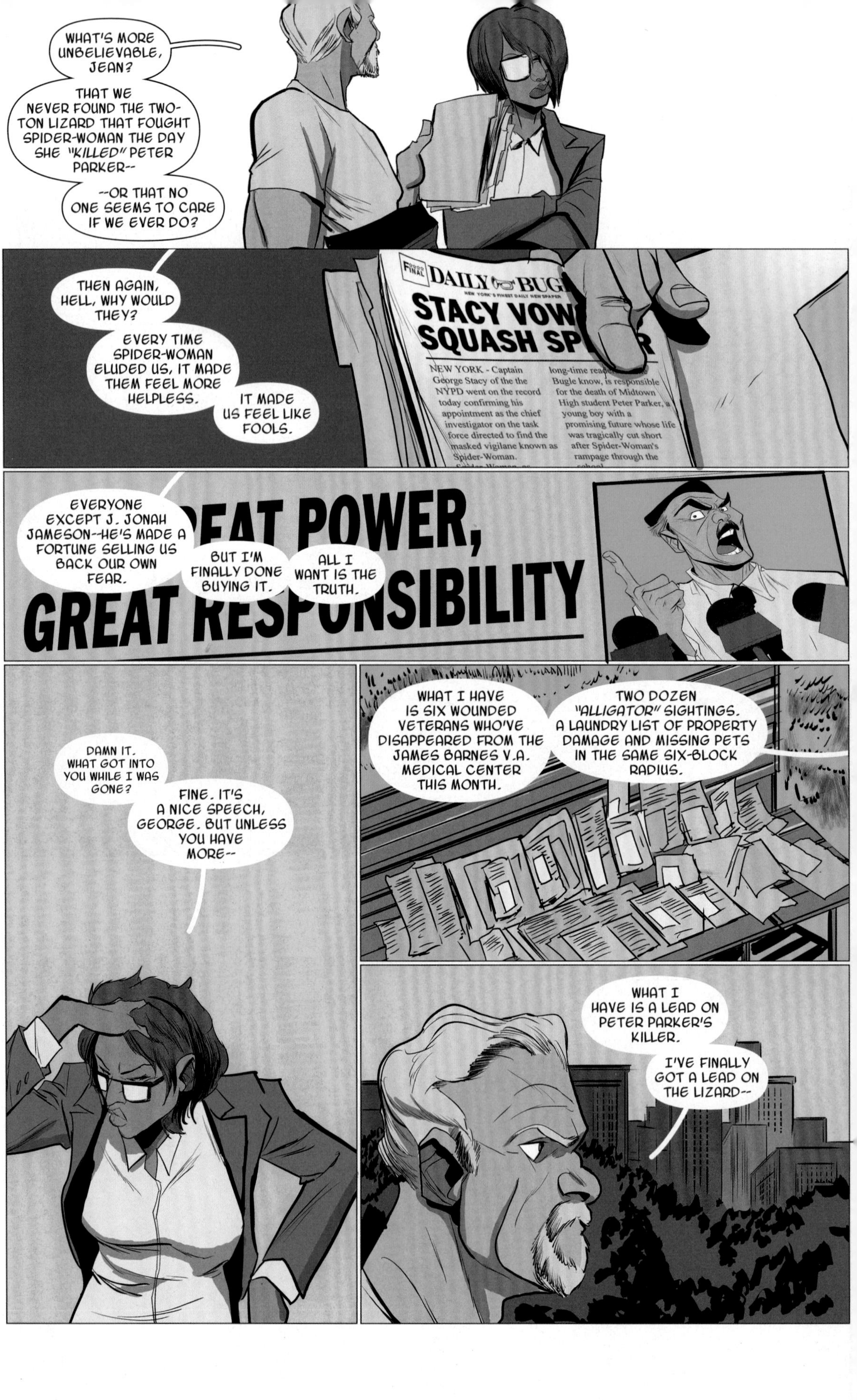

WHAT'S MORE UNBELIEVABLE, JEAN?
THAT WE NEVER FOUND THE TWO-TON LIZARD THAT FOUGHT SPIDER-WOMAN THE DAY SHE "KILLED" PETER PARKER--
--OR THAT NO ONE SEEMS TO CARE IF WE EVER DO?
THEN AGAIN, HELL, WHY WOULD THEY?
EVERY TIME SPIDER-WOMAN ELUDED US, IT MADE THEM FEEL MORE HELPLESS.
IT MADE US FEEL LIKE FOOLS.
FINAL
DAILY BUG
NEW YORK'S FINEST DAILY NEWSPAPER
STACY VOW
SQUASH SP
NEW YORK - Captain George Stacy of the the NYPD went on the record today confirming his appointment as the chief investigator on the task force directed to find the masked vigilane known as Spider-Woman.
long-time reade Bugle know, is responsible for the death of Midtown High student Peter Parker, a young boy with a promising future whose life was tragically cut short after Spider-Woman's rampage through the
EVERYONE EXCEPT J. JONAH JAMESON--HE'S MADE A FORTUNE SELLING US BACK OUR OWN FEAR.
BUT I'M FINALLY DONE BUYING IT.
ALL I WANT IS THE TRUTH.
EAT POWER,
GREAT RESPONSIBILITY
DAMN IT. WHAT GOT INTO YOU WHILE I WAS GONE?
FINE. IT'S A NICE SPEECH, GEORGE. BUT UNLESS YOU HAVE MORE--
WHAT I HAVE IS SIX WOUNDED VETERANS WHO'VE DISAPPEARED FROM THE JAMES BARNES V.A. MEDICAL CENTER THIS MONTH.
TWO DOZEN "ALLIGATOR" SIGHTINGS. A LAUNDRY LIST OF PROPERTY DAMAGE AND MISSING PETS IN THE SAME SIX-BLOCK RADIUS.
WHAT I HAVE IS A LEAD ON PETER PARKER'S KILLER.
I'VE FINALLY GOT A LEAD ON THE LIZARD--

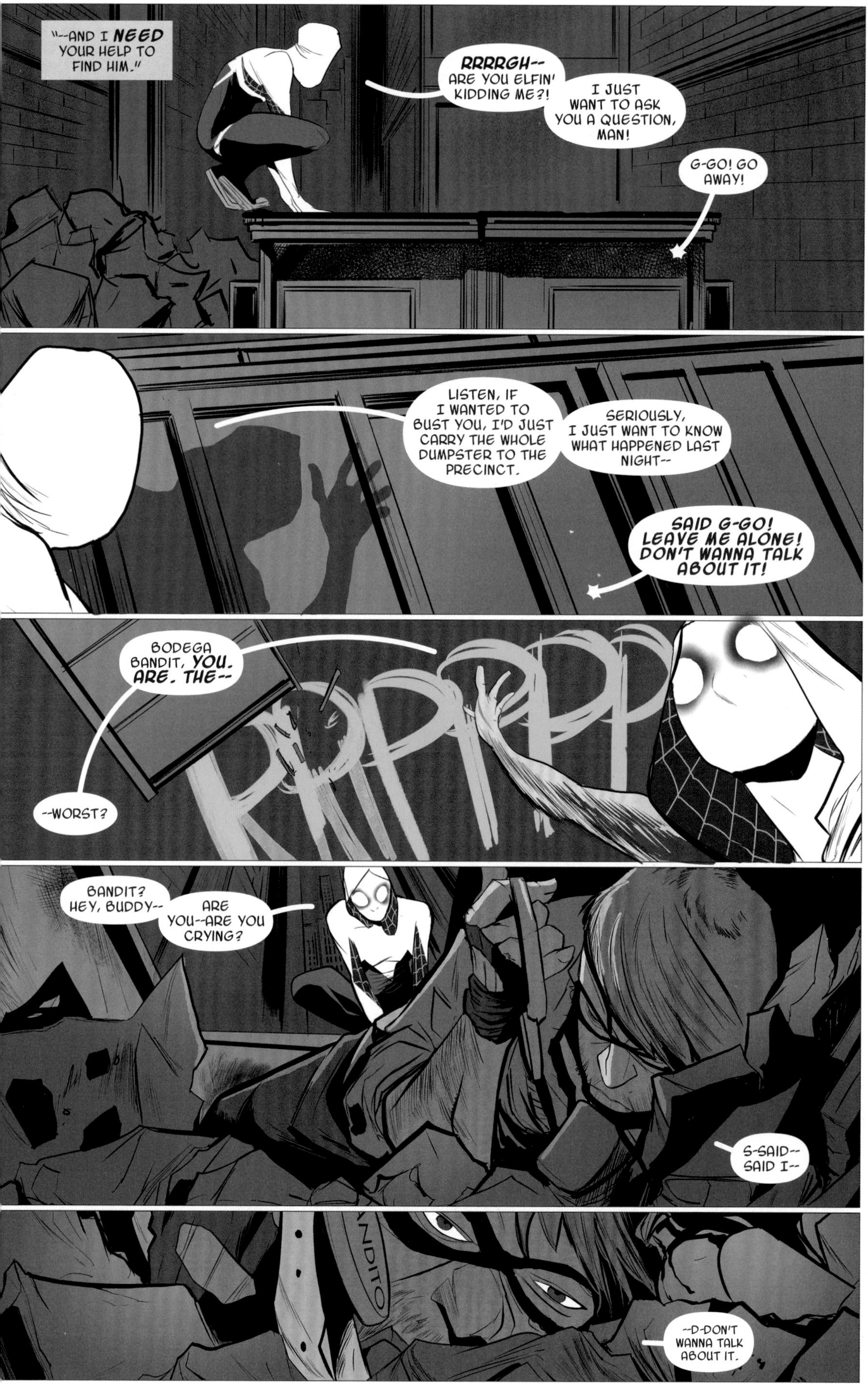
"--AND I NEED YOUR HELP TO FIND HIM."
RRRRGH-- ARE YOU ELFIN' KIDDING ME?!
I JUST WANT TO ASK YOU A QUESTION, MAN!
G-GO! GO AWAY!
LISTEN, IF I WANTED TO BUST YOU, I'D JUST CARRY THE WHOLE DUMPSTER TO THE PRECINCT.
SERIOUSLY, I JUST WANT TO KNOW WHAT HAPPENED LAST NIGHT--
SAID G-GO! LEAVE ME ALONE! DON'T WANNA TALK ABOUT IT!
BODEGA BANDIT, YOU. ARE. THE--
RRIPPPP
--WORST?
BANDIT? HEY, BUDDY--
ARE YOU--ARE YOU CRYING?
S-SAID-- SAID I--
--D-DON'T WANNA TALK ABOUT IT.

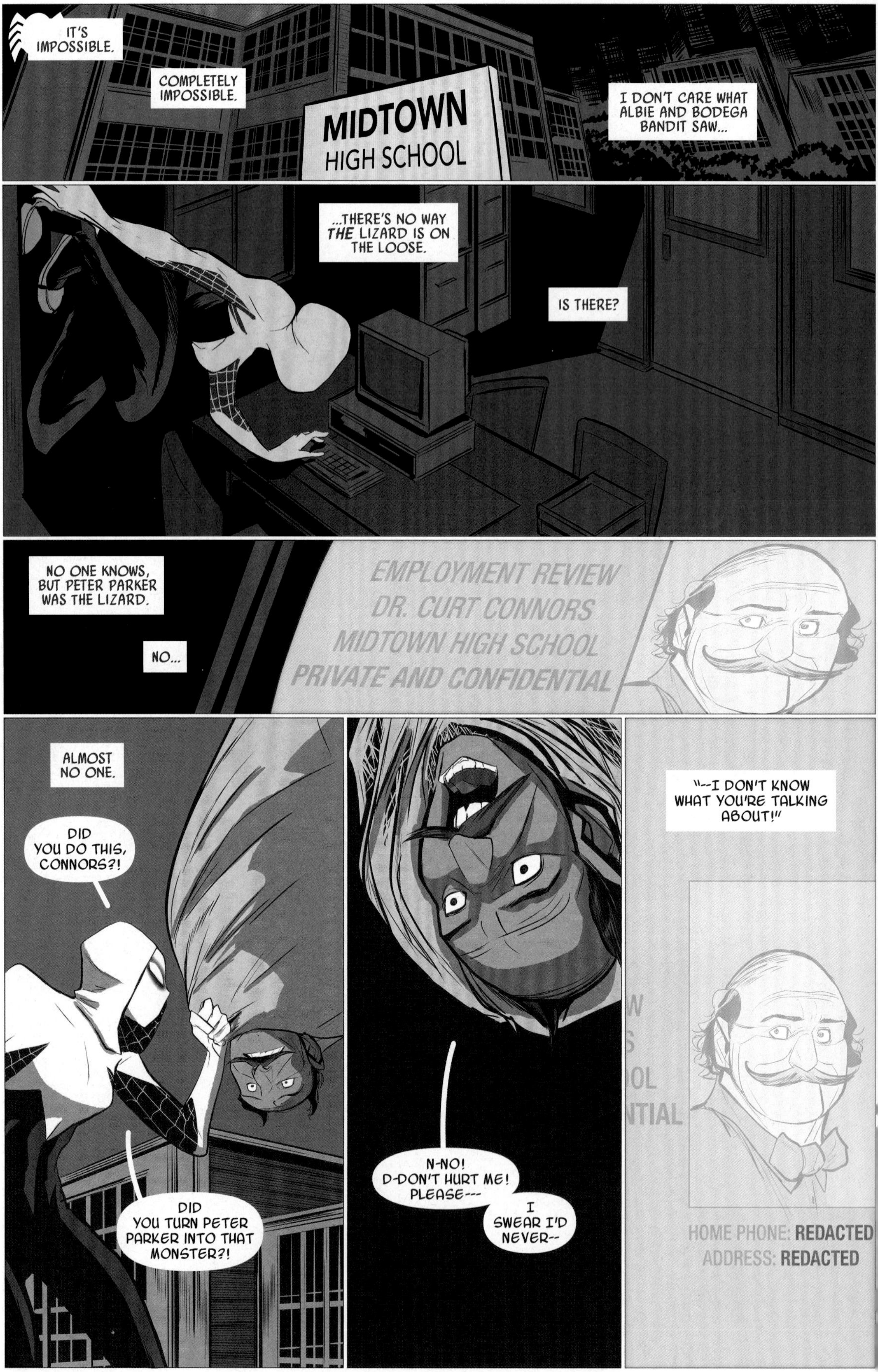
IT'S IMPOSSIBLE.
COMPLETELY IMPOSSIBLE.
MIDTOWN HIGH SCHOOL
I DON'T CARE WHAT ALBIE AND BODEGA BANDIT SAW...
...THERE'S NO WAY THE LIZARD IS ON THE LOOSE.
IS THERE?
NO ONE KNOWS, BUT PETER PARKER WAS THE LIZARD.
NO...
EMPLOYMENT REVIEW
DR. CURT CONNORS
MIDTOWN HIGH SCHOOL
PRIVATE AND CONFIDENTIAL
ALMOST NO ONE.
DID YOU DO THIS, CONNORS?!
DID YOU TURN PETER PARKER INTO THAT MONSTER?!
N-NO! D-DON'T HURT ME! PLEASE---
I SWEAR I'D NEVER--
"--I DON'T KNOW WHAT YOU'RE TALKING ABOUT!"
HOME PHONE: REDACTED
ADDRESS: REDACTED

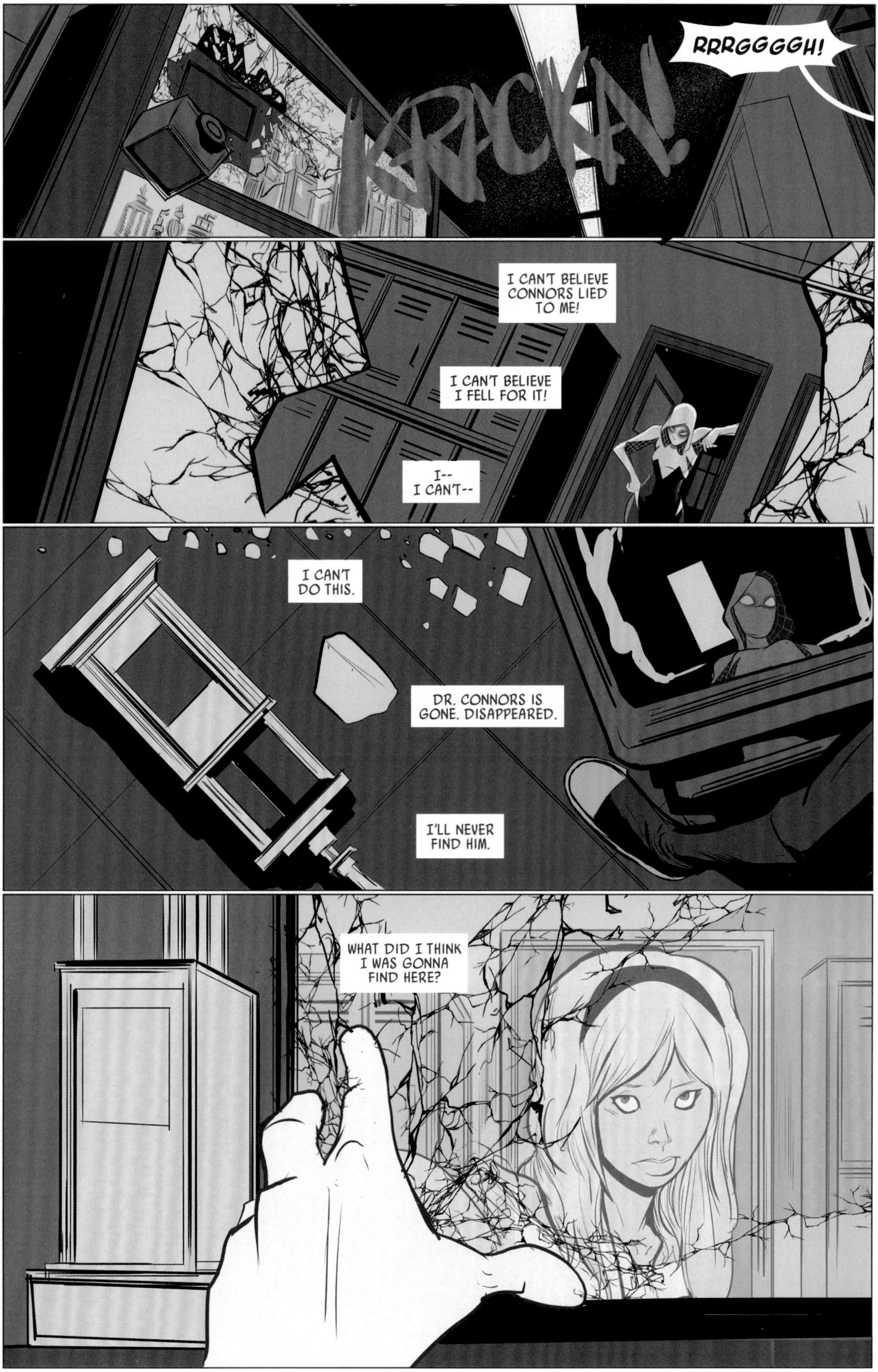
KRACKA!
RRRGGGGH!
I CAN'T BELIEVE CONNORS LIED TO ME!
I CAN'T BELIEVE I FELL FOR IT!
I-- I CAN'T--
I CAN'T DO THIS.
DR. CONNORS IS GONE. DISAPPEARED.
I'LL NEVER FIND HIM.
WHAT DID I THINK I WAS GONNA FIND HERE?

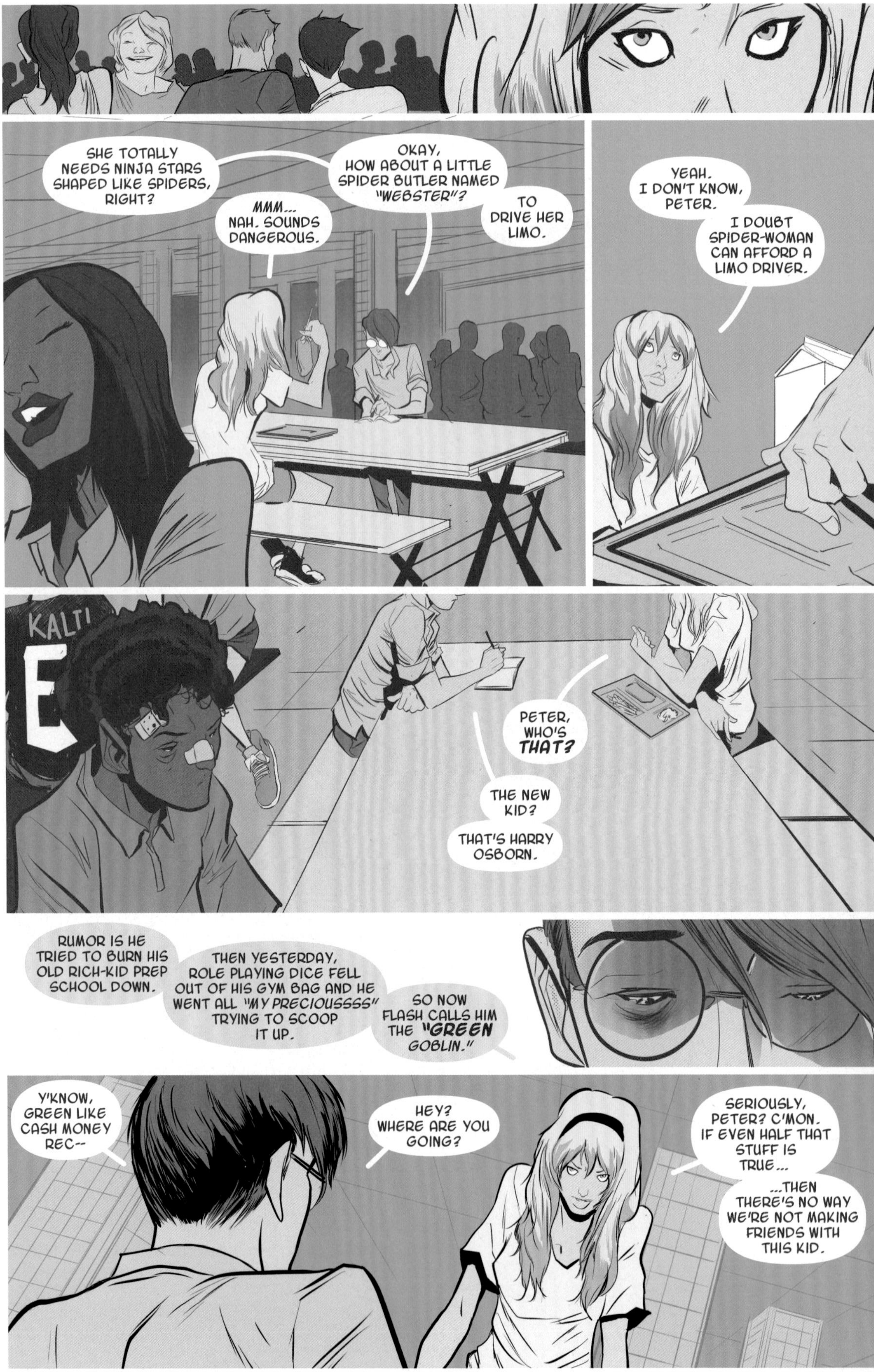
SHE TOTALLY NEEDS NINJA STARS SHAPED LIKE SPIDERS, RIGHT?
MMM... NAH. SOUNDS DANGEROUS.
OKAY, HOW ABOUT A LITTLE SPIDER BUTLER NAMED "WEBSTER"?
TO DRIVE HER LIMO.
YEAH. I DON'T KNOW, PETER.
I DOUBT SPIDER-WOMAN CAN AFFORD A LIMO DRIVER.
KALTI
PETER, WHO'S THAT?
THE NEW KID?
THAT'S HARRY OSBORN.
RUMOR IS HE TRIED TO BURN HIS OLD RICH-KID PREP SCHOOL DOWN.
THEN YESTERDAY, ROLE PLAYING DICE FELL OUT OF HIS GYM BAG AND HE WENT ALL "MY PRECIOUSSSS" TRYING TO SCOOP IT UP.
SO NOW FLASH CALLS HIM THE "GREEN GOBLIN."
Y'KNOW, GREEN LIKE CASH MONEY REC--
HEY? WHERE ARE YOU GOING?
SERIOUSLY, PETER? C'MON. IF EVEN HALF THAT STUFF IS TRUE...
...THEN THERE'S NO WAY WE'RE NOT MAKING FRIENDS WITH THIS KID.

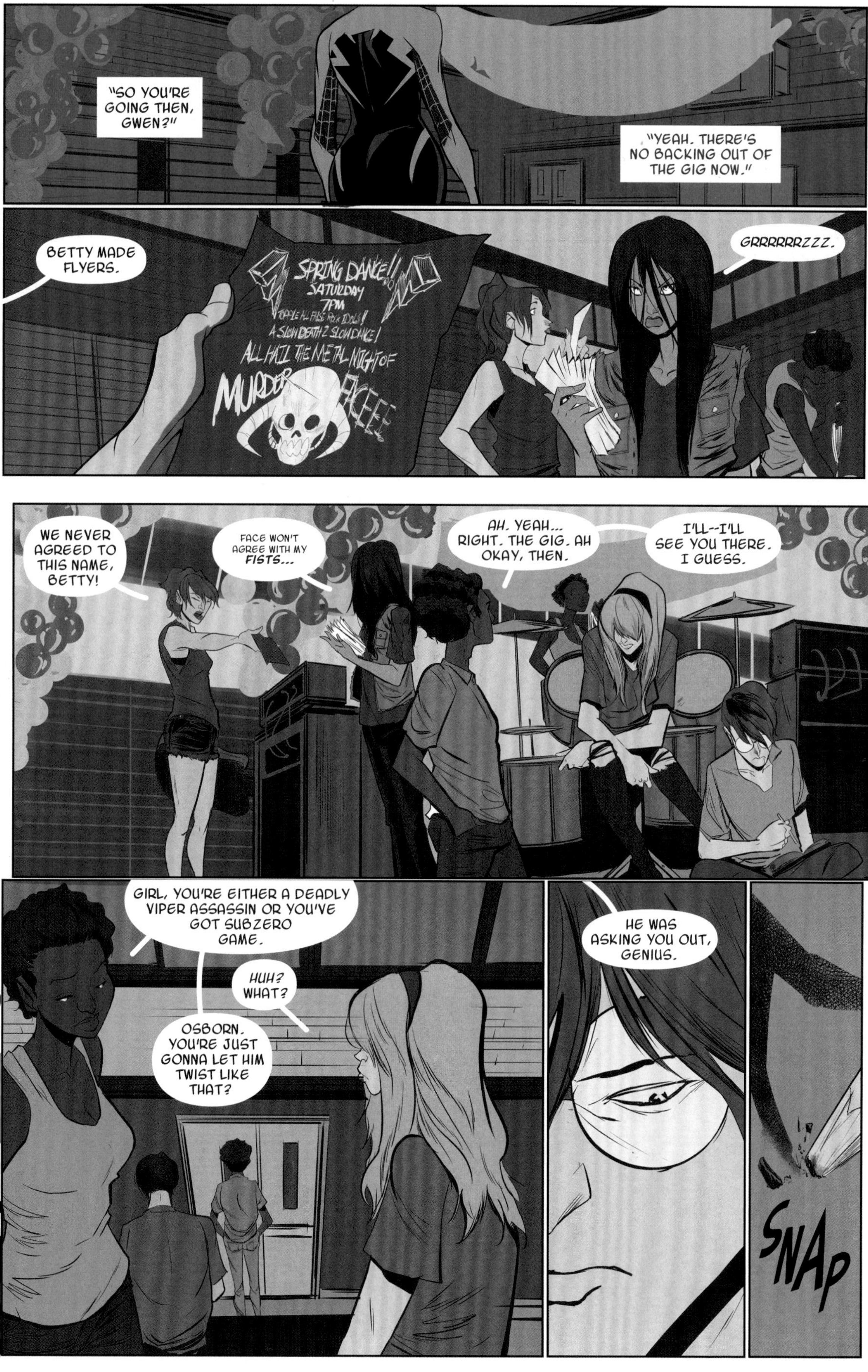
"SO YOU'RE GOING THEN, GWEN?"
"YEAH. THERE'S NO BACKING OUT OF THE GIG NOW."
BETTY MADE FLYERS.
GRRRRRRZZZ.
SPRING DANCE!! SATURDAY 7PM
TOPPLE ALL FALSE ROCK IDOLS!!
A SLOW DEATH 2 SLOW DANCE!
ALL HAIL THE METAL MIGHT OF MURDER FACEEE
WE NEVER AGREED TO THIS NAME, BETTY!
FACE WON'T AGREE WITH MY FISTS...
AH. YEAH... RIGHT. THE GIG. AH OKAY, THEN.
I'LL--I'LL SEE YOU THERE. I GUESS.
GIRL, YOU'RE EITHER A DEADLY VIPER ASSASSIN OR YOU'VE GOT SUBZERO GAME.
HUH? WHAT?
OSBORN. YOU'RE JUST GONNA LET HIM TWIST LIKE THAT?
HE WAS ASKING YOU OUT, GENIUS.
SNAP

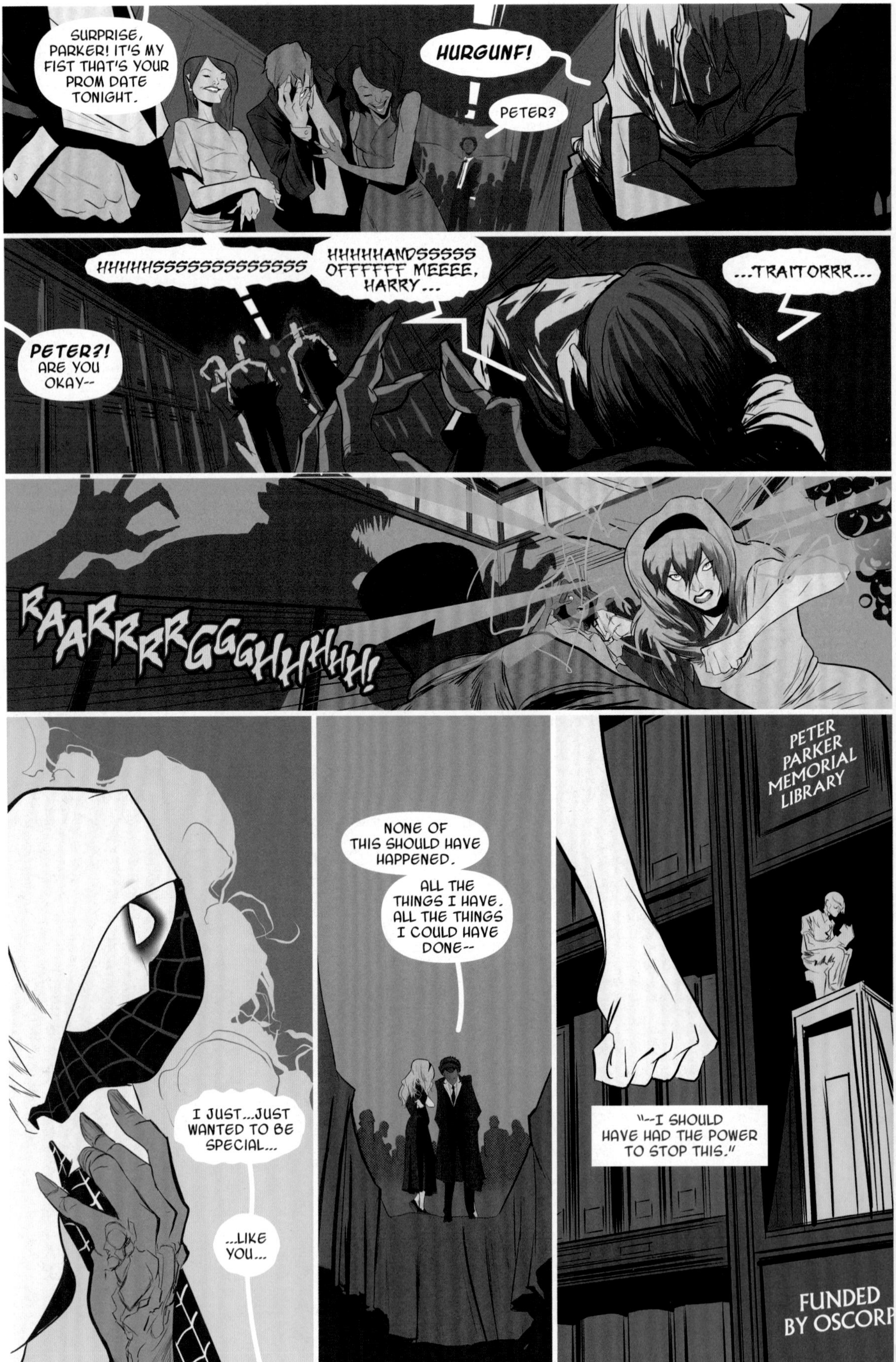

SURPRISE, PARKER! IT'S MY FIST THAT'S YOUR PROM DATE TONIGHT.
HURGUNF!
PETER?
HHHHHSSSSSSSSSSSSSS
HHHHHANDSSSSS OFFFFFF MEEEE, HARRY...
...TRAITORRR...
PETER?! ARE YOU OKAY--
RAARRRRGGGHHHHH!
I JUST...JUST WANTED TO BE SPECIAL...
...LIKE YOU...
NONE OF THIS SHOULD HAVE HAPPENED.
ALL THE THINGS I HAVE. ALL THE THINGS I COULD HAVE DONE--
PETER PARKER MEMORIAL LIBRARY
"--I SHOULD HAVE HAD THE POWER TO STOP THIS."
FUNDED BY OSCORP

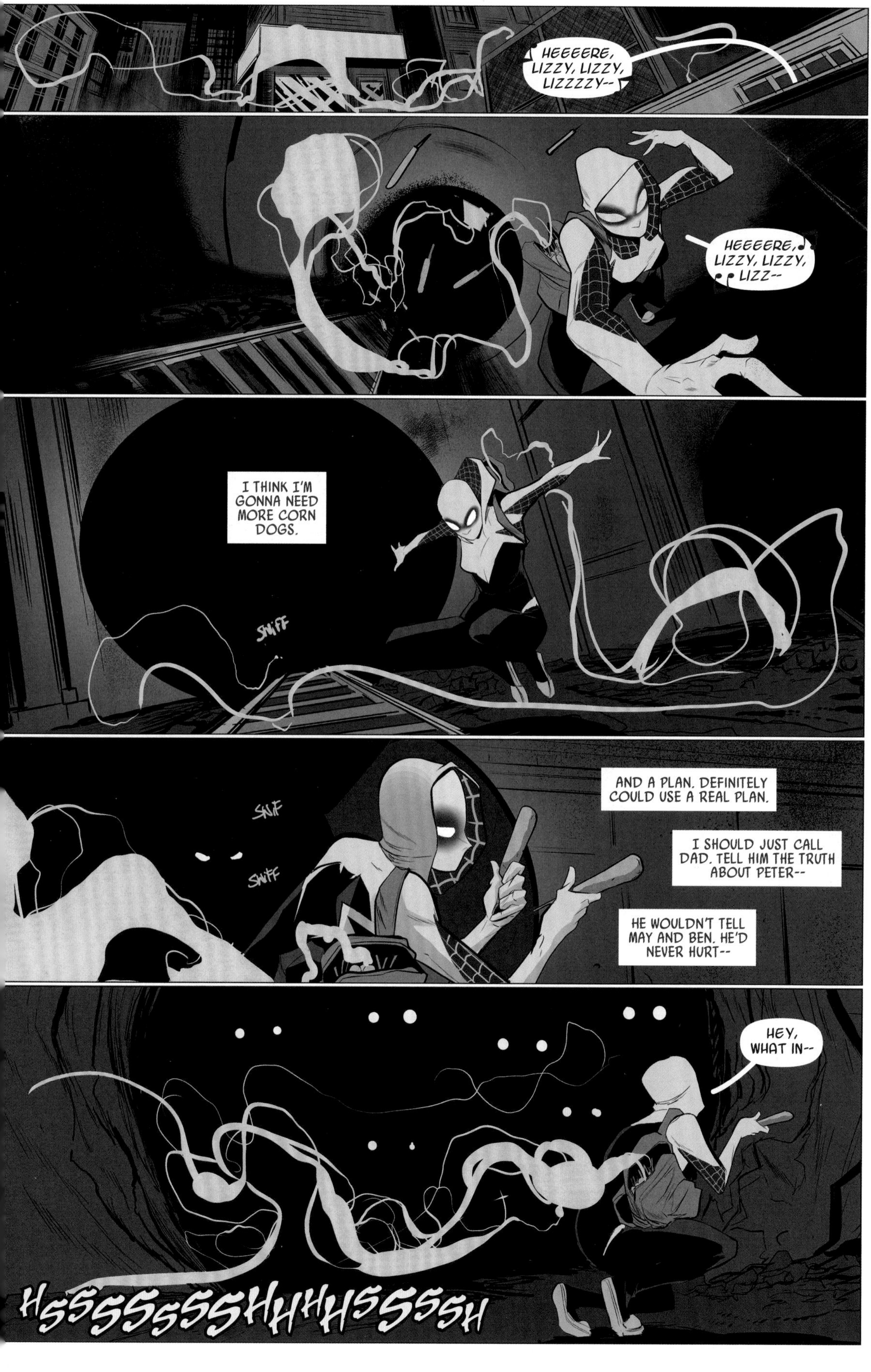
HEEEERE, LIZZY, LIZZY, LIZZZZY--
HEEEERE, LIZZY, LIZZY, LIZZ--
I THINK I'M GONNA NEED MORE CORN DOGS.
SNIFF
AND A PLAN. DEFINITELY COULD USE A REAL PLAN.
SNIFF
SNIFF
I SHOULD JUST CALL DAD. TELL HIM THE TRUTH ABOUT PETER--
HE WOULDN'T TELL MAY AND BEN. HE'D NEVER HURT--
HEY, WHAT IN--
HSSSSSSSHHHHSSSSSH

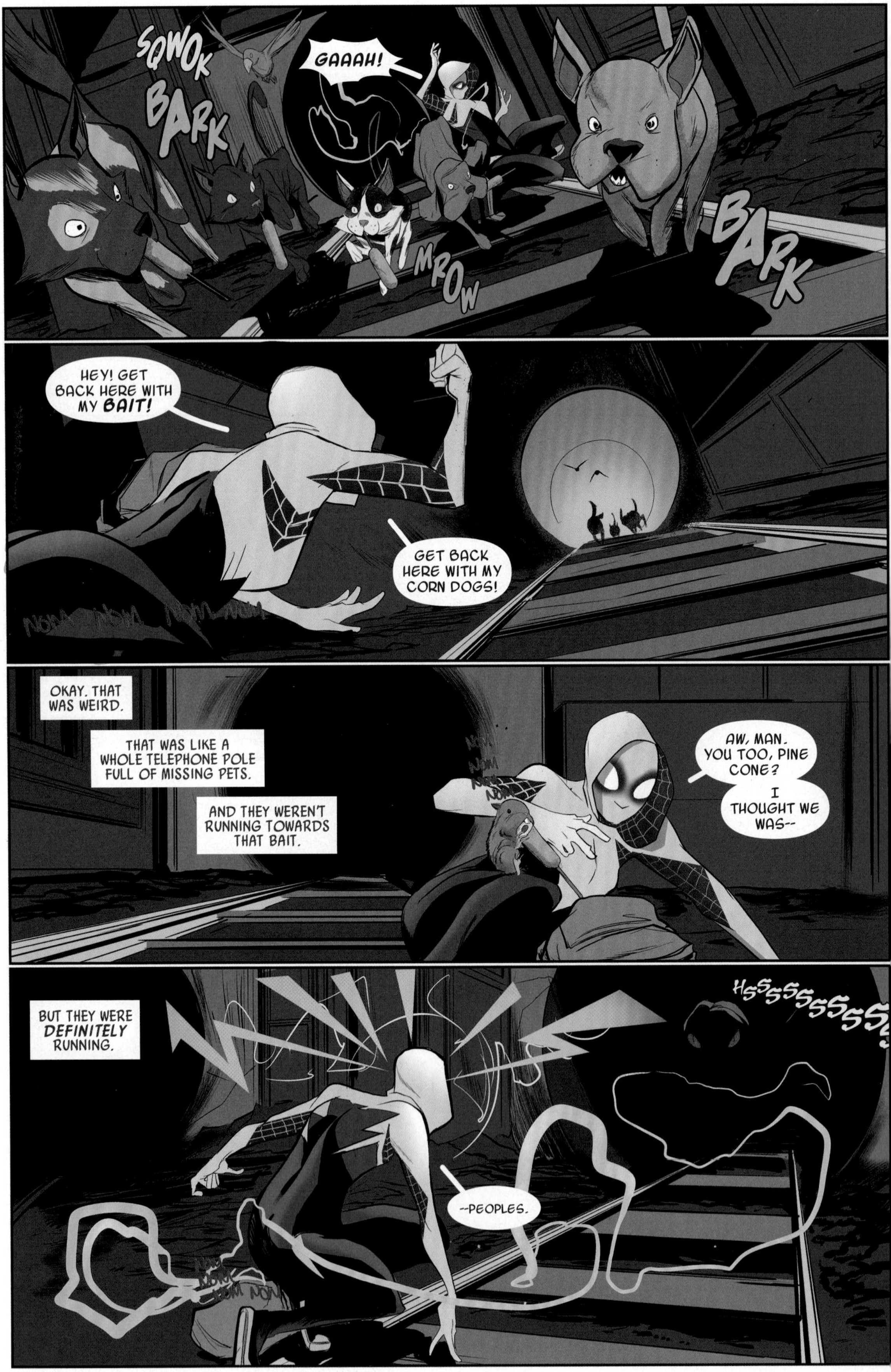

SQWOK
BARK
GAAAH!
MROW
BARK
HEY! GET BACK HERE WITH MY BAIT!
GET BACK HERE WITH MY CORN DOGS!
NOM NOM NOM NOM
OKAY. THAT WAS WEIRD.
THAT WAS LIKE A WHOLE TELEPHONE POLE FULL OF MISSING PETS.
AND THEY WEREN'T RUNNING TOWARDS THAT BAIT.
AW, MAN. YOU TOO, PINE CONE?
I THOUGHT WE WAS--
BUT THEY WERE DEFINITELY RUNNING.
HSSSSSSSSS
--PEOPLES.

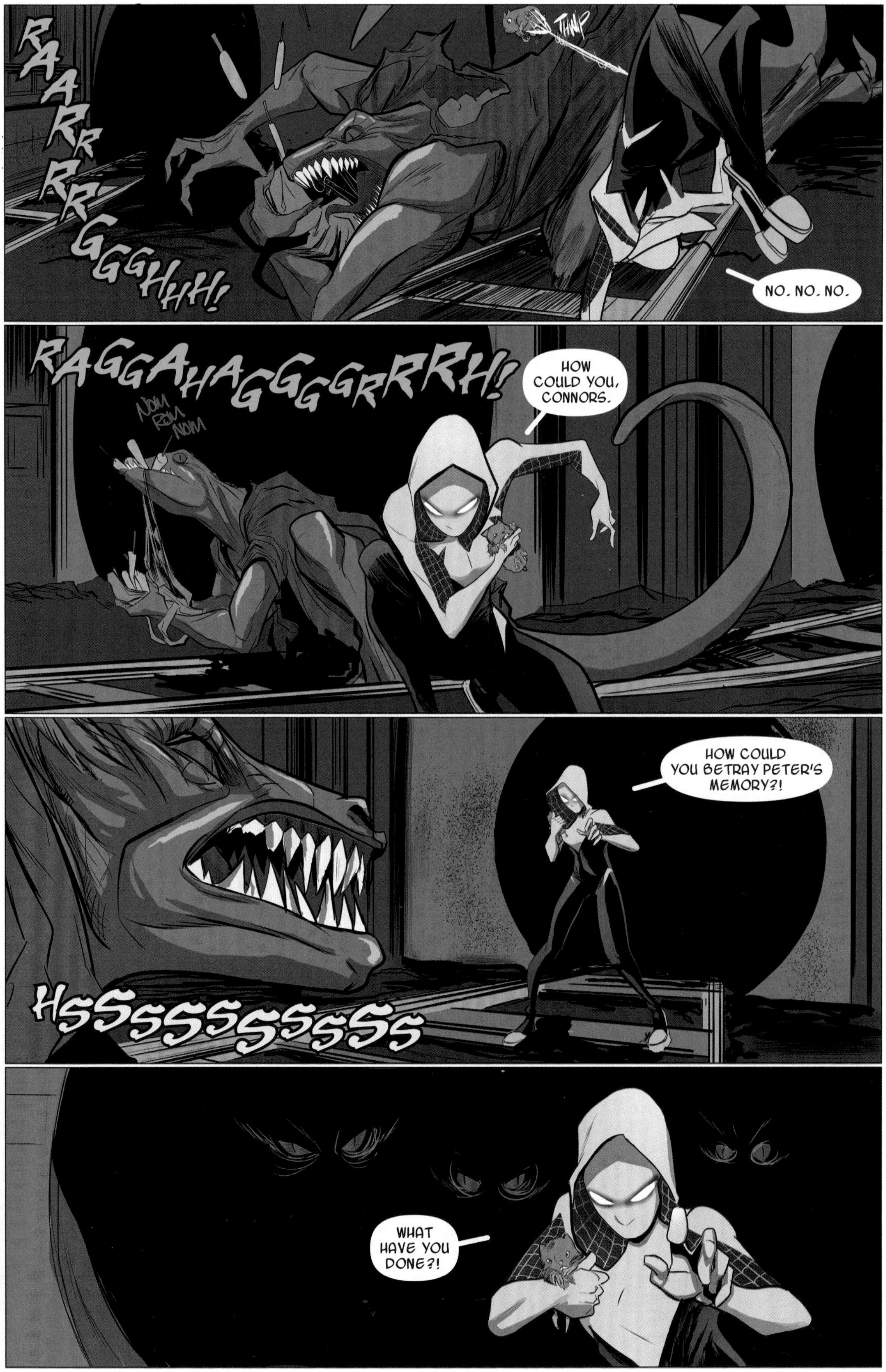
THWIP
RAARRRRGGGHHH!
NO. NO. NO.
RAGGAHAGGGGRRRH!
HOW COULD YOU, CONNORS.
HOW COULD YOU BETRAY PETER'S MEMORY?!
HSSSSSSSSSSS
WHAT HAVE YOU DONE?!

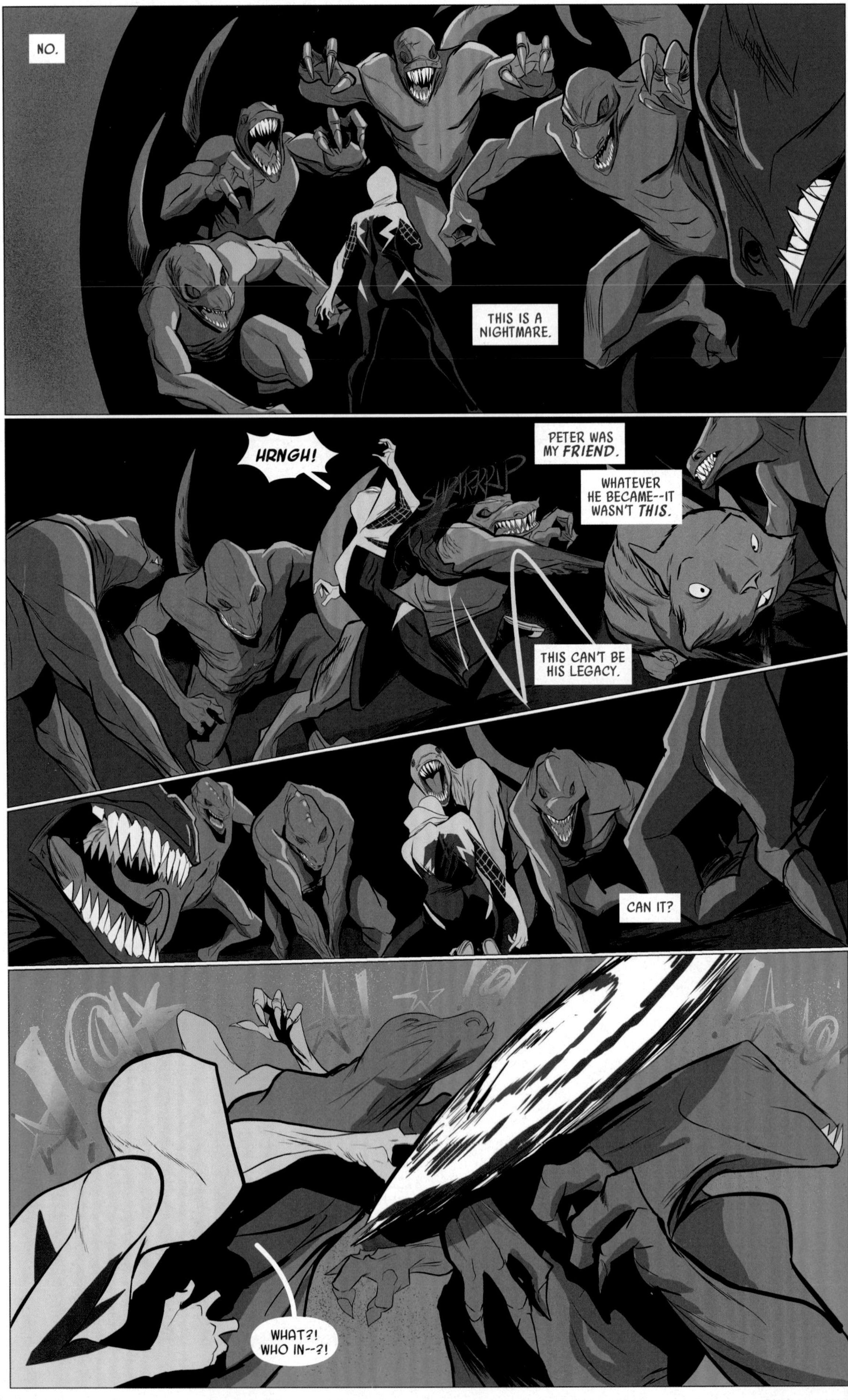
NO.
THIS IS A NIGHTMARE.
HRNGH!
PETER WAS MY *FRIEND*.
WHATEVER HE BECAME--IT WASN'T *THIS*.
THIS CAN'T BE HIS LEGACY.
CAN IT?
WHAT?! WHO IN--?!

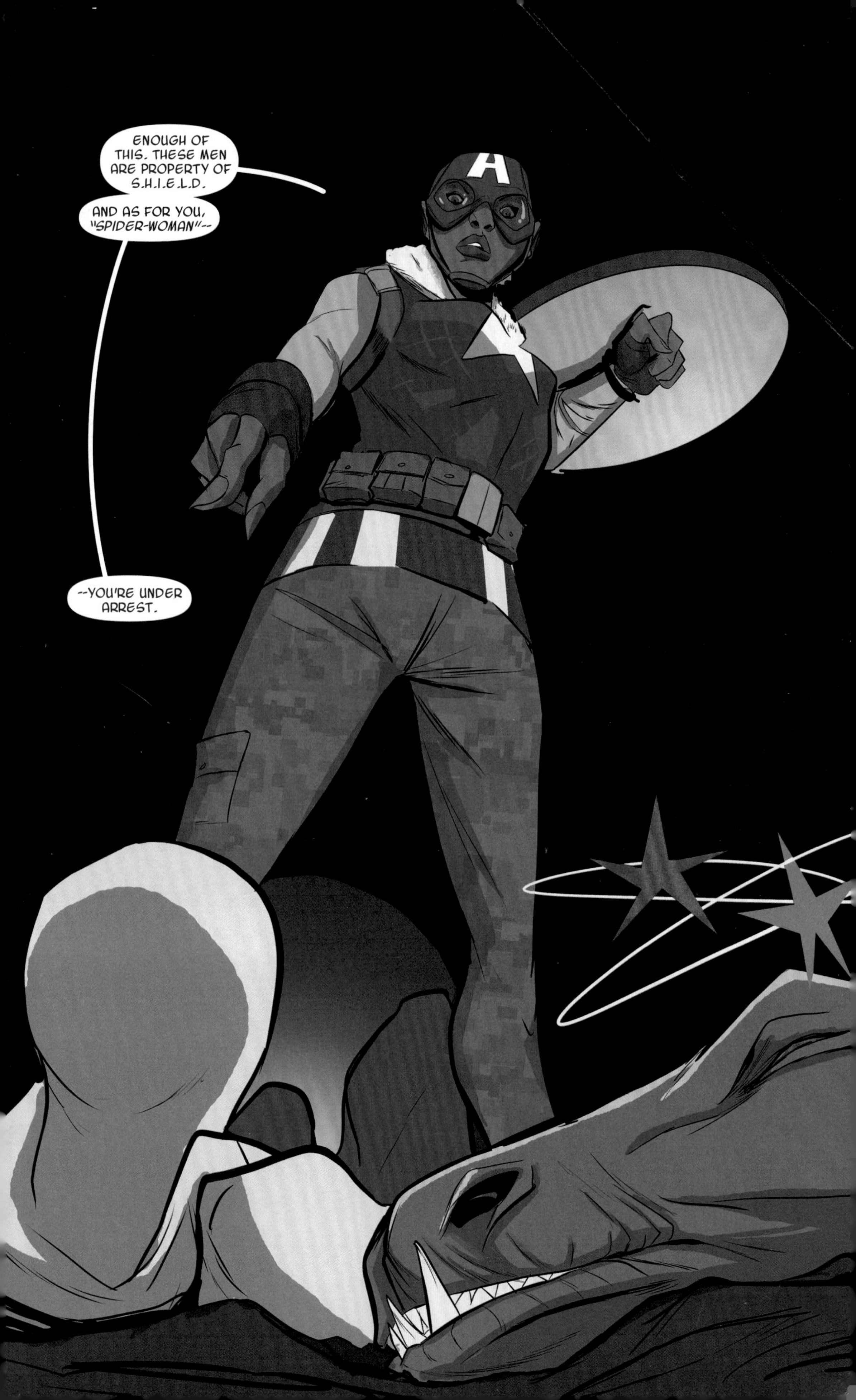
ENOUGH OF THIS. THESE MEN ARE PROPERTY OF S.H.I.E.L.D.
AND AS FOR YOU, "SPIDER-WOMAN"--
--YOU'RE UNDER ARREST.

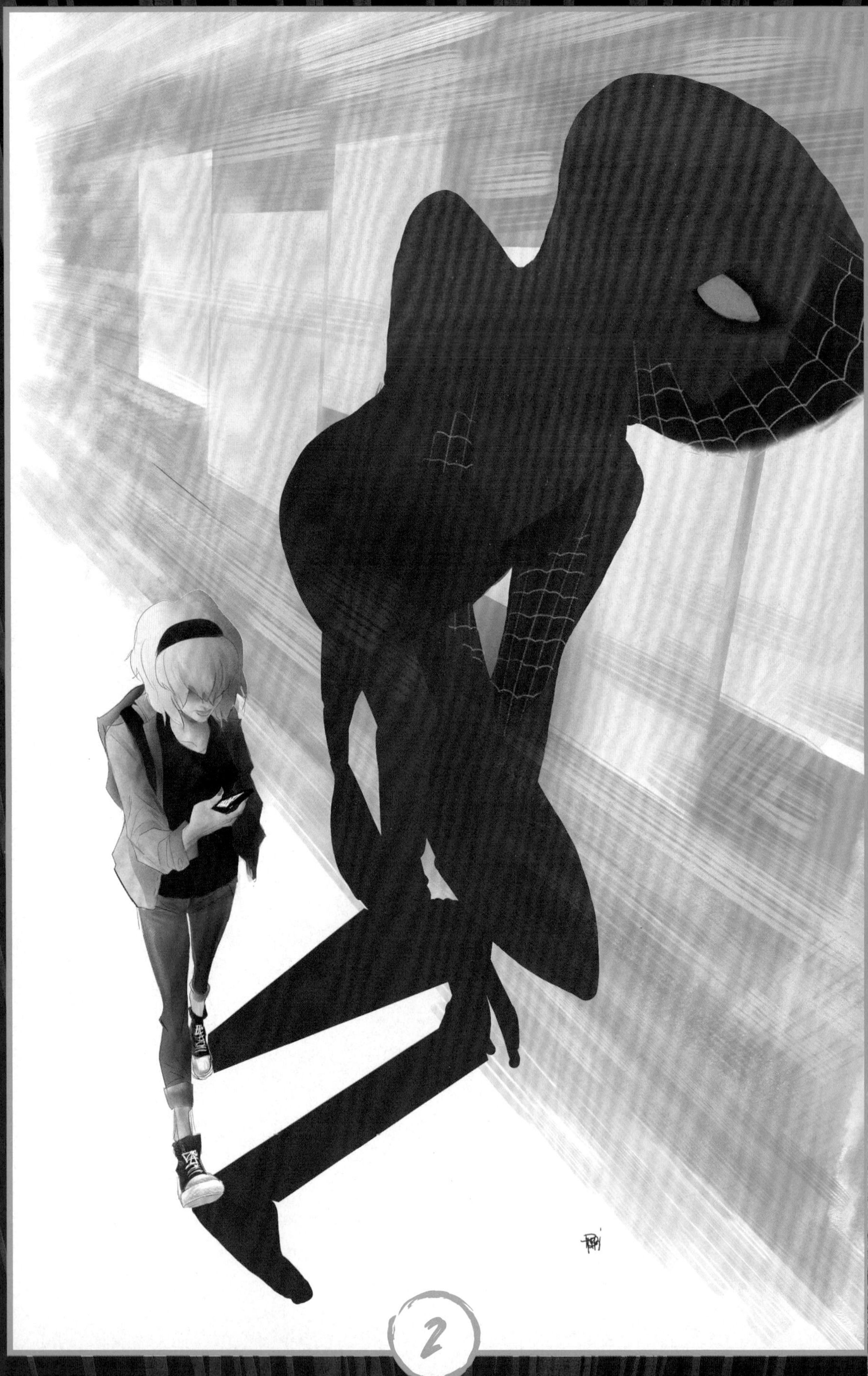
2

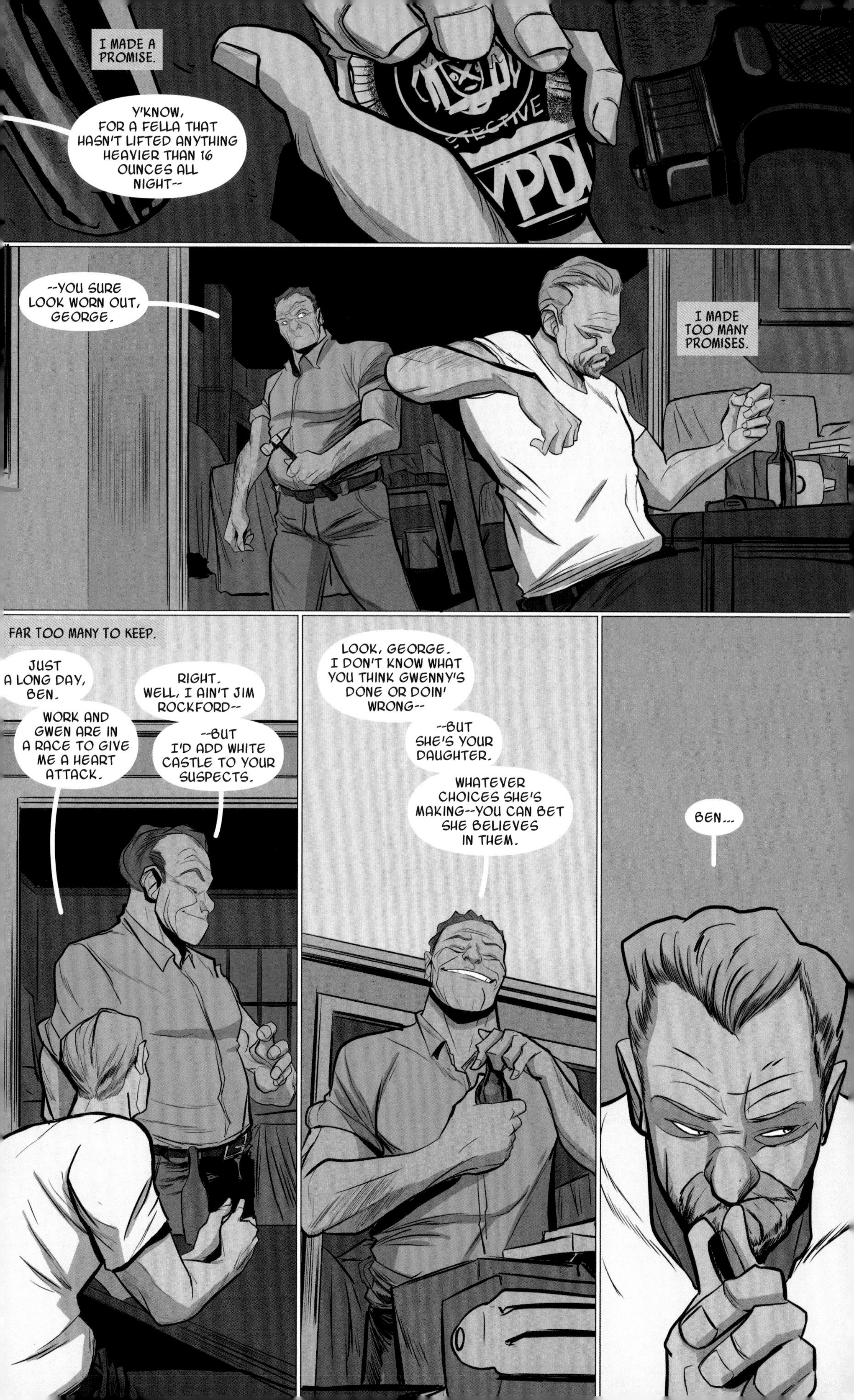
I MADE A PROMISE.
Y'KNOW, FOR A FELLA THAT HASN'T LIFTED ANYTHING HEAVIER THAN 16 OUNCES ALL NIGHT--
DETECTIVE
NYPD
--YOU SURE LOOK WORN OUT, GEORGE.
I MADE TOO MANY PROMISES.
FAR TOO MANY TO KEEP.
JUST A LONG DAY, BEN.
WORK AND GWEN ARE IN A RACE TO GIVE ME A HEART ATTACK.
RIGHT. WELL, I AIN'T JIM ROCKFORD--
--BUT I'D ADD WHITE CASTLE TO YOUR SUSPECTS.
LOOK, GEORGE. I DON'T KNOW WHAT YOU THINK GWENNY'S DONE OR DOIN' WRONG--
--BUT SHE'S YOUR DAUGHTER.
WHATEVER CHOICES SHE'S MAKING--YOU CAN BET SHE BELIEVES IN THEM.
BEN...

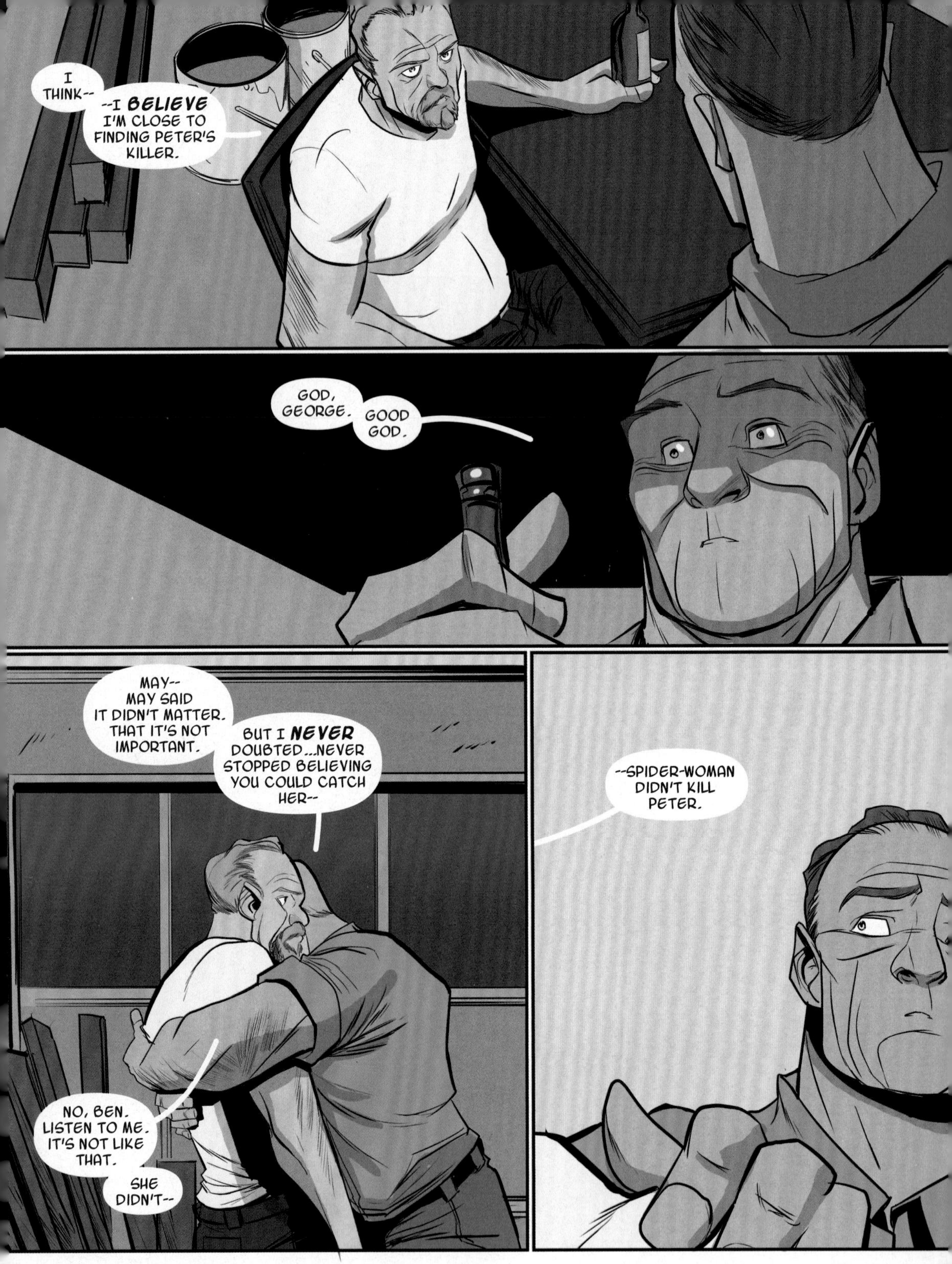
I THINK--
--I BELIEVE I'M CLOSE TO FINDING PETER'S KILLER.
GOD, GEORGE.
GOOD GOD.
MAY-- MAY SAID IT DIDN'T MATTER. THAT IT'S NOT IMPORTANT.
BUT I NEVER DOUBTED...NEVER STOPPED BELIEVING YOU COULD CATCH HER--
NO, BEN. LISTEN TO ME. IT'S NOT LIKE THAT.
SHE DIDN'T--
--SPIDER-WOMAN DIDN'T KILL PETER.

GREATER POWER

PART TWO

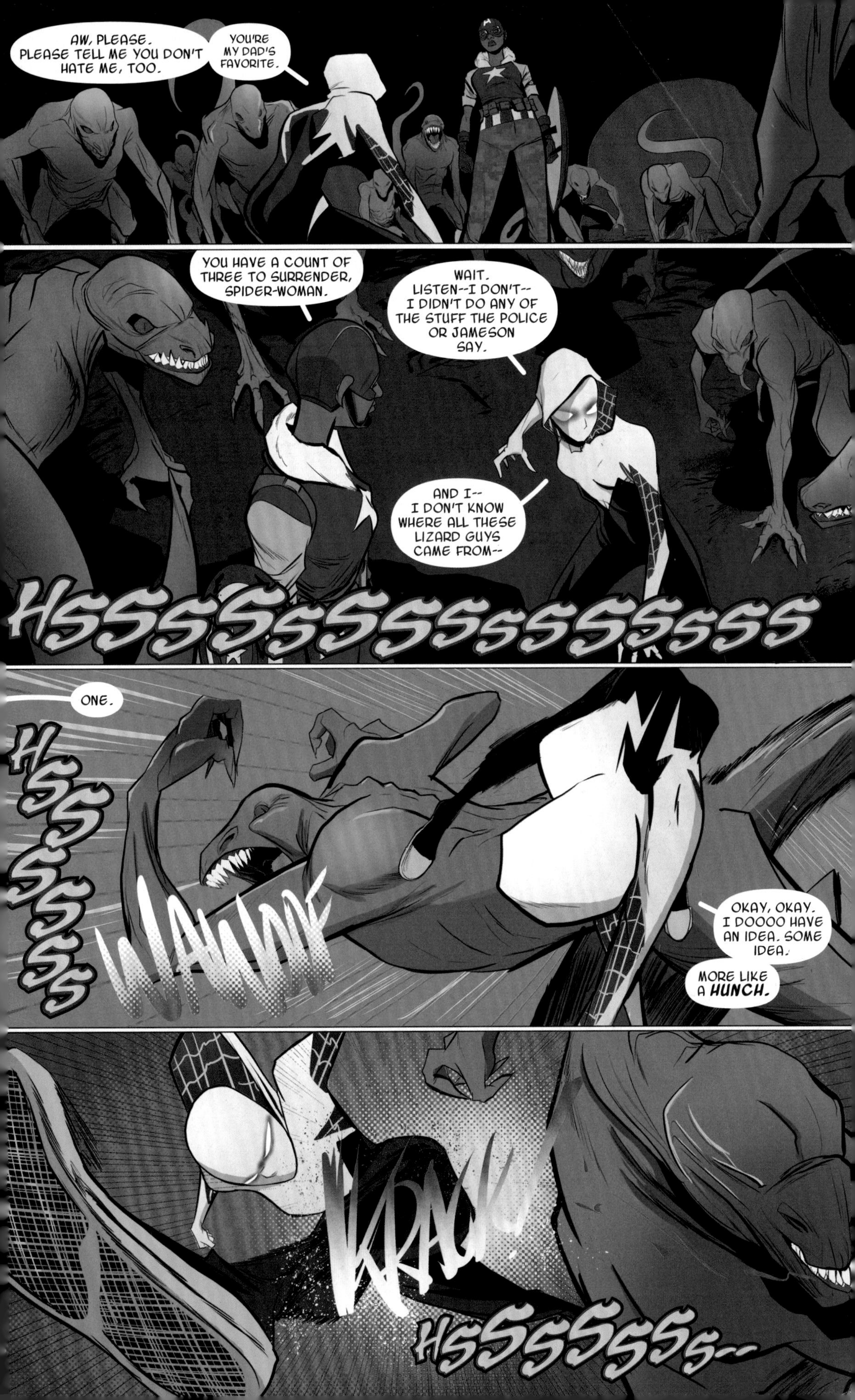
AW, PLEASE. PLEASE TELL ME YOU DON'T HATE ME, TOO.
YOU'RE MY DAD'S FAVORITE.
YOU HAVE A COUNT OF THREE TO SURRENDER, SPIDER-WOMAN.
WAIT. LISTEN--I DON'T-- I DIDN'T DO ANY OF THE STUFF THE POLICE OR JAMESON SAY.
AND I-- I DON'T KNOW WHERE ALL THESE LIZARD GUYS CAME FROM--
HSSSSsSSSSsSSSSsss
ONE.
HSSSSSSS
OKAY, OKAY. I DOOOO HAVE AN IDEA. SOME IDEA.
MORE LIKE A **HUNCH.**
HSSSSSSSs--

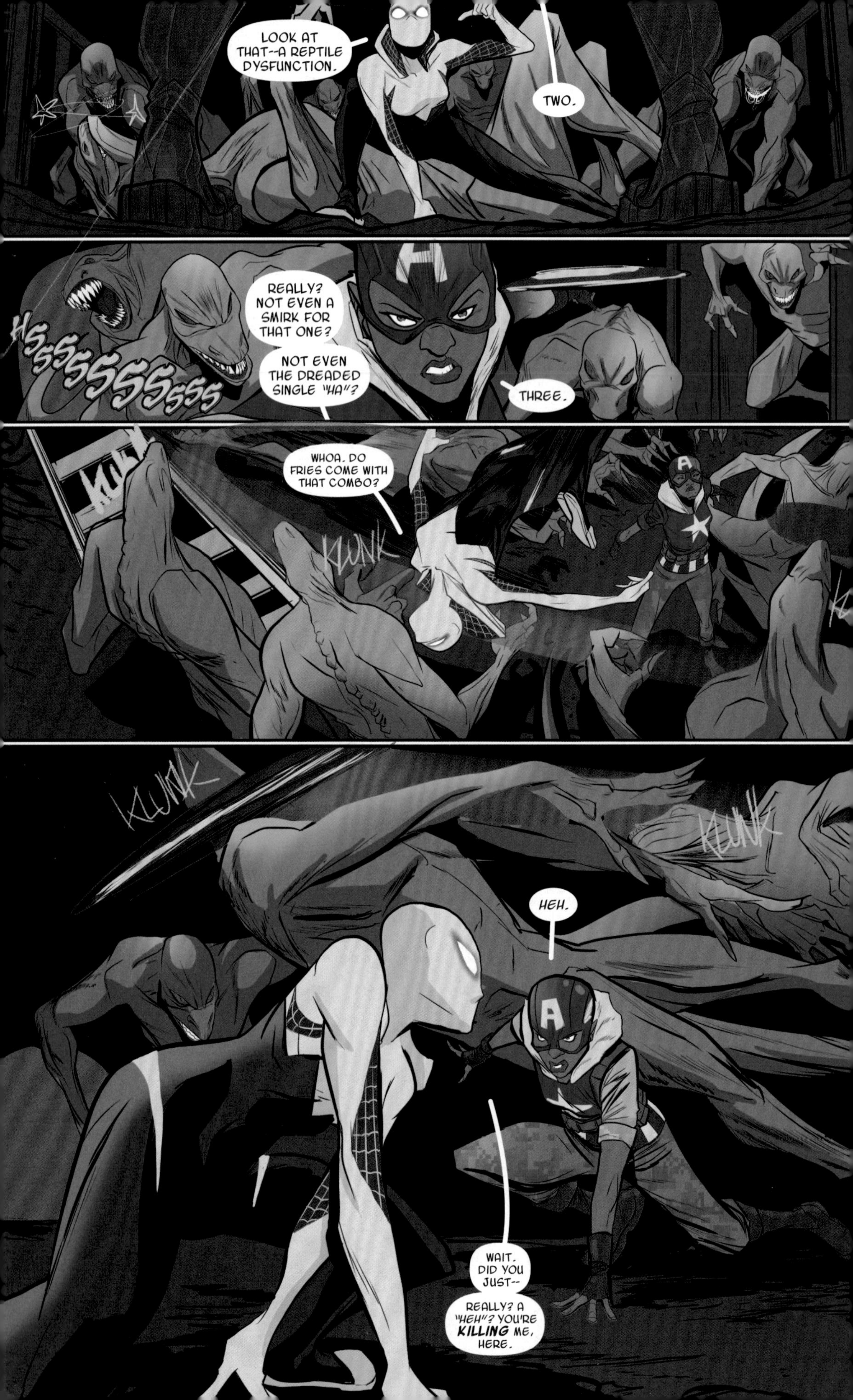
LOOK AT THAT--A REPTILE DYSFUNCTION.
TWO.
HSSSSSSSSSSS
REALLY? NOT EVEN A SMIRK FOR THAT ONE?
NOT EVEN THE DREADED SINGLE "HA"?
THREE.
WHOA. DO FRIES COME WITH THAT COMBO?
KLUNK
KLUNK
KLUNK
HEH.
WAIT. DID YOU JUST--
REALLY? A "HEH"? YOU'RE **KILLING** ME, HERE.

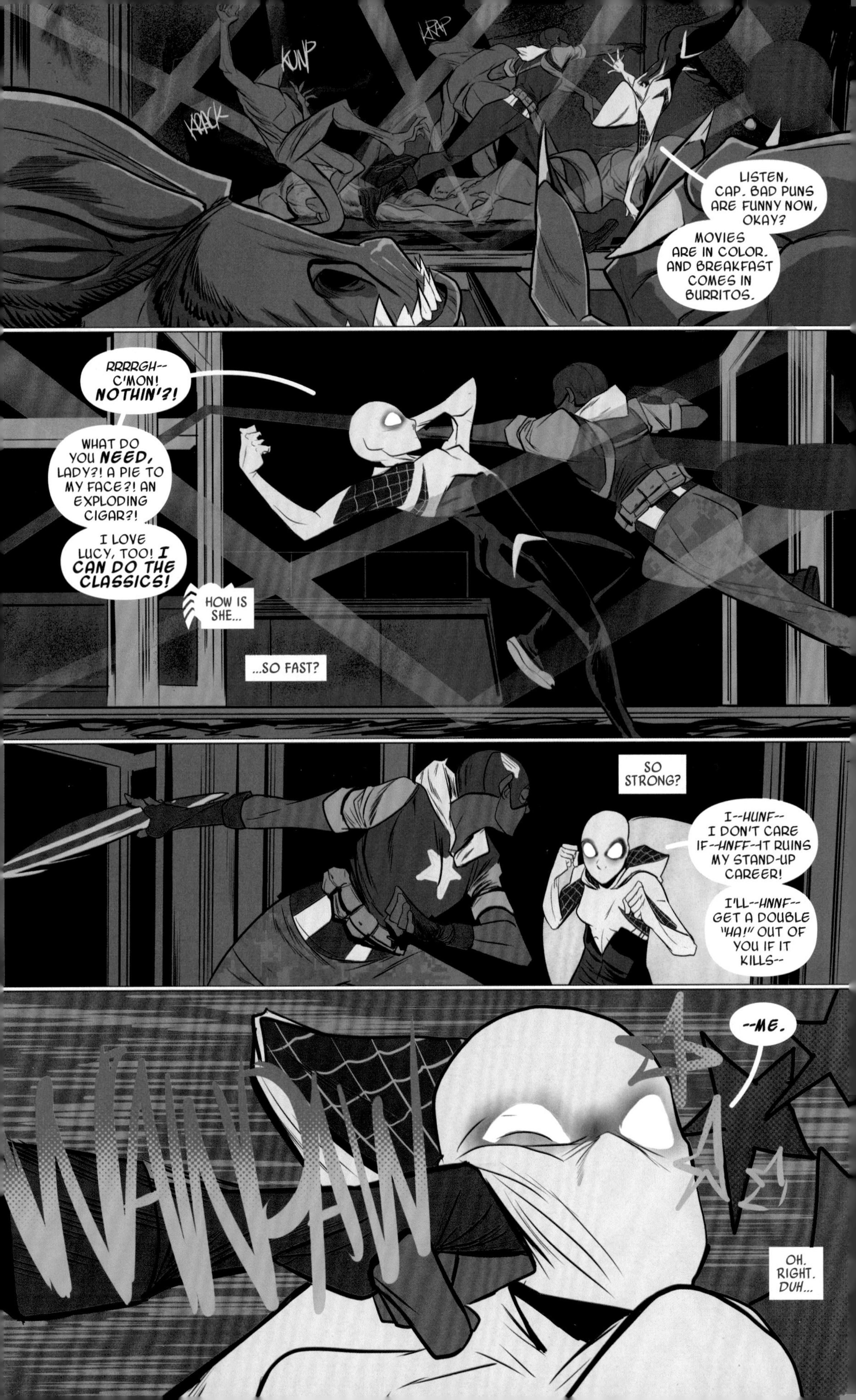
KUNP
KRAP
KRACK
LISTEN, CAP. BAD PUNS ARE FUNNY NOW, OKAY?
MOVIES ARE IN COLOR. AND BREAKFAST COMES IN BURRITOS.
RRRRGH-- C'MON! NOTHIN'?!
WHAT DO YOU NEED, LADY?! A PIE TO MY FACE?! AN EXPLODING CIGAR?!
I LOVE LUCY, TOO! I CAN DO THE CLASSICS!
HOW IS SHE...
...SO FAST?
SO STRONG?
I--HUNF-- I DON'T CARE IF--HNFF--IT RUINS MY STAND-UP CAREER!
I'LL--HNNF-- GET A DOUBLE "HA!" OUT OF YOU IF IT KILLS--
--ME.
WAMPAM
OH. RIGHT. DUH...

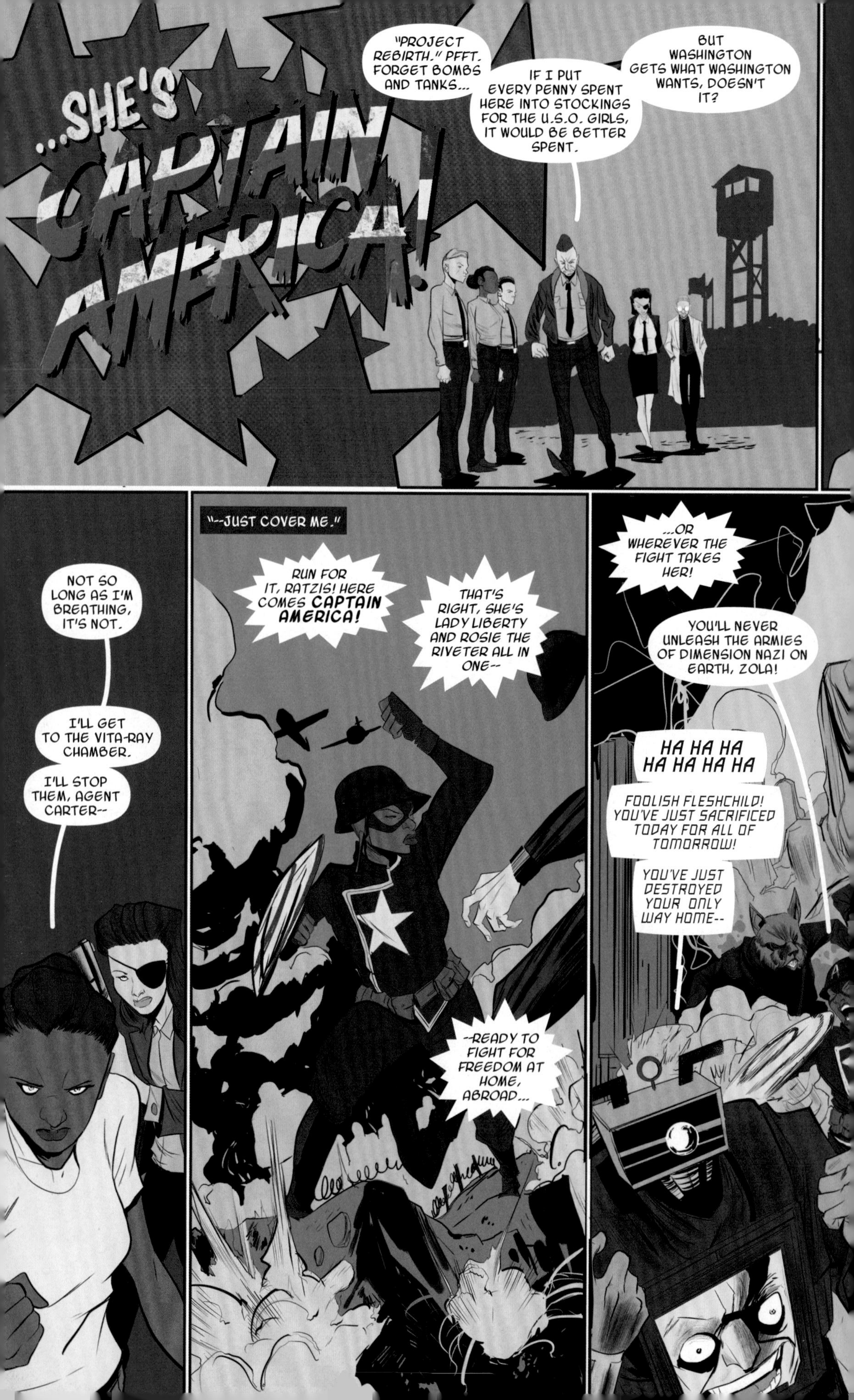
...SHE'S CAPTAIN AMERICA!
"PROJECT REBIRTH." PFFT. FORGET BOMBS AND TANKS...
IF I PUT EVERY PENNY SPENT HERE INTO STOCKINGS FOR THE U.S.O. GIRLS, IT WOULD BE BETTER SPENT.
BUT WASHINGTON GETS WHAT WASHINGTON WANTS, DOESN'T IT?
NOT SO LONG AS I'M BREATHING, IT'S NOT.
I'LL GET TO THE VITA-RAY CHAMBER.
I'LL STOP THEM, AGENT CARTER--
"--JUST COVER ME."
RUN FOR IT, RATZIS! HERE COMES CAPTAIN AMERICA!
THAT'S RIGHT, SHE'S LADY LIBERTY AND ROSIE THE RIVETER ALL IN ONE--
--READY TO FIGHT FOR FREEDOM AT HOME, ABROAD...
...OR WHEREVER THE FIGHT TAKES HER!
YOU'LL NEVER UNLEASH THE ARMIES OF DIMENSION NAZI ON EARTH, ZOLA!
HA HA HA HA HA HA HA
FOOLISH FLESHCHILD! YOU'VE JUST SACRIFICED TODAY FOR ALL OF TOMORROW!
YOU'VE JUST DESTROYED YOUR ONLY WAY HOME--

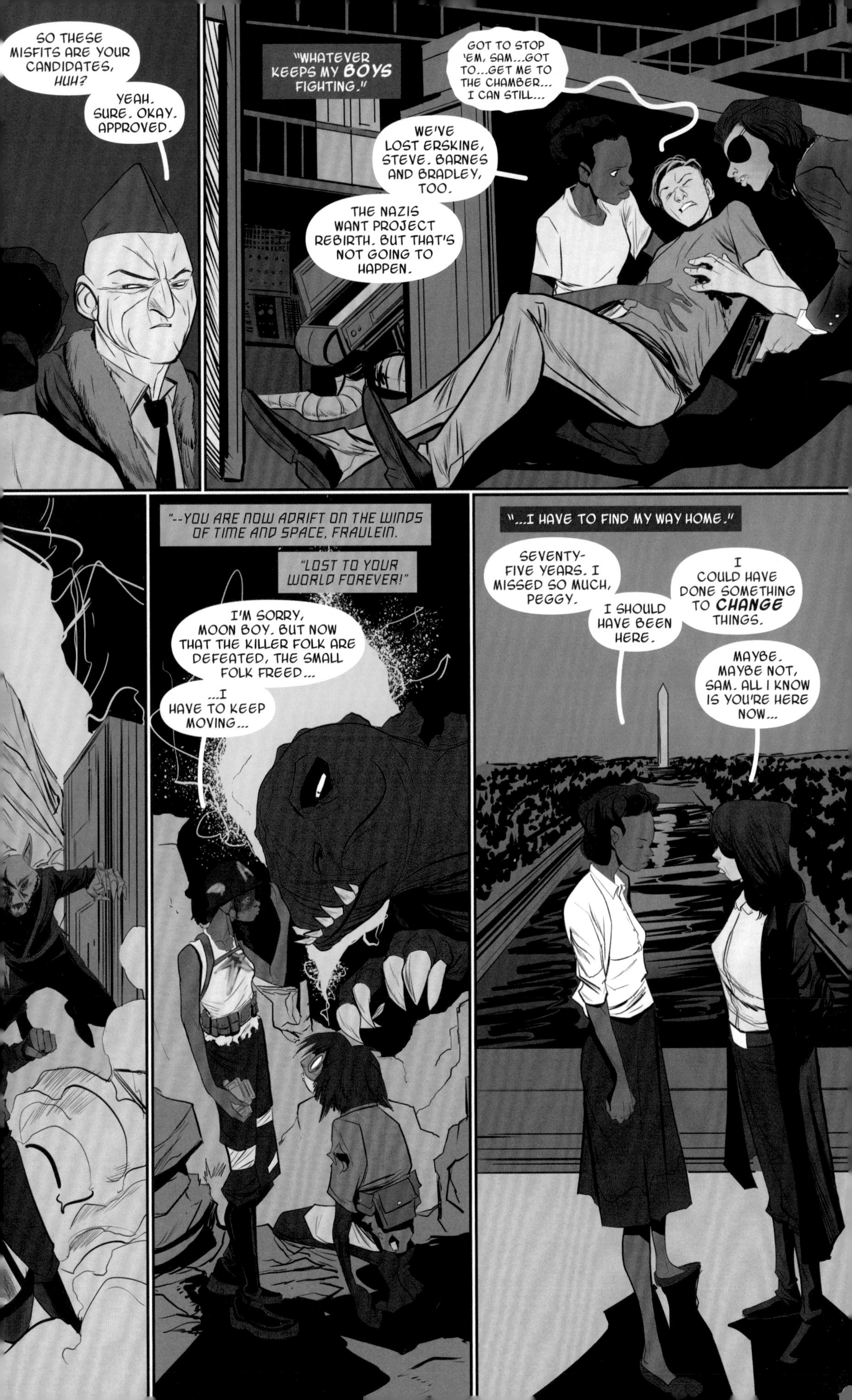
SO THESE MISFITS ARE YOUR CANDIDATES, HUH?
YEAH. SURE. OKAY. APPROVED.
"WHATEVER KEEPS MY BOYS FIGHTING."
GOT TO STOP 'EM, SAM...GOT TO...GET ME TO THE CHAMBER... I CAN STILL...
WE'VE LOST ERSKINE, STEVE. BARNES AND BRADLEY, TOO.
THE NAZIS WANT PROJECT REBIRTH. BUT THAT'S NOT GOING TO HAPPEN.
"--YOU ARE NOW ADRIFT ON THE WINDS OF TIME AND SPACE, FRAULEIN.
"LOST TO YOUR WORLD FOREVER!"
I'M SORRY, MOON BOY. BUT NOW THAT THE KILLER FOLK ARE DEFEATED, THE SMALL FOLK FREED...
...I HAVE TO KEEP MOVING...
"...I HAVE TO FIND MY WAY HOME."
SEVENTY-FIVE YEARS. I MISSED SO MUCH, PEGGY.
I SHOULD HAVE BEEN HERE.
I COULD HAVE DONE SOMETHING TO CHANGE THINGS.
MAYBE. MAYBE NOT, SAM. ALL I KNOW IS YOU'RE HERE NOW...

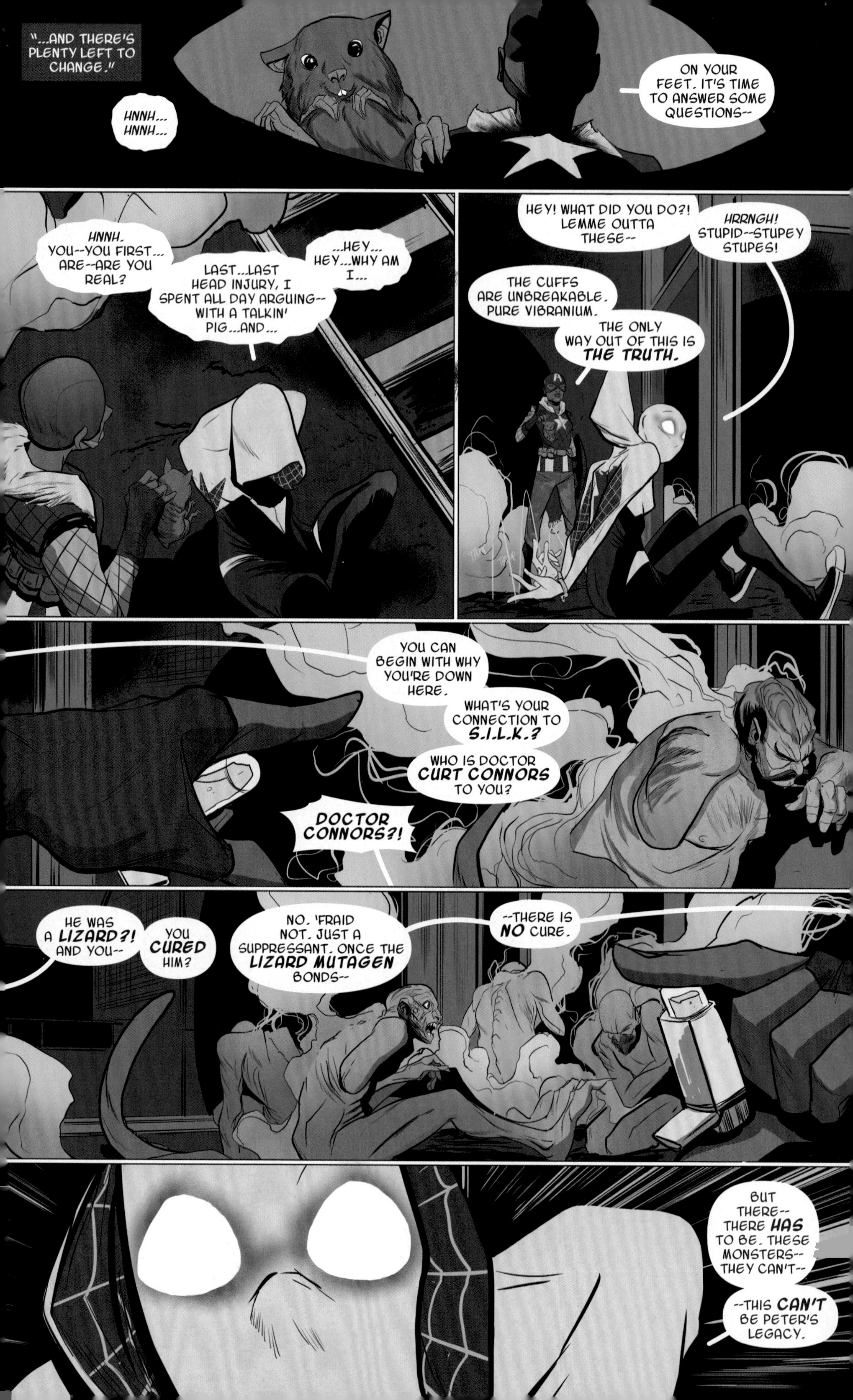

"...AND THERE'S PLENTY LEFT TO CHANGE."
HNNH... HNNH...
ON YOUR FEET. IT'S TIME TO ANSWER SOME QUESTIONS--
HNNH. YOU--YOU FIRST... ARE--ARE YOU REAL?
LAST...LAST HEAD INJURY, I SPENT ALL DAY ARGUING--WITH A TALKIN' PIG...AND...
...HEY... HEY...WHY AM I...
HEY! WHAT DID YOU DO?! LEMME OUTTA THESE--
HRRNGH! STUPID--STUPEY STUPES!
THE CUFFS ARE UNBREAKABLE. PURE VIBRANIUM.
THE ONLY WAY OUT OF THIS IS THE TRUTH.
YOU CAN BEGIN WITH WHY YOU'RE DOWN HERE.
WHAT'S YOUR CONNECTION TO S.I.L.K.?
WHO IS DOCTOR CURT CONNORS TO YOU?
DOCTOR CONNORS?!
HE WAS A LIZARD?! AND YOU--
YOU CURED HIM?
NO. 'FRAID NOT. JUST A SUPPRESSANT. ONCE THE LIZARD MUTAGEN BONDS--
--THERE IS NO CURE.
BUT THERE--THERE HAS TO BE. THESE MONSTERS--THEY CAN'T--
--THIS CAN'T BE PETER'S LEGACY.

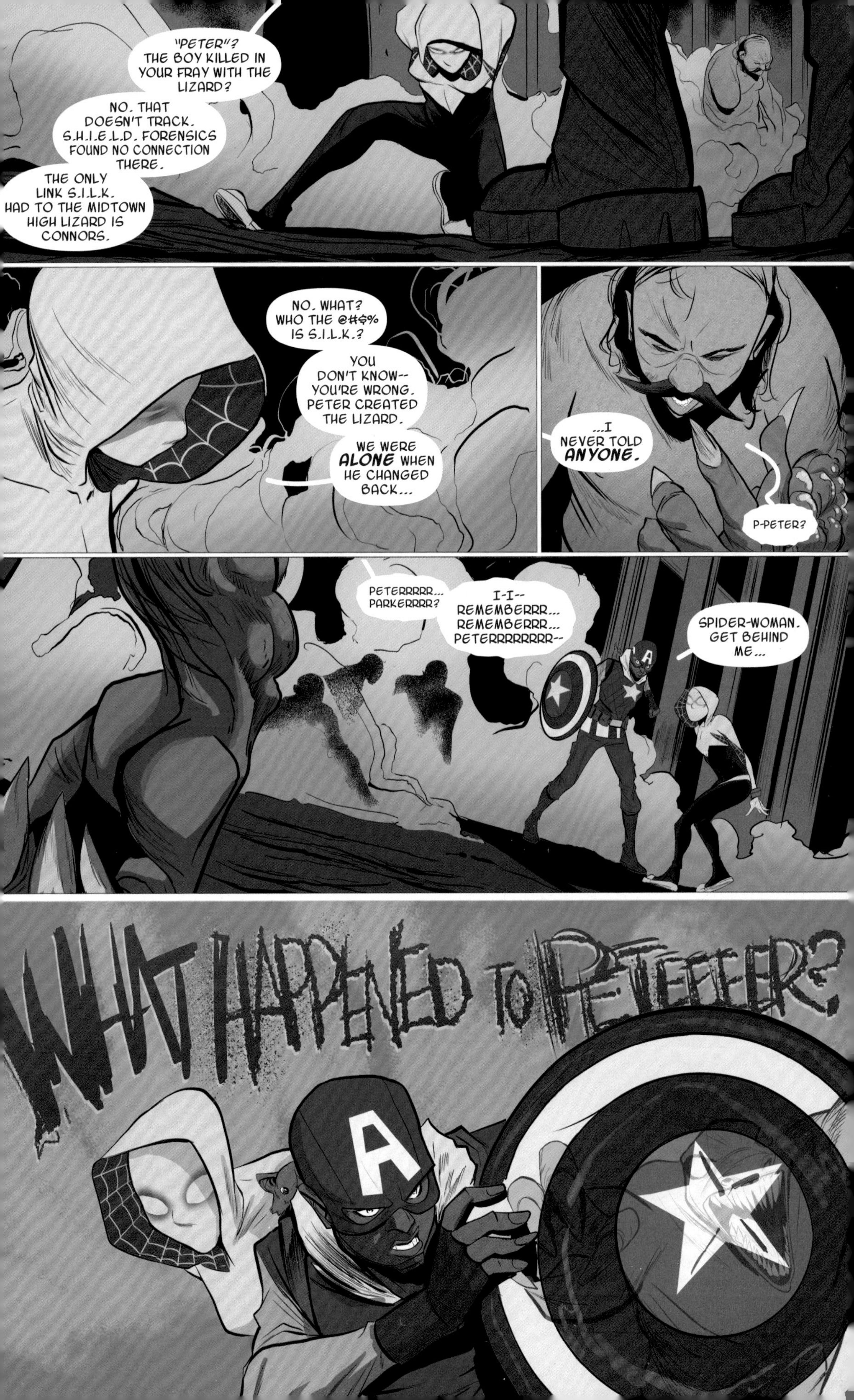
"PETER"? THE BOY KILLED IN YOUR FRAY WITH THE LIZARD?
NO. THAT DOESN'T TRACK. S.H.I.E.L.D. FORENSICS FOUND NO CONNECTION THERE.
THE ONLY LINK S.I.L.K. HAD TO THE MIDTOWN HIGH LIZARD IS CONNORS.
NO. WHAT? WHO THE @#$% IS S.I.L.K.?
YOU DON'T KNOW-- YOU'RE WRONG. PETER CREATED THE LIZARD.
WE WERE ALONE WHEN HE CHANGED BACK...
...I NEVER TOLD ANYONE.
P-PETER?
PETERRRRR... PARKERRRR?
I-I-- REMEMBERRR... REMEMBERRR... PETERRRRRRRR--
SPIDER-WOMAN. GET BEHIND ME...
WHAT HAPPENED TO PETEEEER?

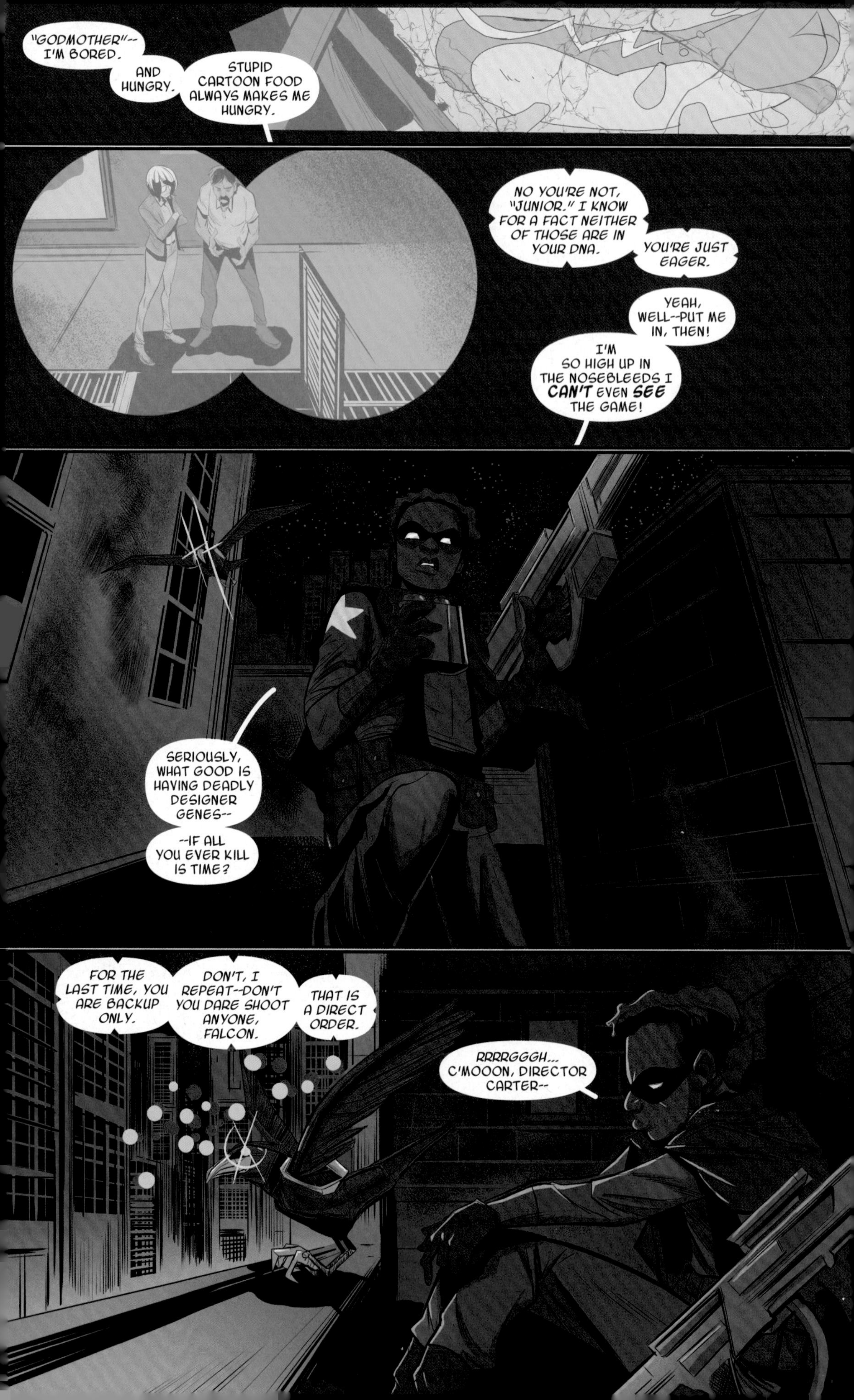
"GODMOTHER"-- I'M BORED.
AND HUNGRY.
STUPID CARTOON FOOD ALWAYS MAKES ME HUNGRY.
NO YOU'RE NOT, "JUNIOR." I KNOW FOR A FACT NEITHER OF THOSE ARE IN YOUR DNA.
YOU'RE JUST EAGER.
YEAH, WELL--PUT ME IN, THEN!
I'M SO HIGH UP IN THE NOSEBLEEDS I CAN'T EVEN SEE THE GAME!
SERIOUSLY, WHAT GOOD IS HAVING DEADLY DESIGNER GENES--
--IF ALL YOU EVER KILL IS TIME?
FOR THE LAST TIME, YOU ARE BACKUP ONLY.
DON'T, I REPEAT--DON'T YOU DARE SHOOT ANYONE, FALCON.
THAT IS A DIRECT ORDER.
RRRRGGGH... C'MOOON, DIRECTOR CARTER--

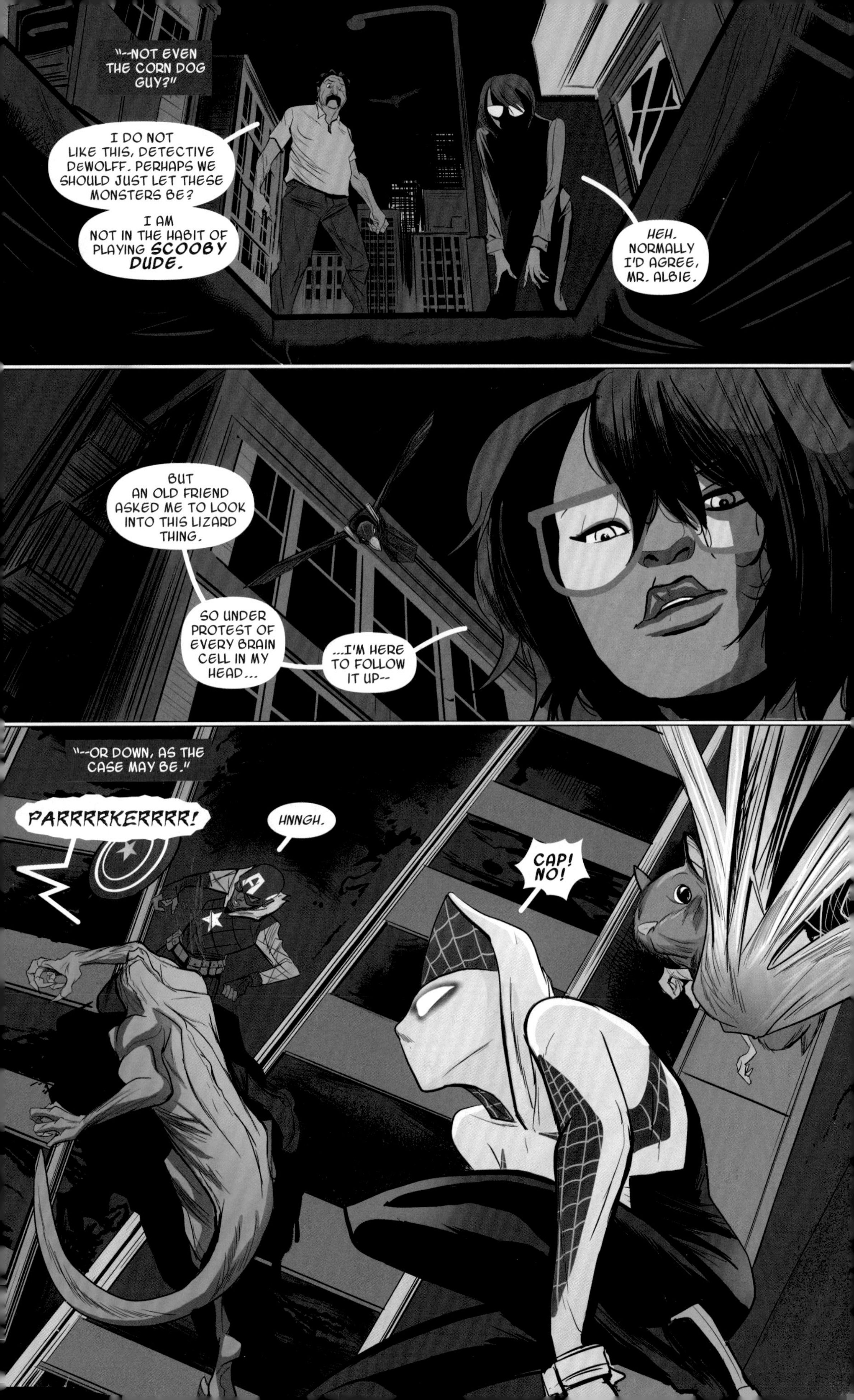
"--NOT EVEN THE CORN DOG GUY?"
I DO NOT LIKE THIS, DETECTIVE DEWOLFF. PERHAPS WE SHOULD JUST LET THESE MONSTERS BE?
I AM NOT IN THE HABIT OF PLAYING SCOOBY DUDE.
HEH. NORMALLY I'D AGREE, MR. ALBIE.
BUT AN OLD FRIEND ASKED ME TO LOOK INTO THIS LIZARD THING.
SO UNDER PROTEST OF EVERY BRAIN CELL IN MY HEAD...
...I'M HERE TO FOLLOW IT UP--
"--OR DOWN, AS THE CASE MAY BE."
PARRRRKERRRR!
HNNGH.
CAP! NO!

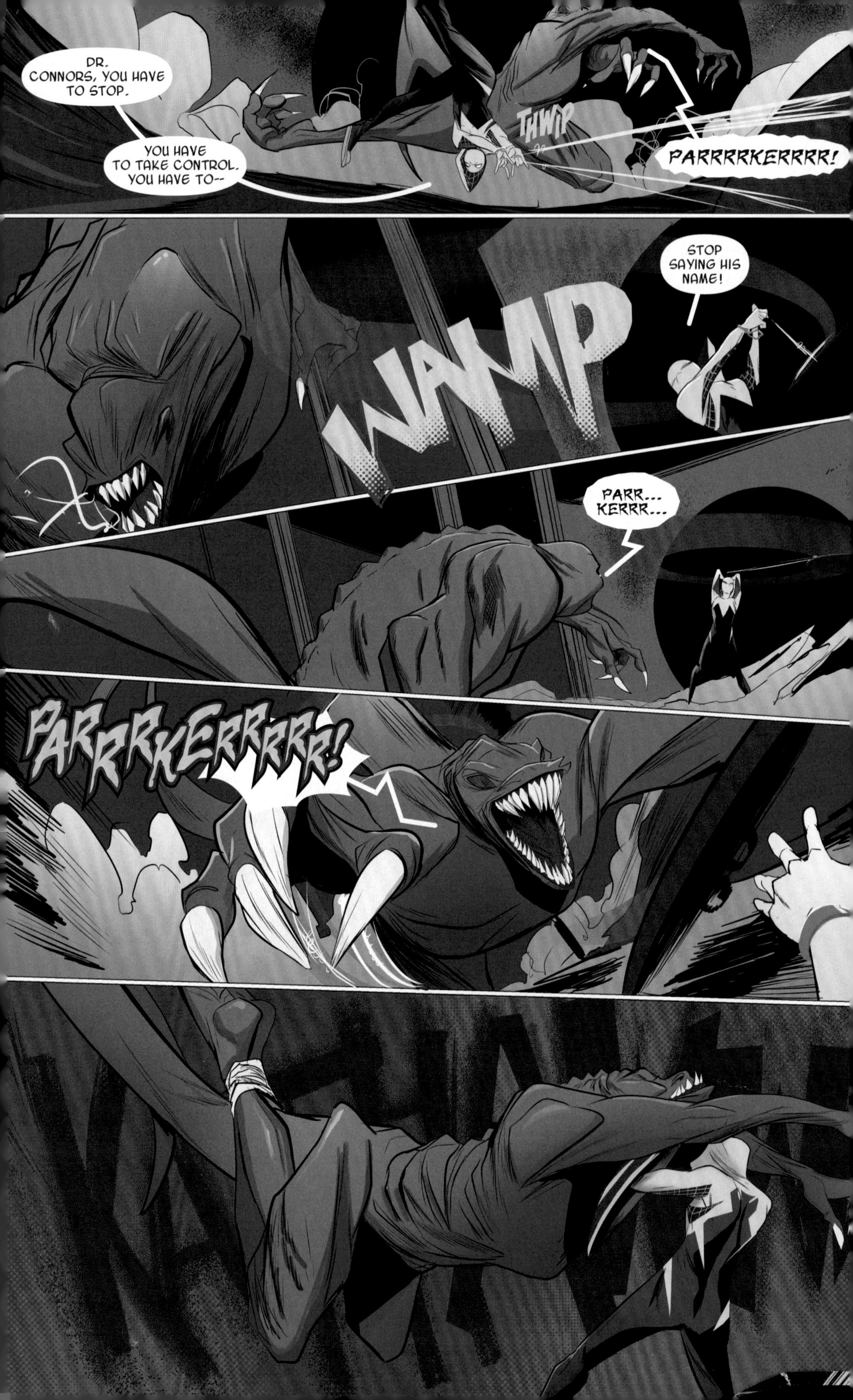
DR. CONNORS, YOU HAVE TO STOP.
YOU HAVE TO TAKE CONTROL. YOU HAVE TO--
THWIP
PARRRRKERRRR!
STOP SAYING HIS NAME!
WAMP
PARR... KERRR...
PARRRKERRRRR!

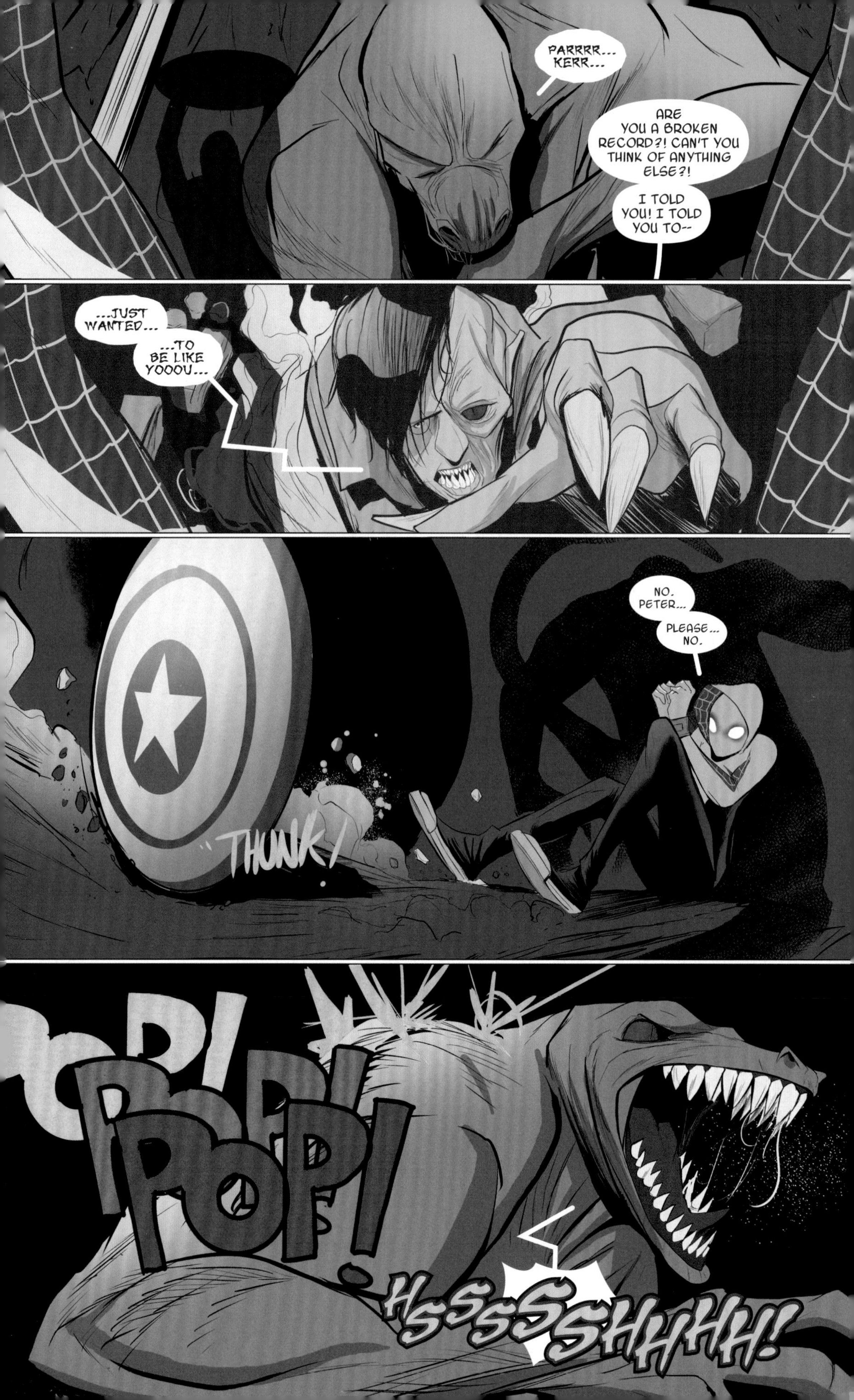
PARRRR... KERR...
ARE YOU A BROKEN RECORD?! CAN'T YOU THINK OF ANYTHING ELSE?!
I TOLD YOU! I TOLD YOU TO--
...JUST WANTED...
...TO BE LIKE YOOOU...
NO. PETER...
PLEASE... NO.
THUNK!
POP! POP! POP!
HSSSSSHHHH!

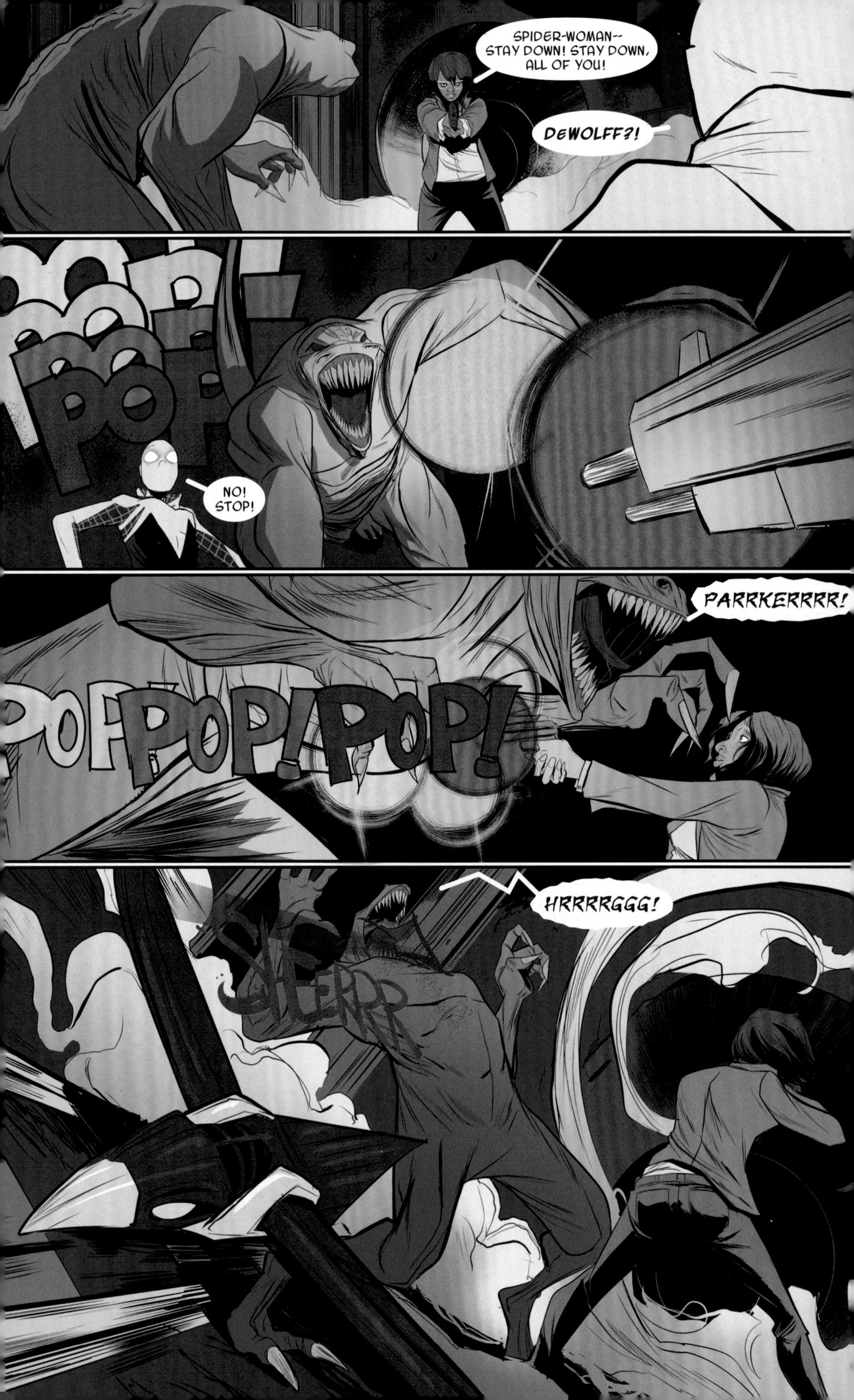
SPIDER-WOMAN-- STAY DOWN! STAY DOWN, ALL OF YOU!
DeWOLFF?!
POP POP POP POP
NO! STOP!
PARRKERRRR!
POP POP! POP!
HRRRRGGG!
SKERRR

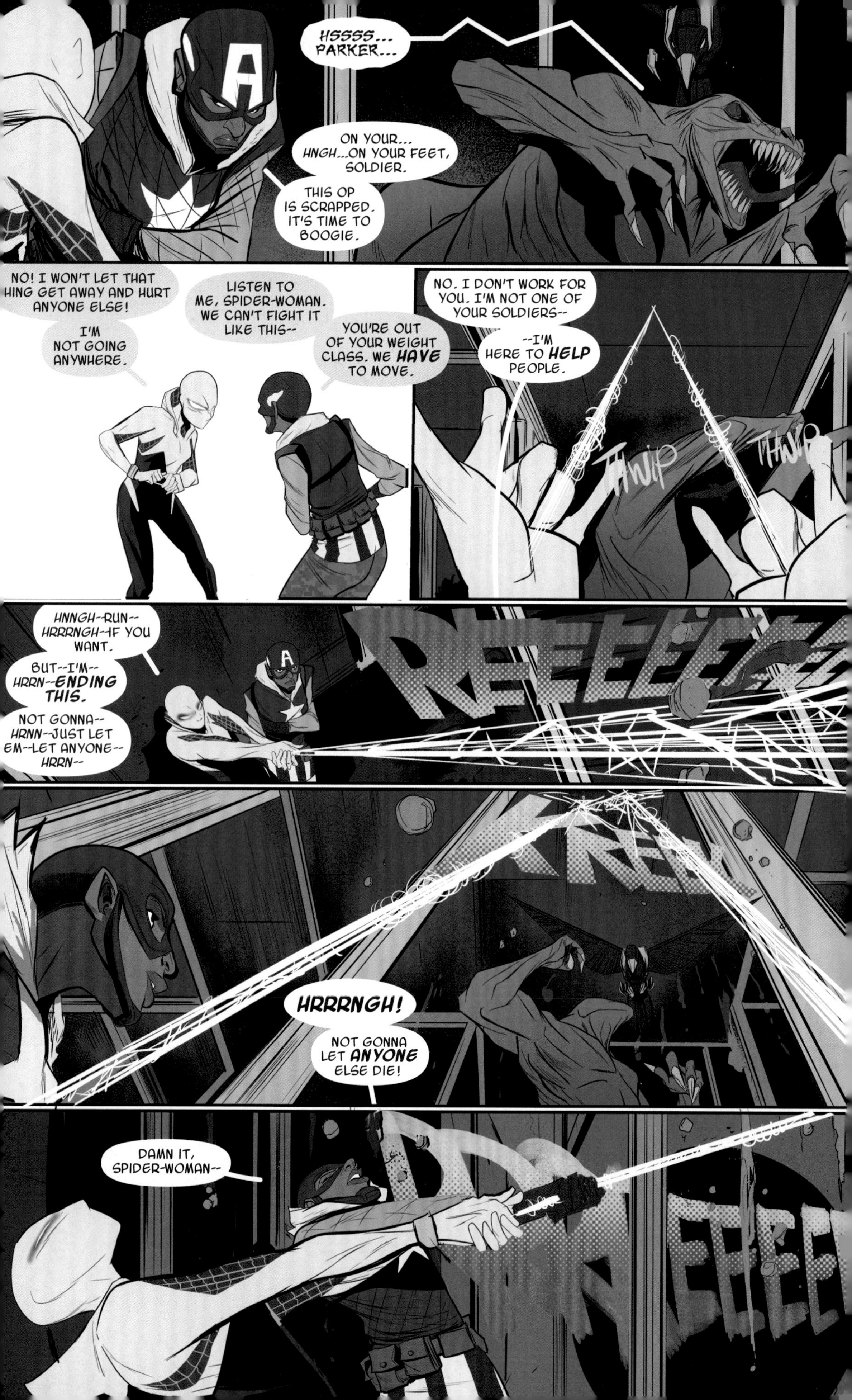
HSSSS... PARKER...
ON YOUR... HNGH...ON YOUR FEET, SOLDIER.
THIS OP IS SCRAPPED. IT'S TIME TO BOOGIE.
NO! I WON'T LET THAT HING GET AWAY AND HURT ANYONE ELSE!
I'M NOT GOING ANYWHERE.
LISTEN TO ME, SPIDER-WOMAN. WE CAN'T FIGHT IT LIKE THIS--
YOU'RE OUT OF YOUR WEIGHT CLASS. WE HAVE TO MOVE.
NO. I DON'T WORK FOR YOU. I'M NOT ONE OF YOUR SOLDIERS--
--I'M HERE TO HELP PEOPLE.
THWIP
THWIP
HNNGH--RUN--HRRRNGH--IF YOU WANT.
BUT--I'M--HRRN--ENDING THIS.
NOT GONNA--HRNN--JUST LET EM--LET ANYONE--HRRN--
REEEEEE
KRAK
HRRRNGH!
NOT GONNA LET ANYONE ELSE DIE!
DAMN IT, SPIDER-WOMAN--
REEEEE

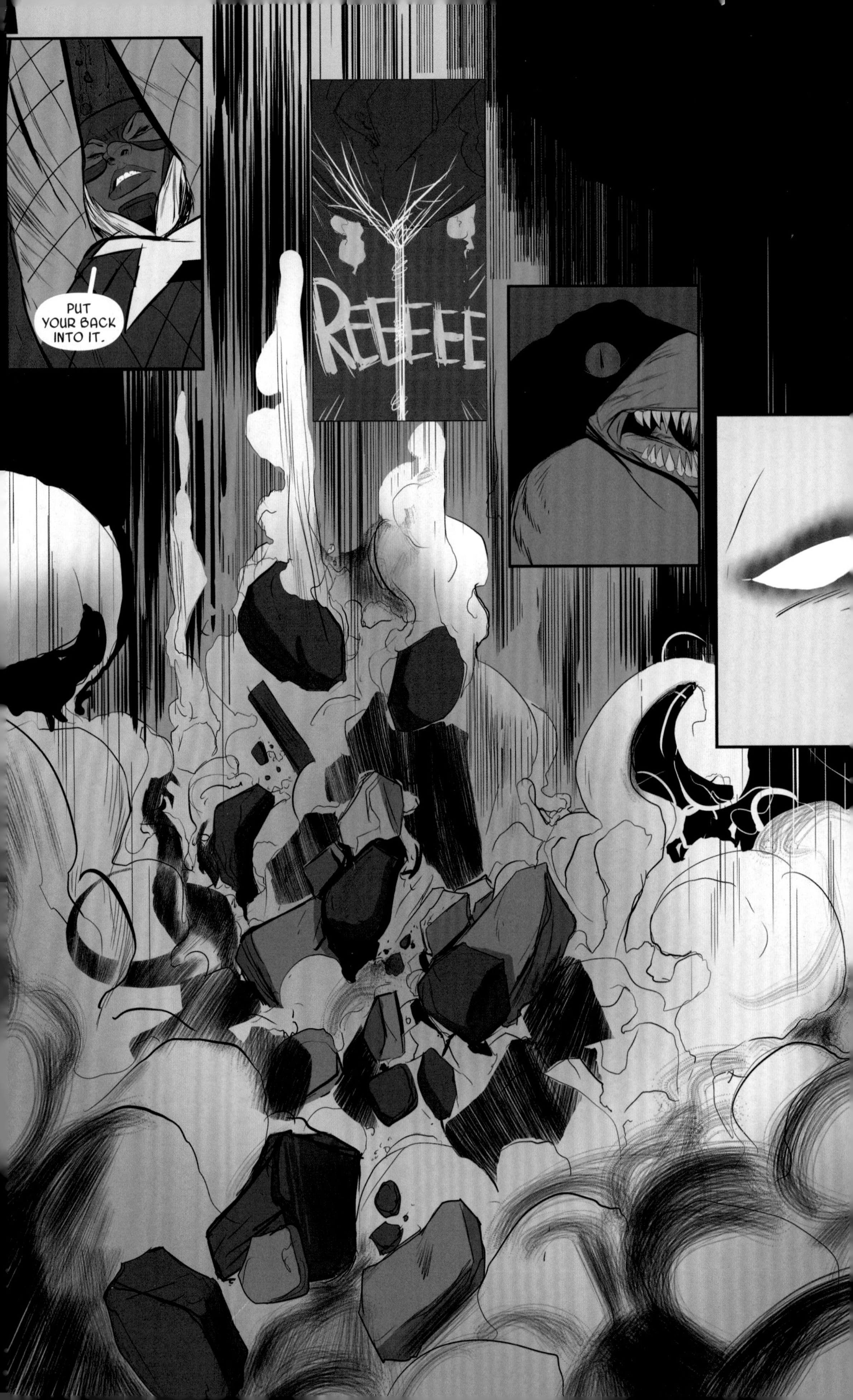
PUT YOUR BACK INTO IT.
REEEEE

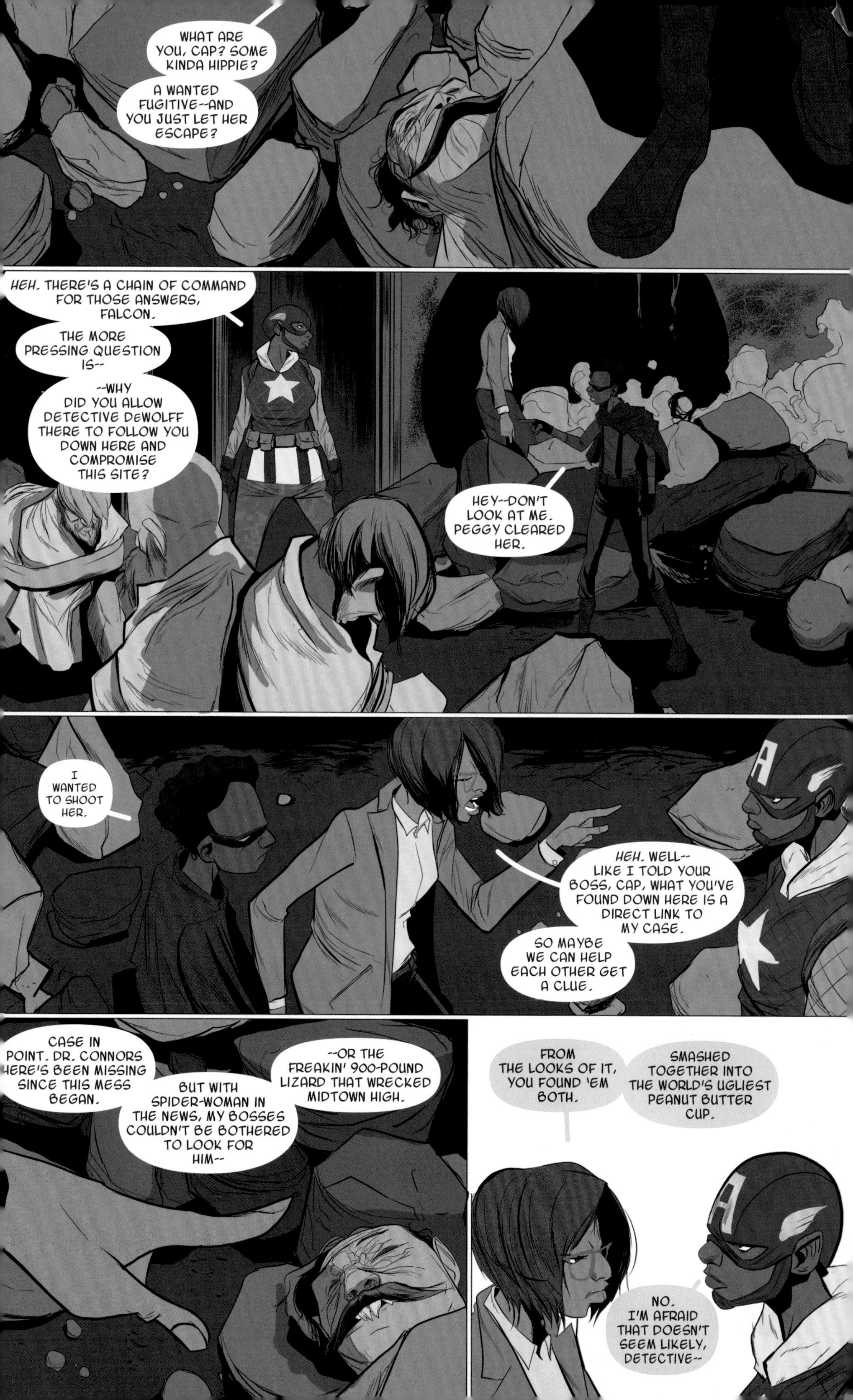

WHAT ARE YOU, CAP? SOME KINDA HIPPIE?
A WANTED FUGITIVE--AND YOU JUST LET HER ESCAPE?
HEH. THERE'S A CHAIN OF COMMAND FOR THOSE ANSWERS, FALCON.
THE MORE PRESSING QUESTION IS--
--WHY DID YOU ALLOW DETECTIVE DeWOLFF THERE TO FOLLOW YOU DOWN HERE AND COMPROMISE THIS SITE?
HEY--DON'T LOOK AT ME. PEGGY CLEARED HER.
I WANTED TO SHOOT HER.
HEH. WELL--LIKE I TOLD YOUR BOSS, CAP, WHAT YOU'VE FOUND DOWN HERE IS A DIRECT LINK TO MY CASE.
SO MAYBE WE CAN HELP EACH OTHER GET A CLUE.
CASE IN POINT. DR. CONNORS HERE'S BEEN MISSING SINCE THIS MESS BEGAN.
BUT WITH SPIDER-WOMAN IN THE NEWS, MY BOSSES COULDN'T BE BOTHERED TO LOOK FOR HIM--
--OR THE FREAKIN' 900-POUND LIZARD THAT WRECKED MIDTOWN HIGH.
FROM THE LOOKS OF IT, YOU FOUND 'EM BOTH.
SMASHED TOGETHER INTO THE WORLD'S UGLIEST PEANUT BUTTER CUP.
NO. I'M AFRAID THAT DOESN'T SEEM LIKELY, DETECTIVE--

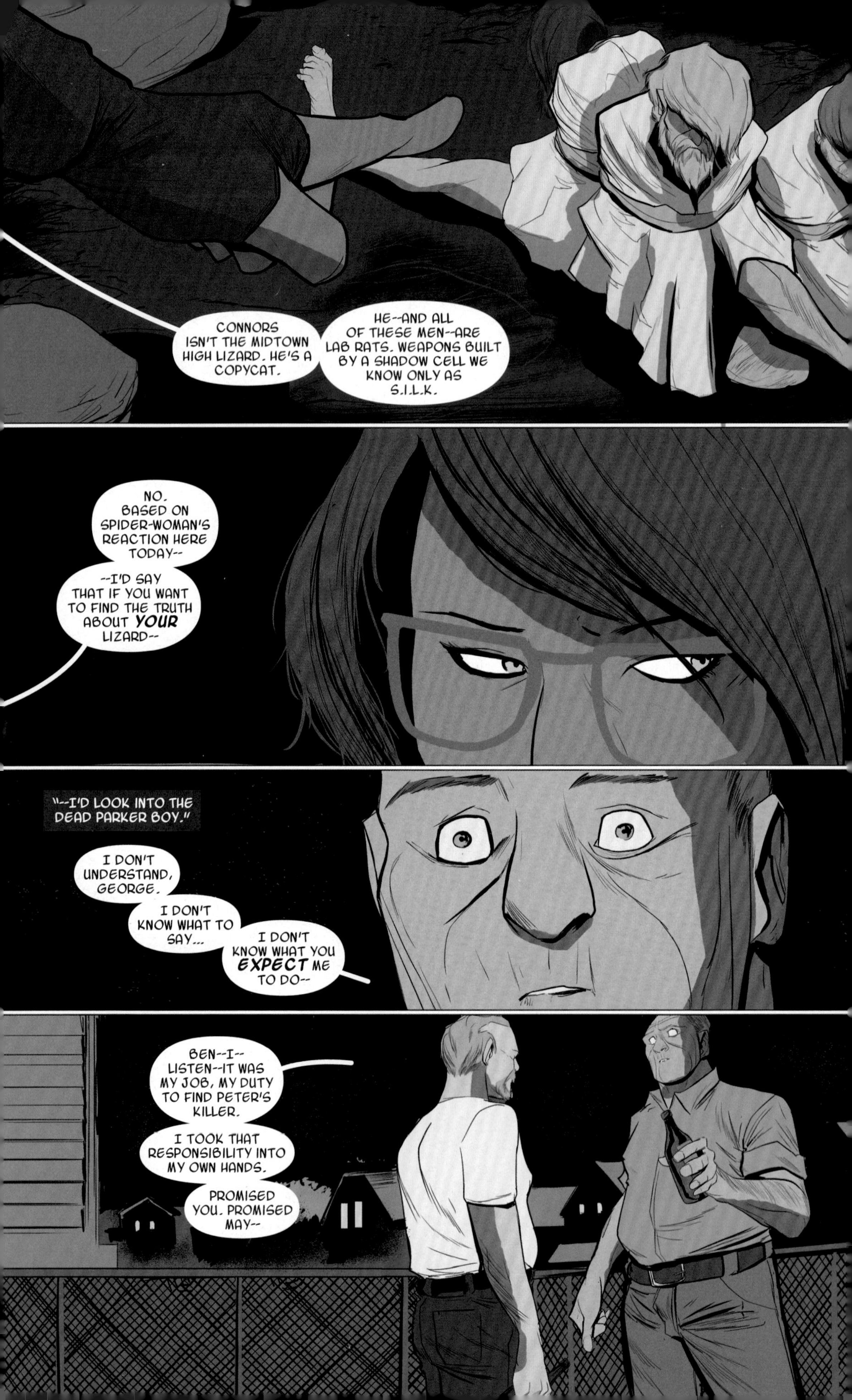
CONNORS ISN'T THE MIDTOWN HIGH LIZARD. HE'S A COPYCAT.
HE--AND ALL OF THESE MEN--ARE LAB RATS. WEAPONS BUILT BY A SHADOW CELL WE KNOW ONLY AS S.I.L.K.
NO. BASED ON SPIDER-WOMAN'S REACTION HERE TODAY--
--I'D SAY THAT IF YOU WANT TO FIND THE TRUTH ABOUT YOUR LIZARD--
"--I'D LOOK INTO THE DEAD PARKER BOY."
I DON'T UNDERSTAND, GEORGE.
I DON'T KNOW WHAT TO SAY...
I DON'T KNOW WHAT YOU EXPECT ME TO DO--
BEN--I--LISTEN--IT WAS MY JOB, MY DUTY TO FIND PETER'S KILLER.
I TOOK THAT RESPONSIBILITY INTO MY OWN HANDS.
PROMISED YOU. PROMISED MAY--

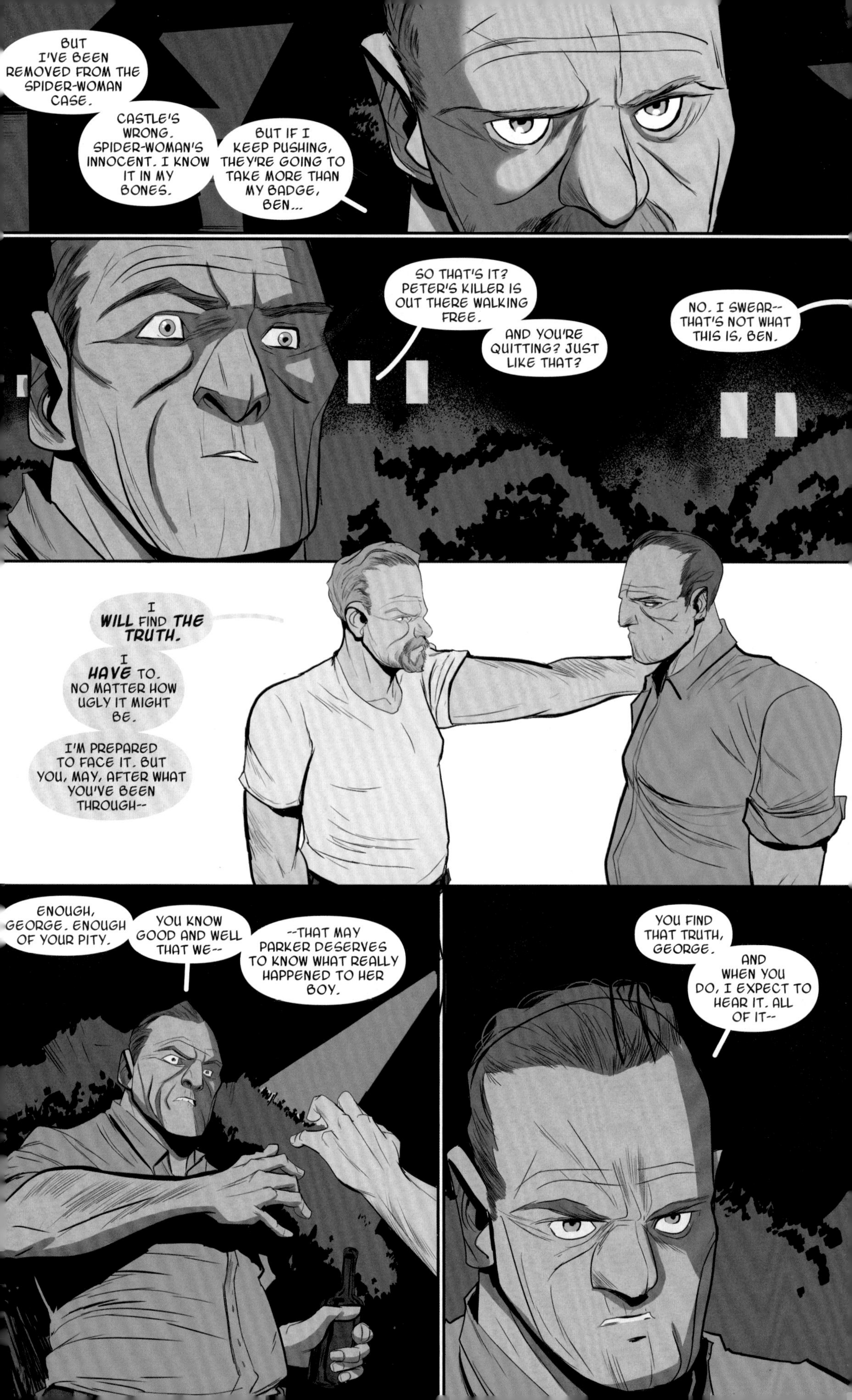
BUT I'VE BEEN REMOVED FROM THE SPIDER-WOMAN CASE.
CASTLE'S WRONG. SPIDER-WOMAN'S INNOCENT. I KNOW IT IN MY BONES.
BUT IF I KEEP PUSHING, THEY'RE GOING TO TAKE MORE THAN MY BADGE, BEN...
SO THAT'S IT? PETER'S KILLER IS OUT THERE WALKING FREE.
AND YOU'RE QUITTING? JUST LIKE THAT?
NO. I SWEAR-- THAT'S NOT WHAT THIS IS, BEN.
I WILL FIND THE TRUTH.
I HAVE TO. NO MATTER HOW UGLY IT MIGHT BE.
I'M PREPARED TO FACE IT. BUT YOU, MAY, AFTER WHAT YOU'VE BEEN THROUGH--
ENOUGH, GEORGE. ENOUGH OF YOUR PITY.
YOU KNOW GOOD AND WELL THAT WE--
--THAT MAY PARKER DESERVES TO KNOW WHAT REALLY HAPPENED TO HER BOY.
YOU FIND THAT TRUTH, GEORGE.
AND WHEN YOU DO, I EXPECT TO HEAR IT. ALL OF IT--

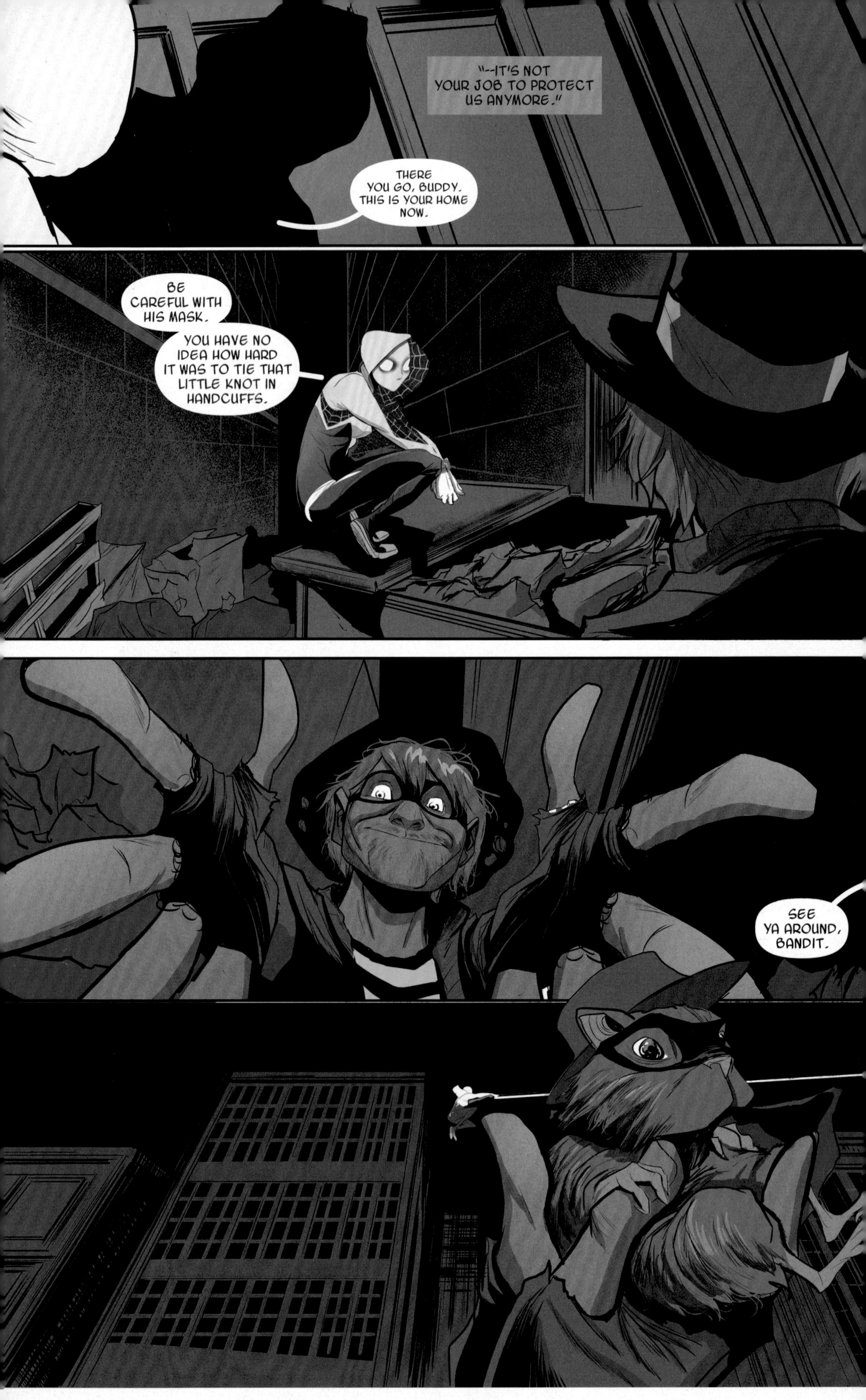
"--IT'S NOT YOUR JOB TO PROTECT US ANYMORE."
THERE YOU GO, BUDDY. THIS IS YOUR HOME NOW.
BE CAREFUL WITH HIS MASK.
YOU HAVE NO IDEA HOW HARD IT WAS TO TIE THAT LITTLE KNOT IN HANDCUFFS.
SEE YA AROUND, BANDIT.

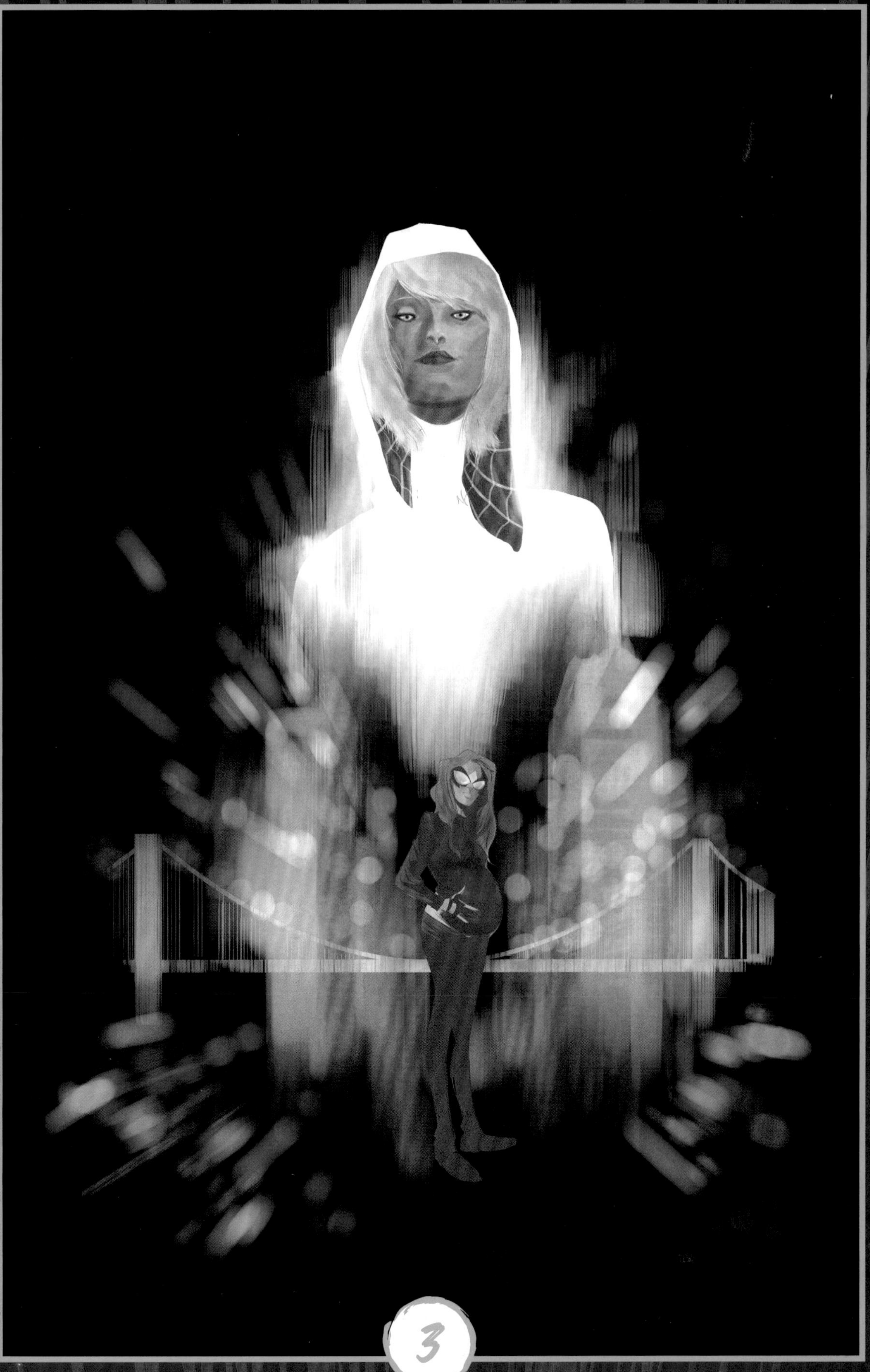

3

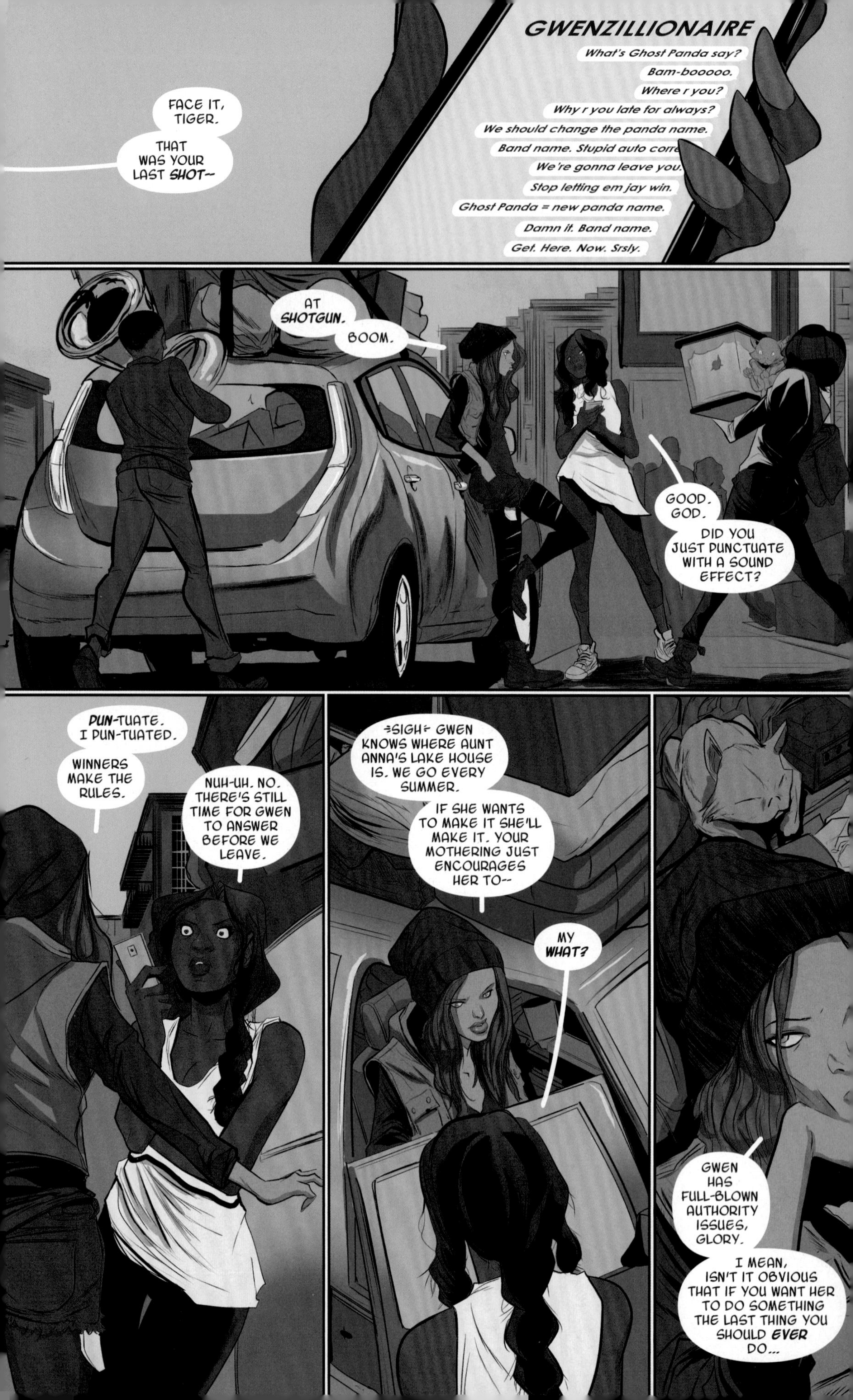

FACE IT, TIGER.
THAT WAS YOUR LAST SHOT--
GWENZILLIONAIRE
What's Ghost Panda say?
Bam-booooo.
Where r you?
Why r you late for always?
We should change the panda name.
Band name. Stupid auto corre
We're gonna leave you.
Stop letting em jay win.
Ghost Panda = new panda name.
Damn it. Band name.
Get. Here. Now. Srsly.
AT SHOTGUN.
BOOM.
GOOD. GOD.
DID YOU JUST PUNCTUATE WITH A SOUND EFFECT?
PUN-TUATE. I PUN-TUATED.
WINNERS MAKE THE RULES.
NUH-UH. NO. THERE'S STILL TIME FOR GWEN TO ANSWER BEFORE WE LEAVE.
=SIGH= GWEN KNOWS WHERE AUNT ANNA'S LAKE HOUSE IS. WE GO EVERY SUMMER.
IF SHE WANTS TO MAKE IT SHE'LL MAKE IT. YOUR MOTHERING JUST ENCOURAGES HER TO--
MY WHAT?
GWEN HAS FULL-BLOWN AUTHORITY ISSUES, GLORY.
I MEAN, ISN'T IT OBVIOUS THAT IF YOU WANT HER TO DO SOMETHING THE LAST THING YOU SHOULD EVER DO...

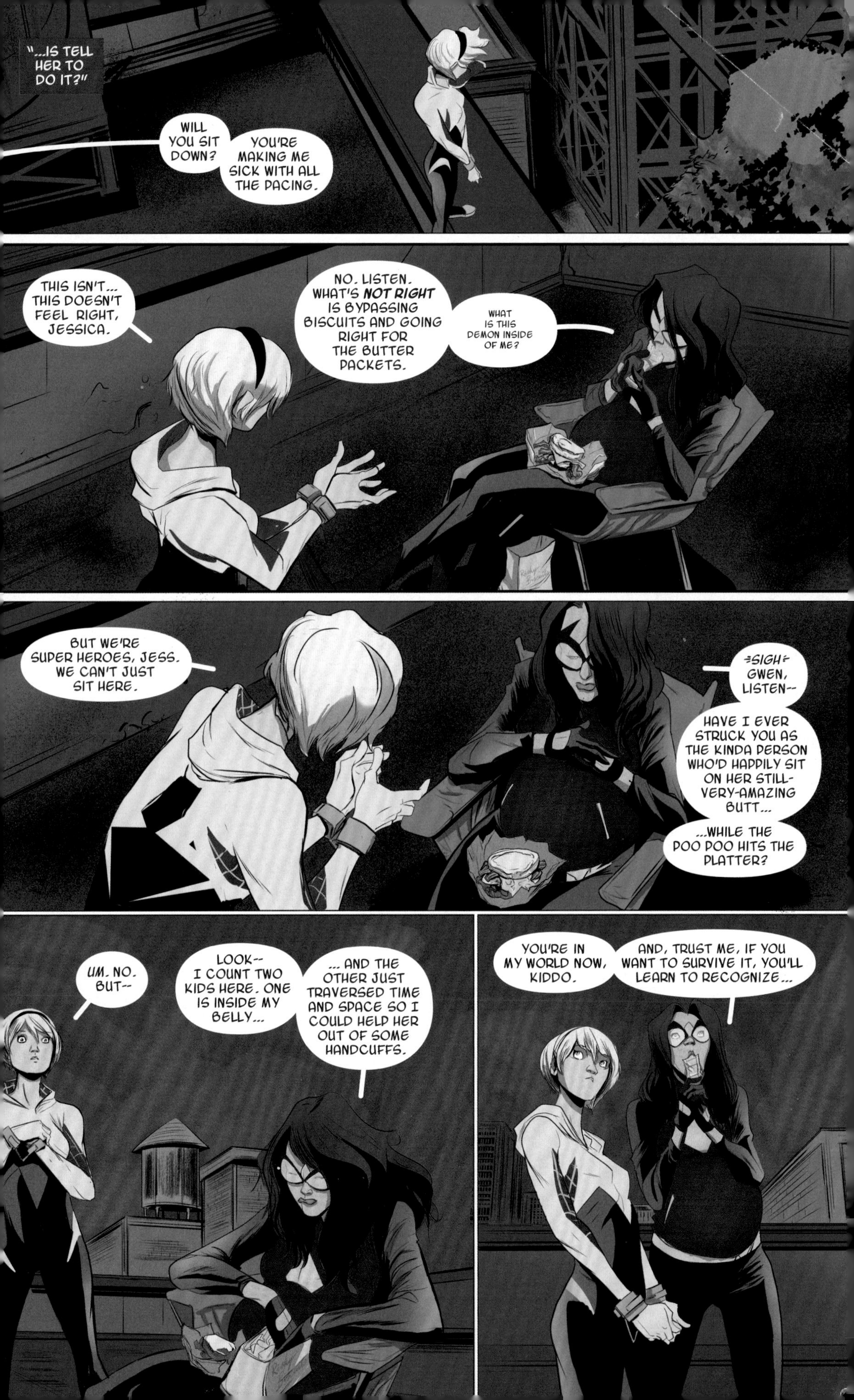
"...IS TELL HER TO DO IT?"
WILL YOU SIT DOWN?
YOU'RE MAKING ME SICK WITH ALL THE PACING.
THIS ISN'T... THIS DOESN'T FEEL RIGHT, JESSICA.
NO. LISTEN. WHAT'S **NOT RIGHT** IS BYPASSING BISCUITS AND GOING RIGHT FOR THE BUTTER PACKETS.
WHAT IS THIS DEMON INSIDE OF ME?
BUT WE'RE SUPER HEROES, JESS. WE CAN'T JUST SIT HERE.
=SIGH= GWEN, LISTEN--
HAVE I EVER STRUCK YOU AS THE KINDA PERSON WHO'D HAPPILY SIT ON HER STILL-VERY-AMAZING BUTT...
...WHILE THE POO POO HITS THE PLATTER?
UM. NO. BUT--
LOOK-- I COUNT TWO KIDS HERE. ONE IS INSIDE MY BELLY...
... AND THE OTHER JUST TRAVERSED TIME AND SPACE SO I COULD HELP HER OUT OF SOME HANDCUFFS.
YOU'RE IN MY WORLD NOW, KIDDO.
AND, TRUST ME, IF YOU WANT TO SURVIVE IT, YOU'LL LEARN TO RECOGNIZE...

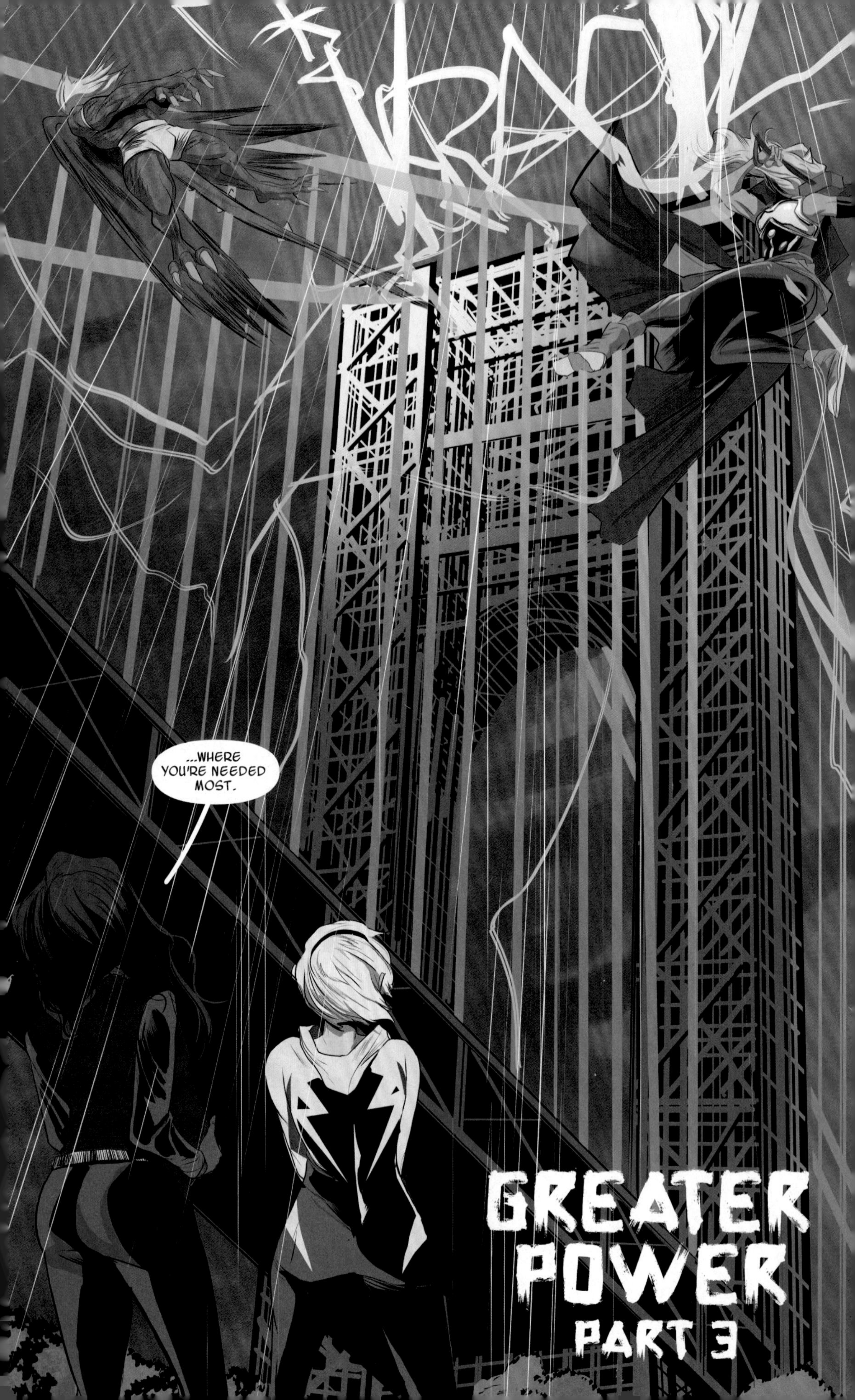
...WHERE YOU'RE NEEDED MOST.
GREATER POWER
PART 3

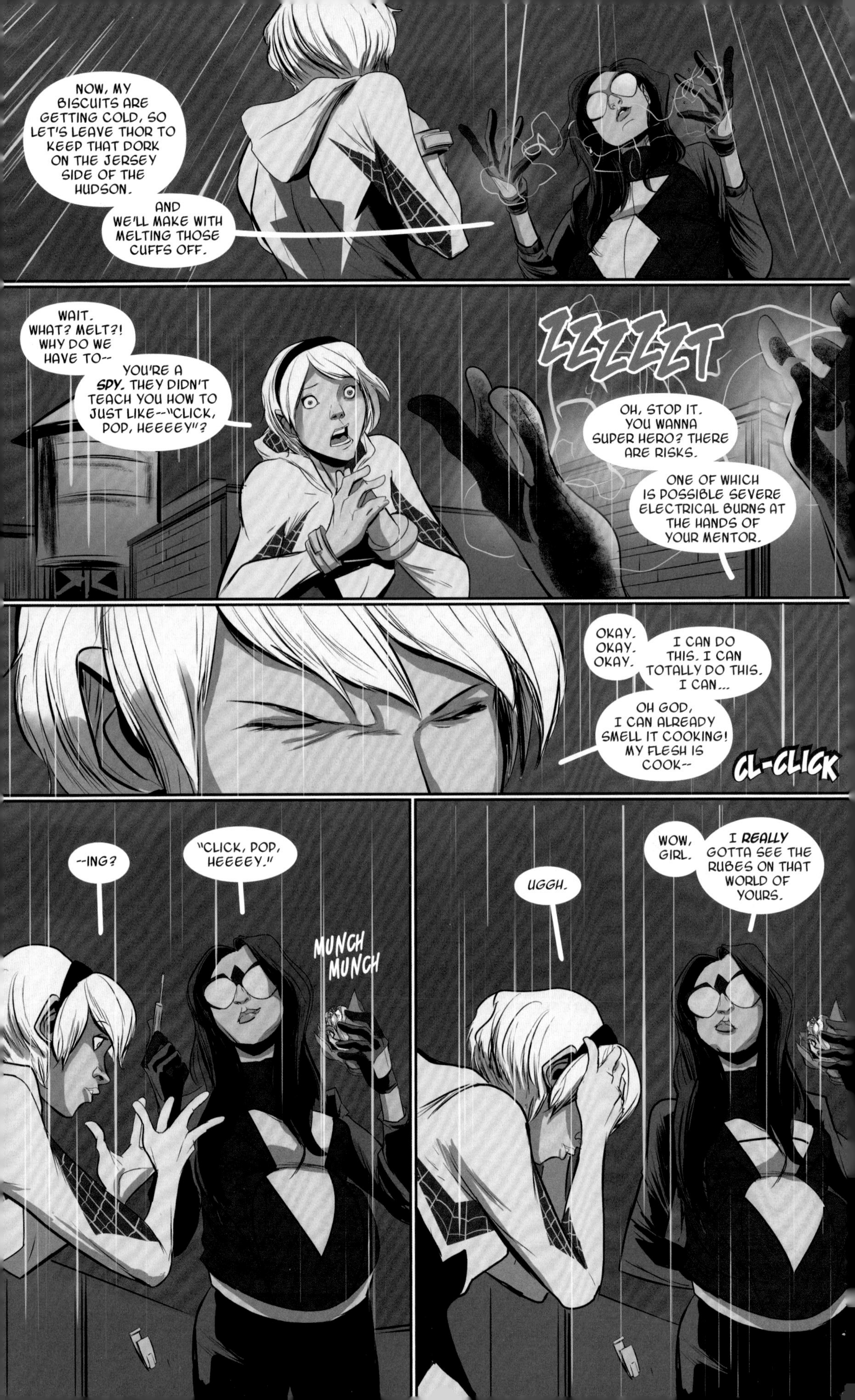
NOW, MY BISCUITS ARE GETTING COLD, SO LET'S LEAVE THOR TO KEEP THAT DORK ON THE JERSEY SIDE OF THE HUDSON.
AND WE'LL MAKE WITH MELTING THOSE CUFFS OFF.
WAIT. WHAT? MELT?! WHY DO WE HAVE TO--
YOU'RE A **SPY.** THEY DIDN'T TEACH YOU HOW TO JUST LIKE--"CLICK, POP, HEEEEY"?
ZZZZZT
OH, STOP IT. YOU WANNA SUPER HERO? THERE ARE RISKS.
ONE OF WHICH IS POSSIBLE SEVERE ELECTRICAL BURNS AT THE HANDS OF YOUR MENTOR.
OKAY. OKAY. OKAY.
I CAN DO THIS. I CAN TOTALLY DO THIS. I CAN...
OH GOD, I CAN ALREADY SMELL IT COOKING! MY FLESH IS COOK--
CL-CLICK
--ING?
"CLICK, POP, HEEEEY."
MUNCH MUNCH
UGGH.
WOW, GIRL.
I **REALLY** GOTTA SEE THE RUBES ON THAT WORLD OF YOURS.

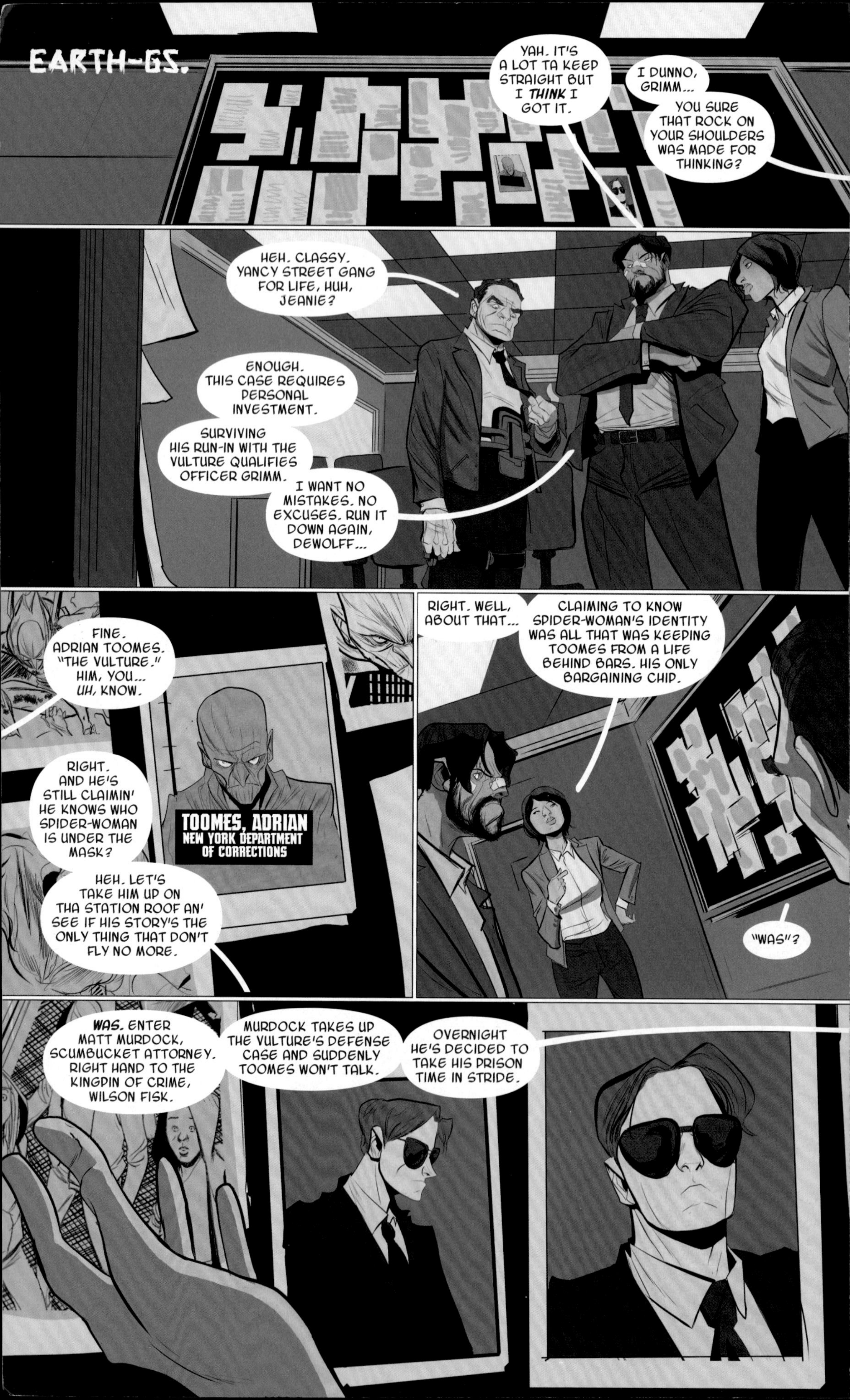
EARTH-65.
YAH. IT'S A LOT TA KEEP STRAIGHT BUT I *THINK* I GOT IT.
I DUNNO, GRIMM...
YOU SURE THAT ROCK ON YOUR SHOULDERS WAS MADE FOR THINKING?
HEH. CLASSY. YANCY STREET GANG FOR LIFE, HUH, JEANIE?
ENOUGH. THIS CASE REQUIRES PERSONAL INVESTMENT.
SURVIVING HIS RUN-IN WITH THE VULTURE QUALIFIES OFFICER GRIMM.
I WANT NO MISTAKES. NO EXCUSES. RUN IT DOWN AGAIN, DEWOLFF...
FINE. ADRIAN TOOMES. "THE VULTURE." HIM, YOU... UH, KNOW.
TOOMES, ADRIAN
NEW YORK DEPARTMENT OF CORRECTIONS
RIGHT. AND HE'S STILL CLAIMIN' HE KNOWS WHO SPIDER-WOMAN IS UNDER THE MASK?
HEH. LET'S TAKE HIM UP ON THA STATION ROOF AN' SEE IF HIS STORY'S THE ONLY THING THAT DON'T FLY NO MORE.
RIGHT. WELL, ABOUT THAT...
CLAIMING TO KNOW SPIDER-WOMAN'S IDENTITY WAS ALL THAT WAS KEEPING TOOMES FROM A LIFE BEHIND BARS. HIS ONLY BARGAINING CHIP.
"WAS"?
WAS. ENTER MATT MURDOCK, SCUMBUCKET ATTORNEY. RIGHT HAND TO THE KINGPIN OF CRIME, WILSON FISK.
MURDOCK TAKES UP THE VULTURE'S DEFENSE CASE AND SUDDENLY TOOMES WON'T TALK.
OVERNIGHT HE'S DECIDED TO TAKE HIS PRISON TIME IN STRIDE.

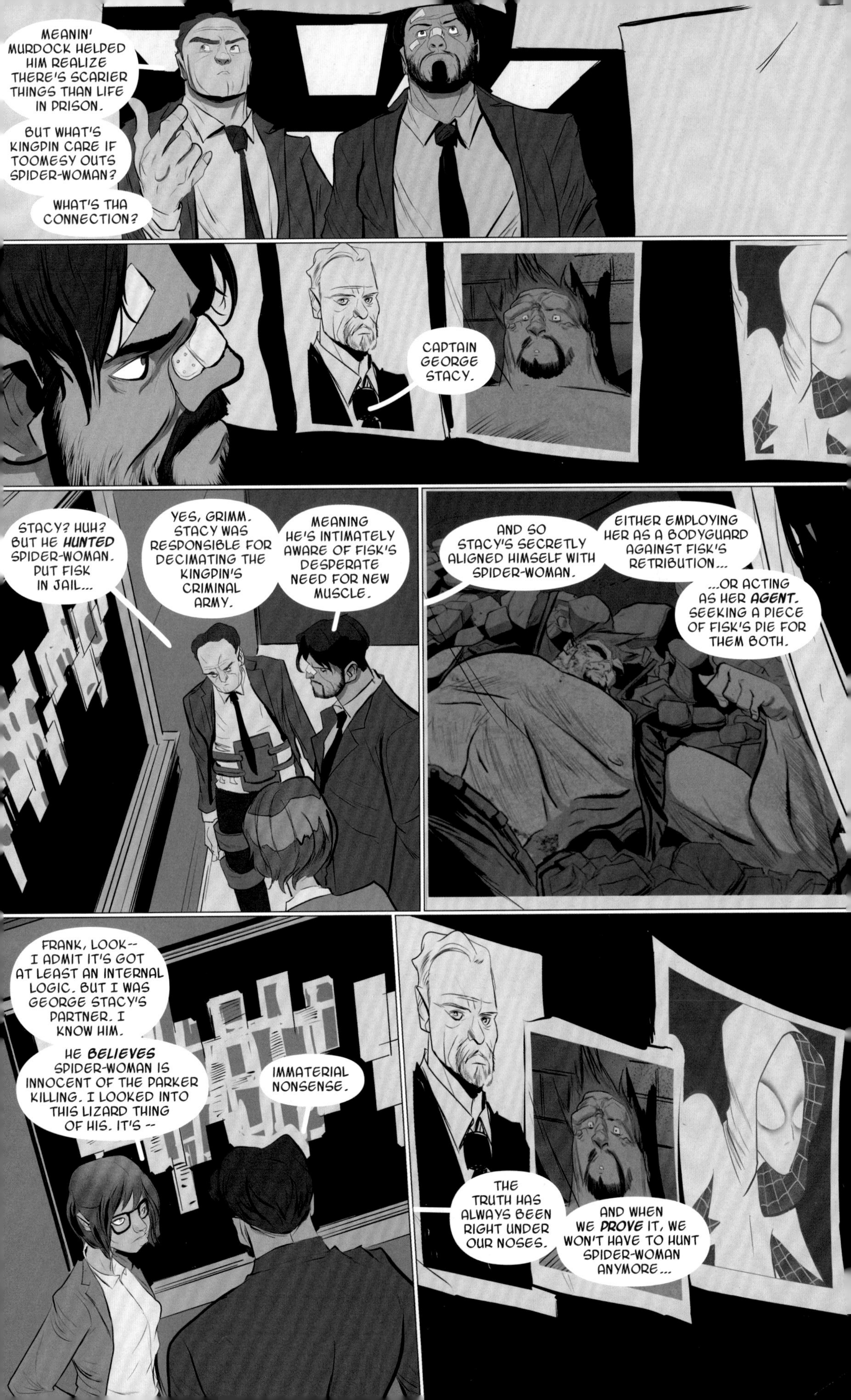
MEANIN' MURDOCK HELPED HIM REALIZE THERE'S SCARIER THINGS THAN LIFE IN PRISON.
BUT WHAT'S KINGPIN CARE IF TOOMESY OUTS SPIDER-WOMAN?
WHAT'S THA CONNECTION?
CAPTAIN GEORGE STACY.
STACY? HUH? BUT HE **HUNTED** SPIDER-WOMAN. PUT FISK IN JAIL...
YES, GRIMM. STACY WAS RESPONSIBLE FOR DECIMATING THE KINGPIN'S CRIMINAL ARMY.
MEANING HE'S INTIMATELY AWARE OF FISK'S DESPERATE NEED FOR NEW MUSCLE.
AND SO STACY'S SECRETLY ALIGNED HIMSELF WITH SPIDER-WOMAN.
EITHER EMPLOYING HER AS A BODYGUARD AGAINST FISK'S RETRIBUTION...
...OR ACTING AS HER **AGENT.** SEEKING A PIECE OF FISK'S PIE FOR THEM BOTH.
FRANK, LOOK-- I ADMIT IT'S GOT AT LEAST AN INTERNAL LOGIC. BUT I WAS GEORGE STACY'S PARTNER. I KNOW HIM.
HE **BELIEVES** SPIDER-WOMAN IS INNOCENT OF THE PARKER KILLING. I LOOKED INTO THIS LIZARD THING OF HIS. IT'S --
IMMATERIAL NONSENSE.
THE TRUTH HAS ALWAYS BEEN RIGHT UNDER OUR NOSES.
AND WHEN WE **PROVE** IT, WE WON'T HAVE TO HUNT SPIDER-WOMAN ANYMORE...

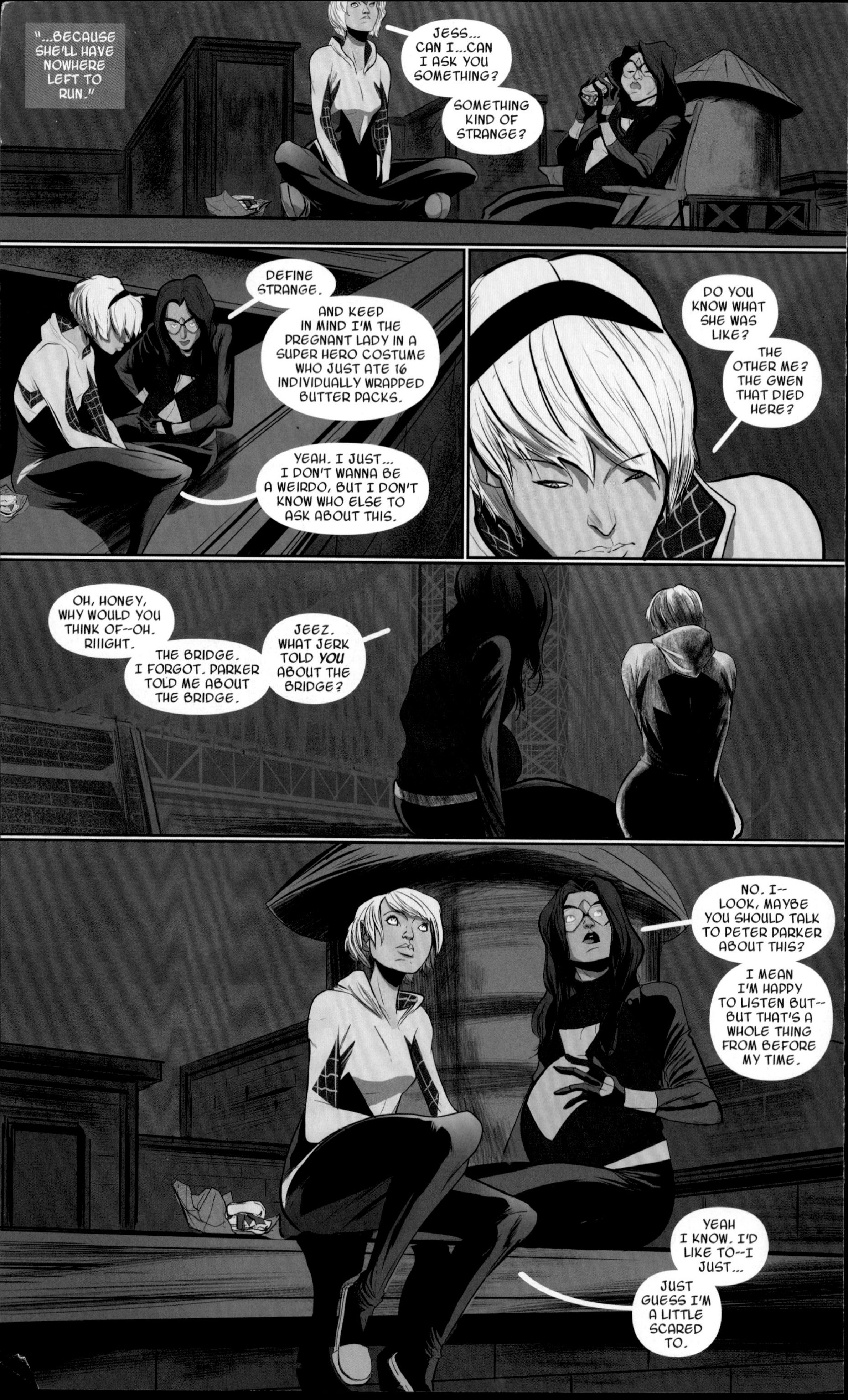
"...BECAUSE SHE'LL HAVE NOWHERE LEFT TO RUN."
JESS... CAN I...CAN I ASK YOU SOMETHING?
SOMETHING KIND OF STRANGE?
DEFINE STRANGE.
AND KEEP IN MIND I'M THE PREGNANT LADY IN A SUPER HERO COSTUME WHO JUST ATE 16 INDIVIDUALLY WRAPPED BUTTER PACKS.
YEAH. I JUST... I DON'T WANNA BE A WEIRDO, BUT I DON'T KNOW WHO ELSE TO ASK ABOUT THIS.
DO YOU KNOW WHAT SHE WAS LIKE?
THE OTHER ME? THE GWEN THAT DIED HERE?
OH, HONEY, WHY WOULD YOU THINK OF--OH. RIIIGHT.
THE BRIDGE. I FORGOT. PARKER TOLD ME ABOUT THE BRIDGE.
JEEZ. WHAT JERK TOLD *YOU* ABOUT THE BRIDGE?
NO. I-- LOOK, MAYBE YOU SHOULD TALK TO PETER PARKER ABOUT THIS?
I MEAN I'M HAPPY TO LISTEN BUT-- BUT THAT'S A WHOLE THING FROM BEFORE MY TIME.
YEAH I KNOW. I'D LIKE TO--I JUST...
JUST GUESS I'M A LITTLE SCARED TO.

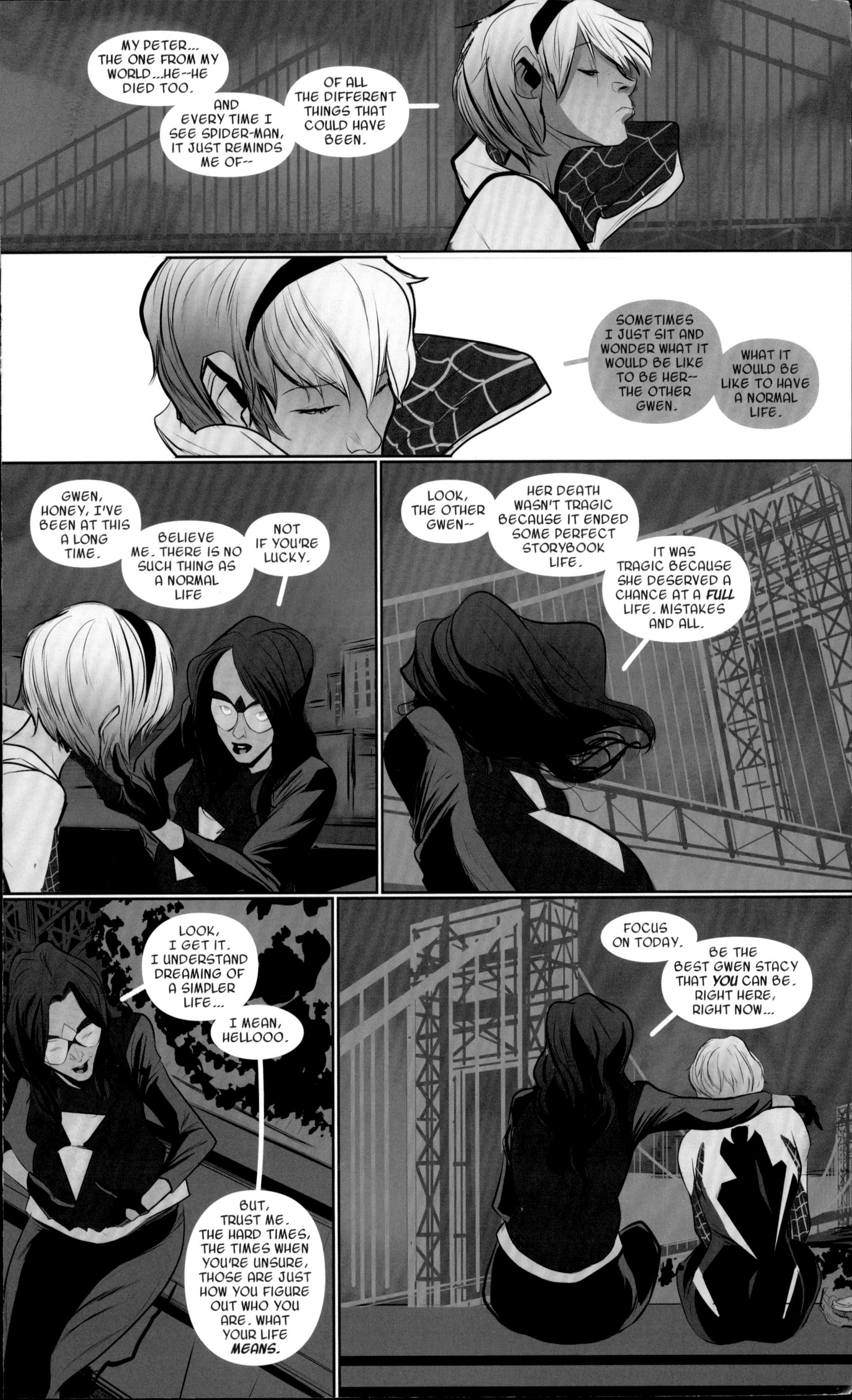
MY PETER... THE ONE FROM MY WORLD...HE--HE DIED TOO.
AND EVERY TIME I SEE SPIDER-MAN, IT JUST REMINDS ME OF--
OF ALL THE DIFFERENT THINGS THAT COULD HAVE BEEN.
SOMETIMES I JUST SIT AND WONDER WHAT IT WOULD BE LIKE TO BE HER-- THE OTHER GWEN.
WHAT IT WOULD BE LIKE TO HAVE A NORMAL LIFE.
GWEN, HONEY, I'VE BEEN AT THIS A LONG TIME.
BELIEVE ME. THERE IS NO SUCH THING AS A NORMAL LIFE
NOT IF YOU'RE LUCKY.
LOOK, THE OTHER GWEN--
HER DEATH WASN'T TRAGIC BECAUSE IT ENDED SOME PERFECT STORYBOOK LIFE.
IT WAS TRAGIC BECAUSE SHE DESERVED A CHANCE AT A **FULL** LIFE. MISTAKES AND ALL.
LOOK, I GET IT. I UNDERSTAND DREAMING OF A SIMPLER LIFE...
I MEAN, HELLOOO.
BUT, TRUST ME. THE HARD TIMES, THE TIMES WHEN YOU'RE UNSURE, THOSE ARE JUST HOW YOU FIGURE OUT WHO YOU ARE. WHAT YOUR LIFE **MEANS.**
FOCUS ON TODAY.
BE THE BEST GWEN STACY THAT **YOU** CAN BE. RIGHT HERE, RIGHT NOW...

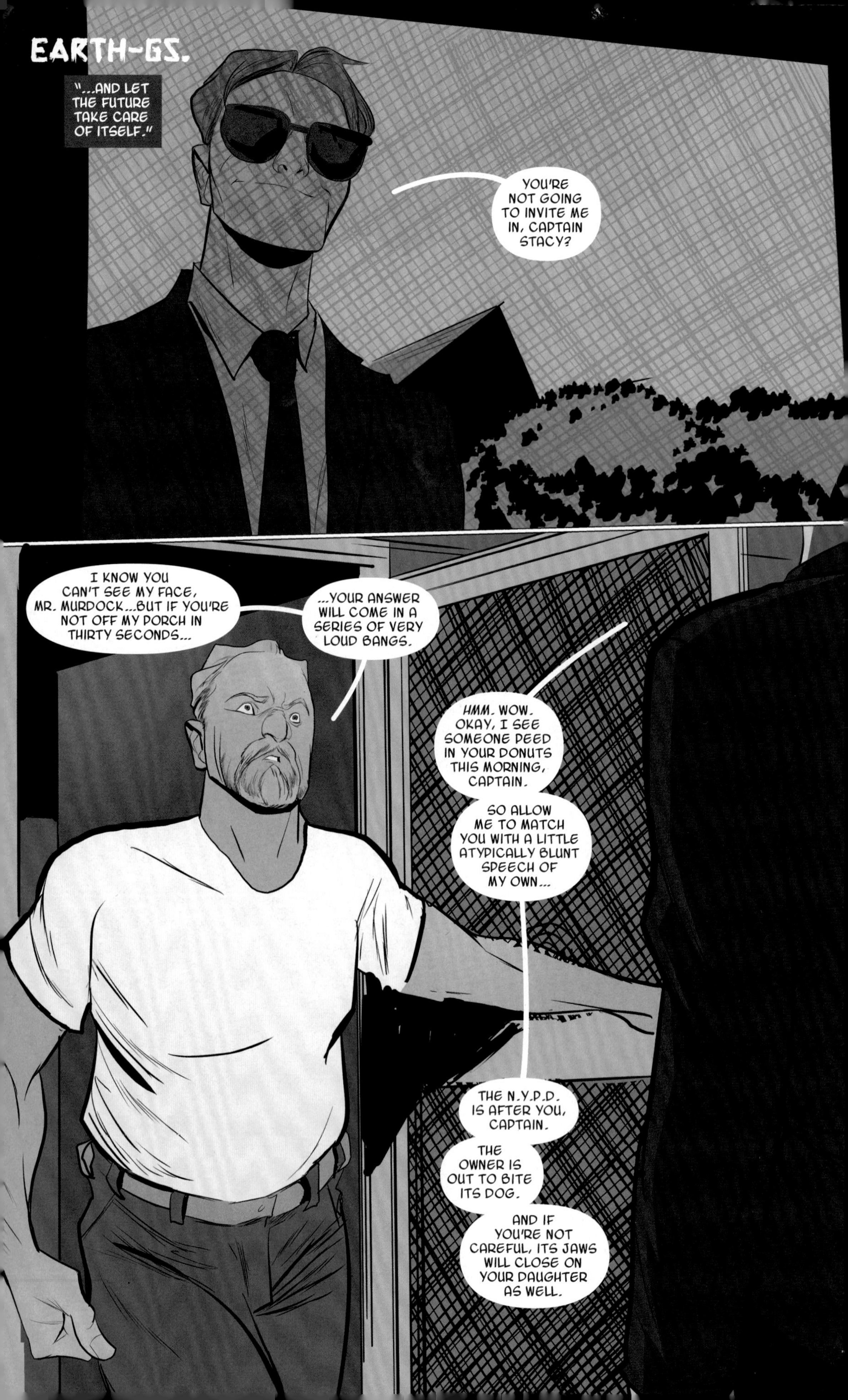
EARTH-65.
"...AND LET THE FUTURE TAKE CARE OF ITSELF."
YOU'RE NOT GOING TO INVITE ME IN, CAPTAIN STACY?
I KNOW YOU CAN'T SEE MY FACE, MR. MURDOCK...BUT IF YOU'RE NOT OFF MY PORCH IN THIRTY SECONDS...
...YOUR ANSWER WILL COME IN A SERIES OF VERY LOUD BANGS.
HMM. WOW. OKAY, I SEE SOMEONE PEED IN YOUR DONUTS THIS MORNING, CAPTAIN.
SO ALLOW ME TO MATCH YOU WITH A LITTLE ATYPICALLY BLUNT SPEECH OF MY OWN...
THE N.Y.P.D. IS AFTER YOU, CAPTAIN.
THE OWNER IS OUT TO BITE ITS DOG.
AND IF YOU'RE NOT CAREFUL, ITS JAWS WILL CLOSE ON YOUR DAUGHTER AS WELL.

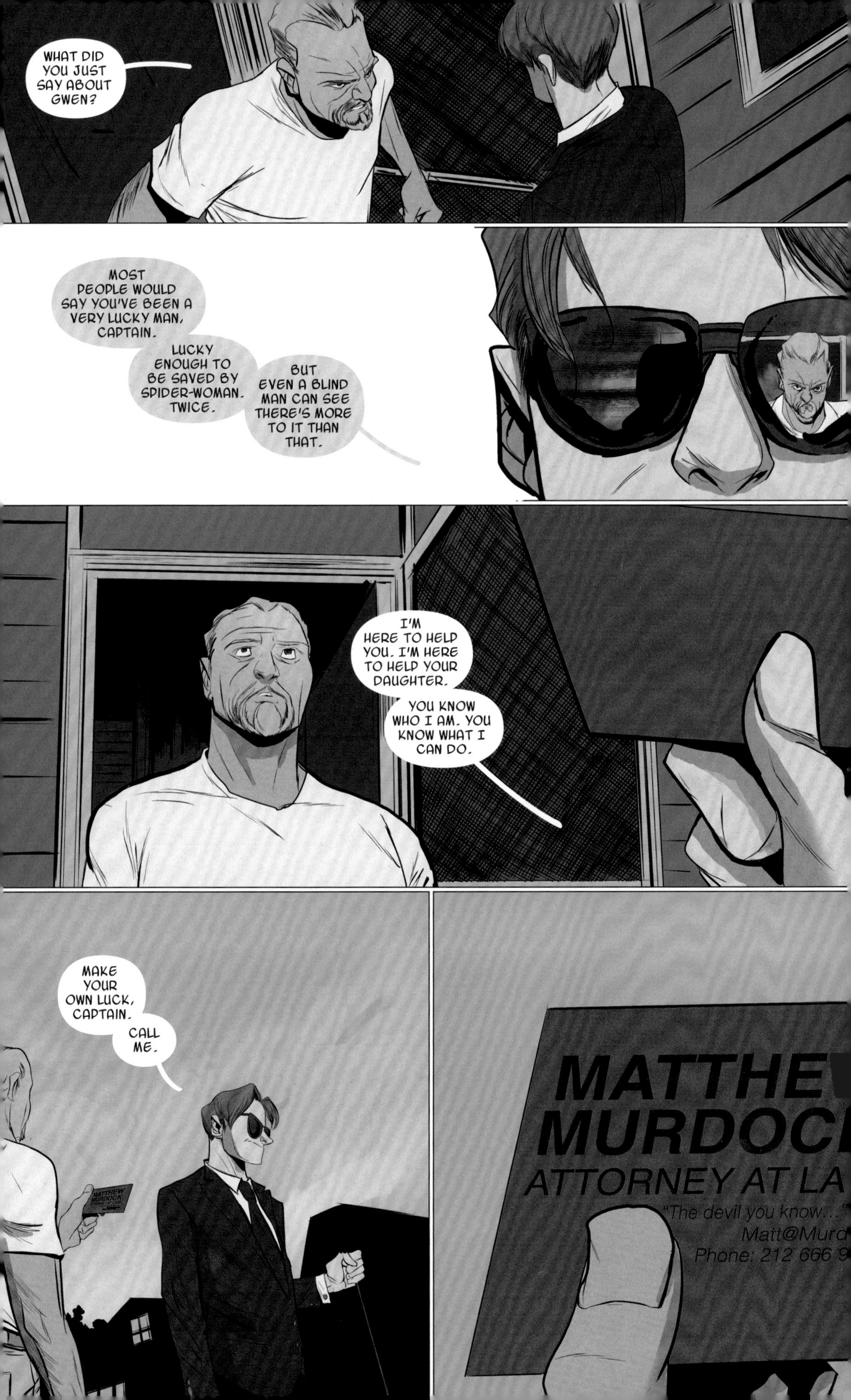
WHAT DID YOU JUST SAY ABOUT GWEN?
MOST PEOPLE WOULD SAY YOU'VE BEEN A VERY LUCKY MAN, CAPTAIN.
LUCKY ENOUGH TO BE SAVED BY SPIDER-WOMAN. TWICE.
BUT EVEN A BLIND MAN CAN SEE THERE'S MORE TO IT THAN THAT.
I'M HERE TO HELP YOU. I'M HERE TO HELP YOUR DAUGHTER.
YOU KNOW WHO I AM. YOU KNOW WHAT I CAN DO.
MAKE YOUR OWN LUCK, CAPTAIN.
CALL ME.
MATTHE
MURDOC
ATTORNEY AT LA
"The devil you know..."
Matt@Murd
Phone: 212 666 9

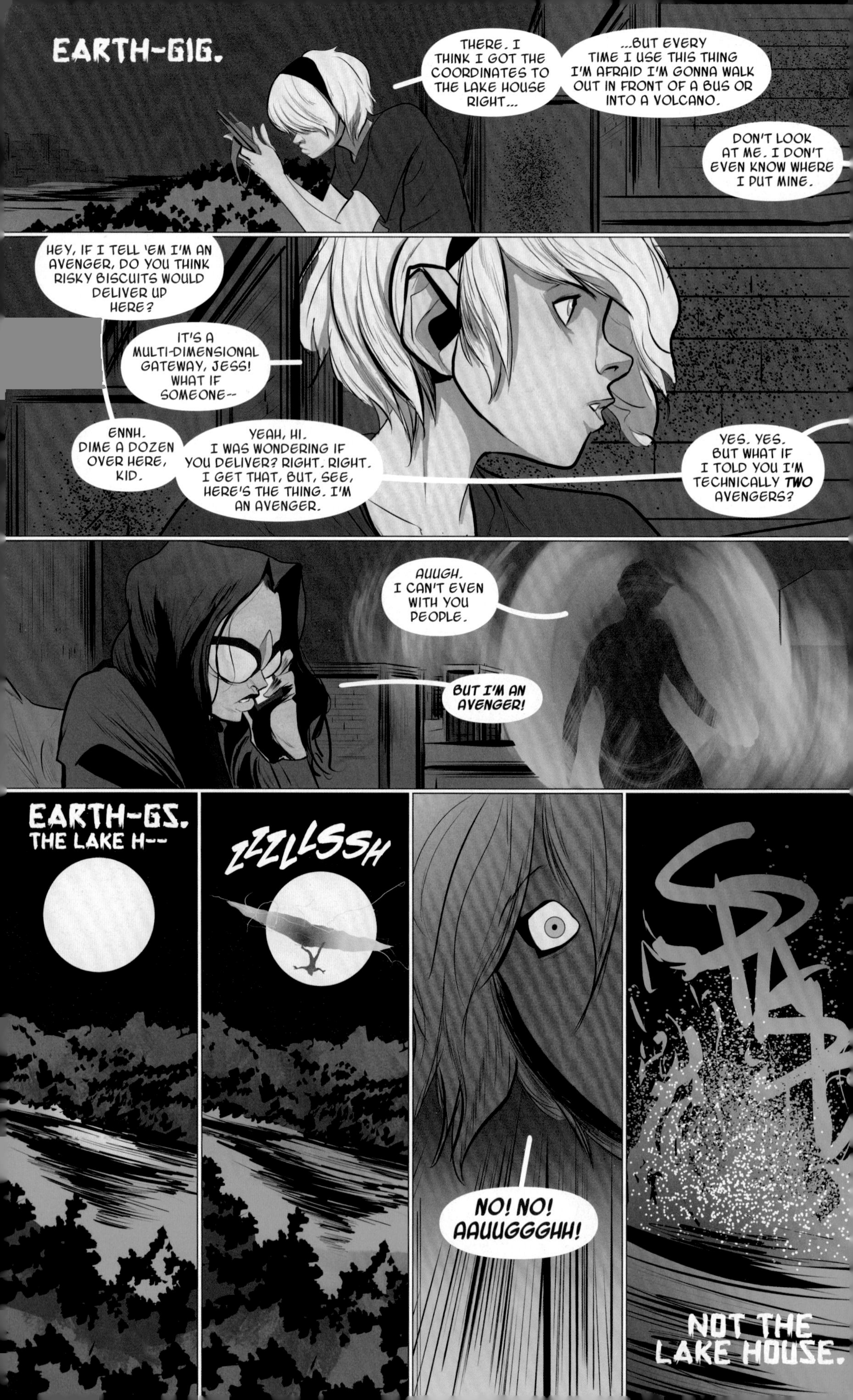
EARTH-616.
THERE. I THINK I GOT THE COORDINATES TO THE LAKE HOUSE RIGHT...
...BUT EVERY TIME I USE THIS THING I'M AFRAID I'M GONNA WALK OUT IN FRONT OF A BUS OR INTO A VOLCANO.
DON'T LOOK AT ME. I DON'T EVEN KNOW WHERE I PUT MINE.
HEY, IF I TELL 'EM I'M AN AVENGER, DO YOU THINK RISKY BISCUITS WOULD DELIVER UP HERE?
IT'S A MULTI-DIMENSIONAL GATEWAY, JESS! WHAT IF SOMEONE--
ENNH. DIME A DOZEN OVER HERE, KID.
YEAH, HI. I WAS WONDERING IF YOU DELIVER? RIGHT. RIGHT. I GET THAT, BUT, SEE, HERE'S THE THING. I'M AN AVENGER.
YES. YES. BUT WHAT IF I TOLD YOU I'M TECHNICALLY **TWO** AVENGERS?
AUUGH. I CAN'T EVEN WITH YOU PEOPLE.
BUT I'M AN AVENGER!
EARTH-65. THE LAKE H--
ZZZLLSSH
NO! NO! AAUUGGGHH!
NOT THE LAKE HOUSE.

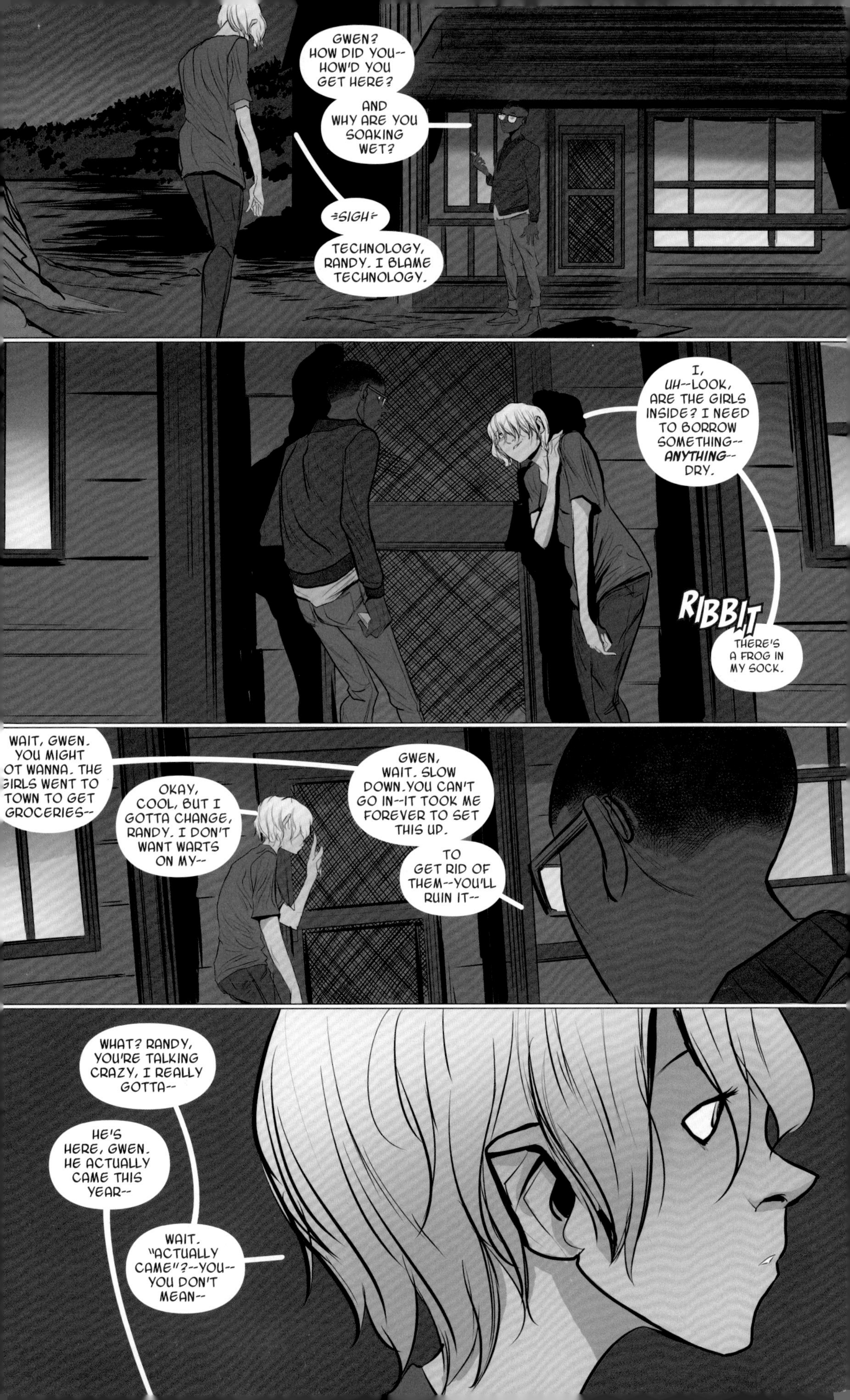
GWEN? HOW DID YOU-- HOW'D YOU GET HERE?
AND WHY ARE YOU SOAKING WET?
SIGH
TECHNOLOGY, RANDY. I BLAME TECHNOLOGY.
I, UH--LOOK, ARE THE GIRLS INSIDE? I NEED TO BORROW SOMETHING--ANYTHING--DRY.
RIBBIT
THERE'S A FROG IN MY SOCK.
WAIT, GWEN. YOU MIGHT OT WANNA. THE IRLS WENT TO TOWN TO GET GROCERIES--
OKAY, COOL, BUT I GOTTA CHANGE, RANDY. I DON'T WANT WARTS ON MY--
GWEN, WAIT. SLOW DOWN. YOU CAN'T GO IN--IT TOOK ME FOREVER TO SET THIS UP.
TO GET RID OF THEM--YOU'LL RUIN IT--
WHAT? RANDY, YOU'RE TALKING CRAZY, I REALLY GOTTA--
HE'S HERE, GWEN. HE ACTUALLY CAME THIS YEAR--
WAIT. "ACTUALLY CAME"?--YOU--YOU DON'T MEAN--

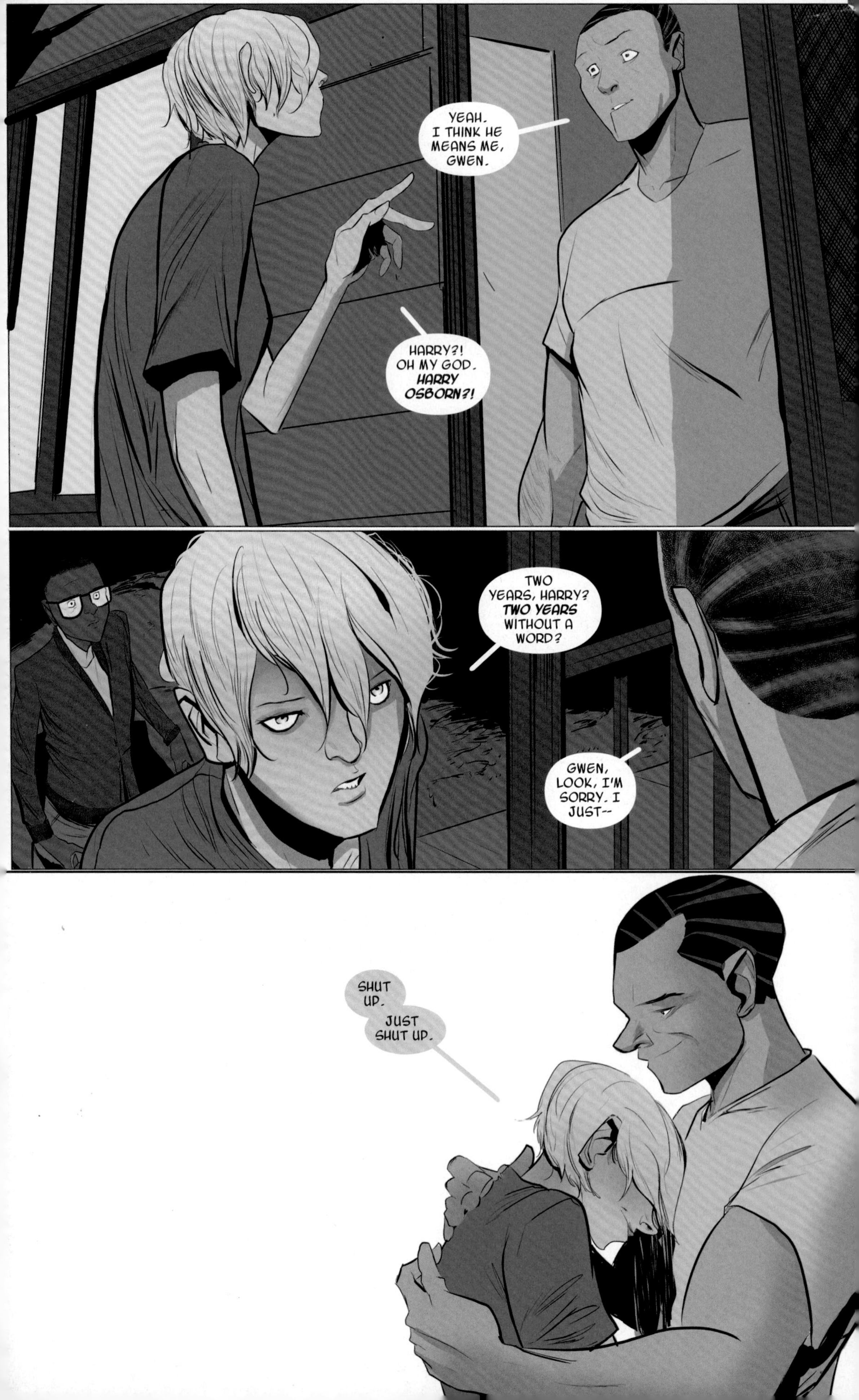
YEAH. I THINK HE MEANS ME, GWEN.
HARRY?! OH MY GOD. HARRY OSBORN?!
TWO YEARS, HARRY? TWO YEARS WITHOUT A WORD?
GWEN, LOOK, I'M SORRY. I JUST--
SHUT UP.
JUST SHUT UP.

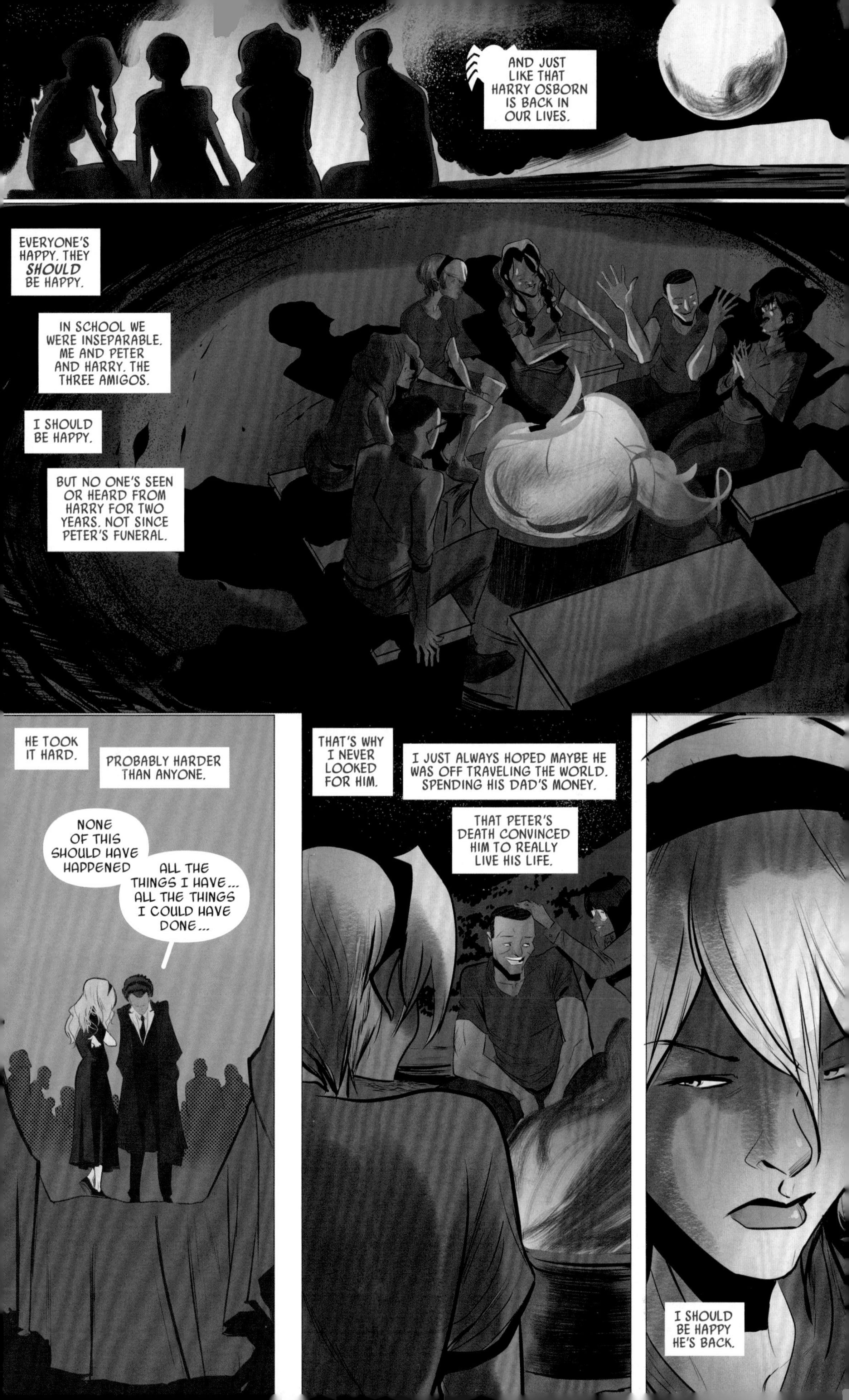
AND JUST LIKE THAT HARRY OSBORN IS BACK IN OUR LIVES.
EVERYONE'S HAPPY. THEY SHOULD BE HAPPY.
IN SCHOOL WE WERE INSEPARABLE. ME AND PETER AND HARRY. THE THREE AMIGOS.
I SHOULD BE HAPPY.
BUT NO ONE'S SEEN OR HEARD FROM HARRY FOR TWO YEARS. NOT SINCE PETER'S FUNERAL.
HE TOOK IT HARD.
PROBABLY HARDER THAN ANYONE.
NONE OF THIS SHOULD HAVE HAPPENED
ALL THE THINGS I HAVE... ALL THE THINGS I COULD HAVE DONE...
THAT'S WHY I NEVER LOOKED FOR HIM.
I JUST ALWAYS HOPED MAYBE HE WAS OFF TRAVELING THE WORLD. SPENDING HIS DAD'S MONEY.
THAT PETER'S DEATH CONVINCED HIM TO REALLY LIVE HIS LIFE.
I SHOULD BE HAPPY HE'S BACK.

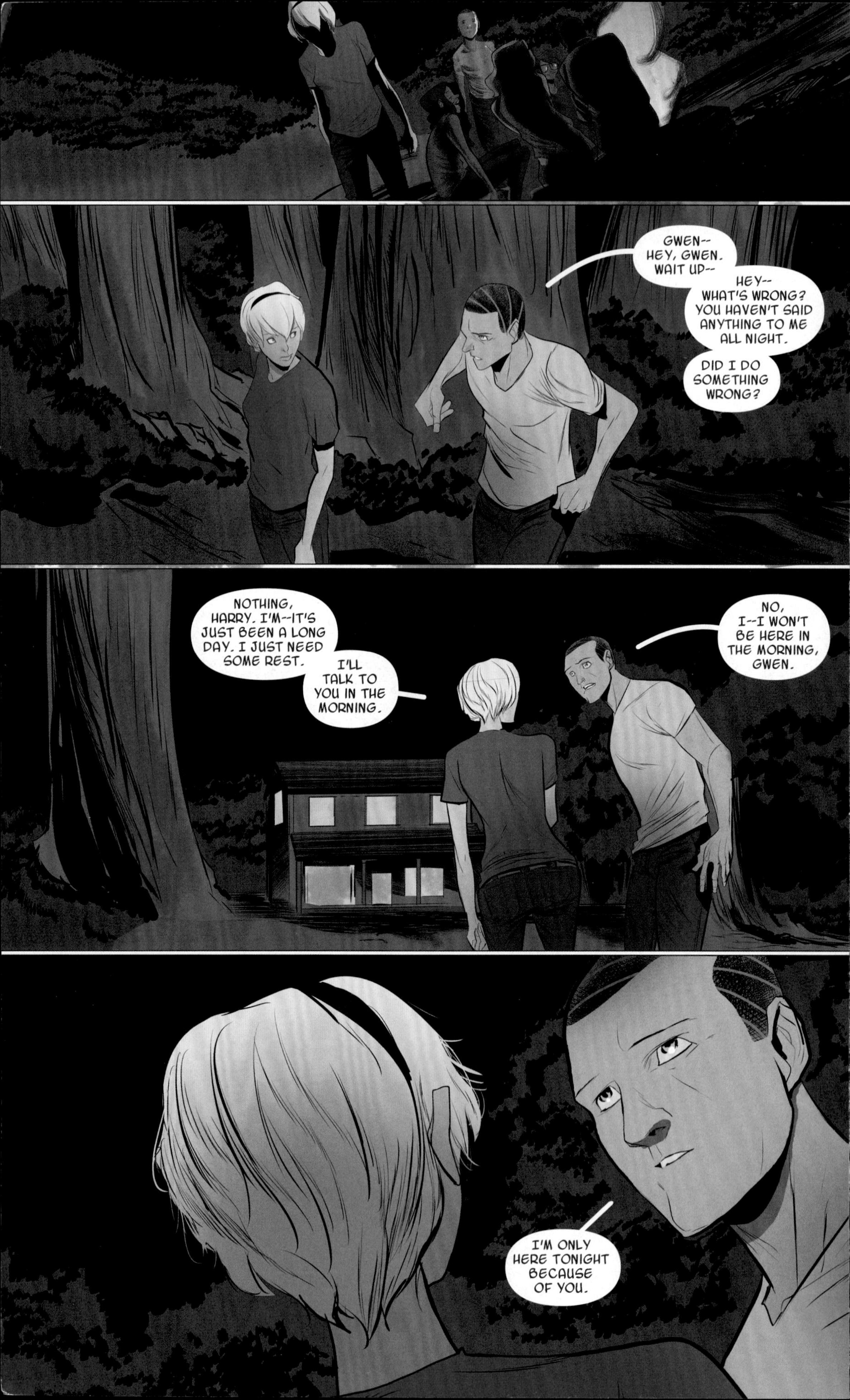
GWEN--
HEY, GWEN.
WAIT UP--
HEY--
WHAT'S WRONG?
YOU HAVEN'T SAID
ANYTHING TO ME
ALL NIGHT.
DID I DO
SOMETHING
WRONG?
NOTHING,
HARRY. I'M--IT'S
JUST BEEN A LONG
DAY. I JUST NEED
SOME REST.
I'LL
TALK TO
YOU IN THE
MORNING.
NO,
I--I WON'T
BE HERE IN
THE MORNING,
GWEN.
I'M ONLY
HERE TONIGHT
BECAUSE
OF YOU.

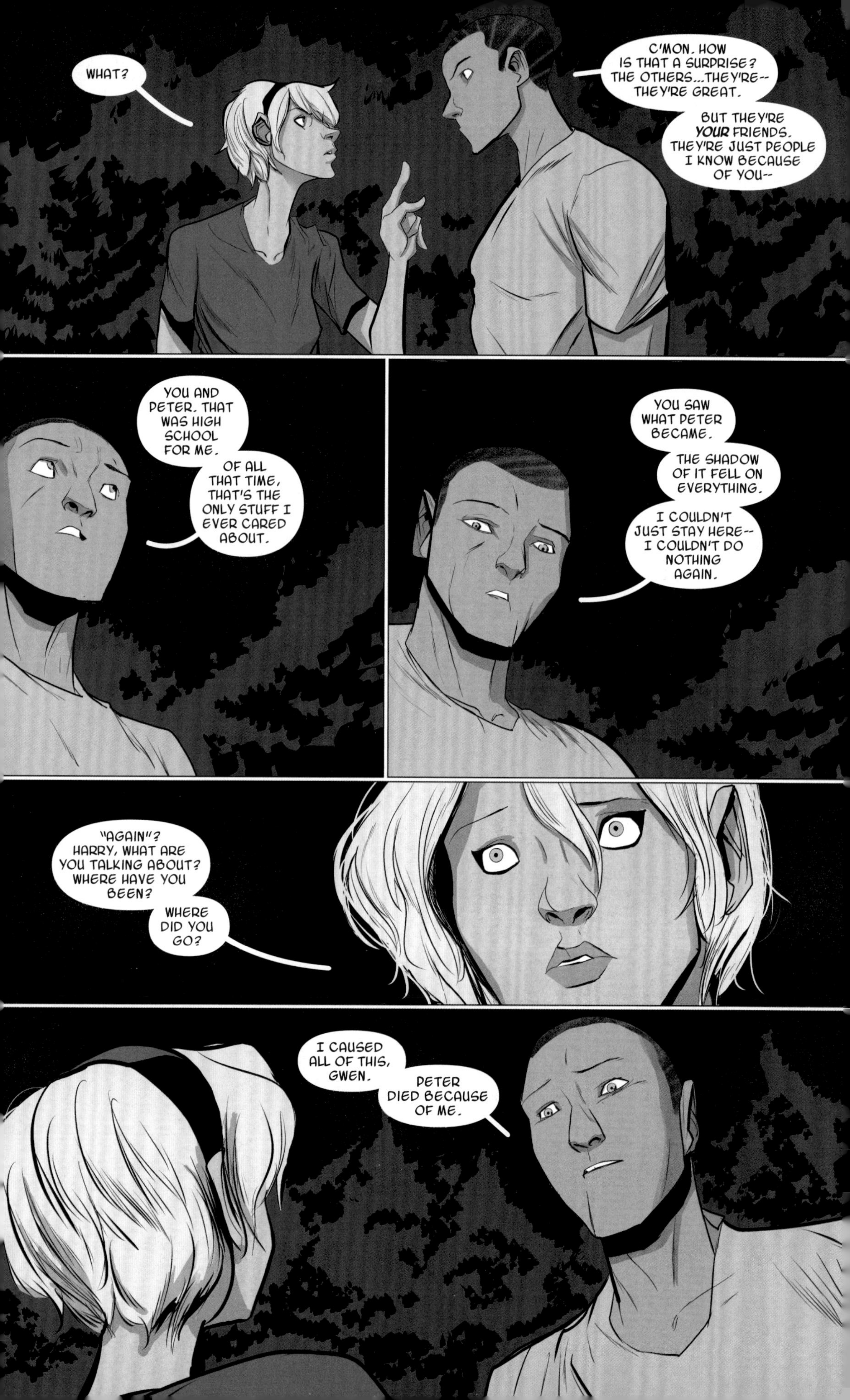
WHAT?
C'MON. HOW IS THAT A SURPRISE? THE OTHERS...THEY'RE-- THEY'RE GREAT.
BUT THEY'RE **YOUR** FRIENDS. THEY'RE JUST PEOPLE I KNOW BECAUSE OF YOU--
YOU AND PETER. THAT WAS HIGH SCHOOL FOR ME.
OF ALL THAT TIME, THAT'S THE ONLY STUFF I EVER CARED ABOUT.
YOU SAW WHAT PETER BECAME.
THE SHADOW OF IT FELL ON EVERYTHING.
I COULDN'T JUST STAY HERE-- I COULDN'T DO NOTHING AGAIN.
"AGAIN"? HARRY, WHAT ARE YOU TALKING ABOUT? WHERE HAVE YOU BEEN?
WHERE DID YOU GO?
I CAUSED ALL OF THIS, GWEN.
PETER DIED BECAUSE OF ME.

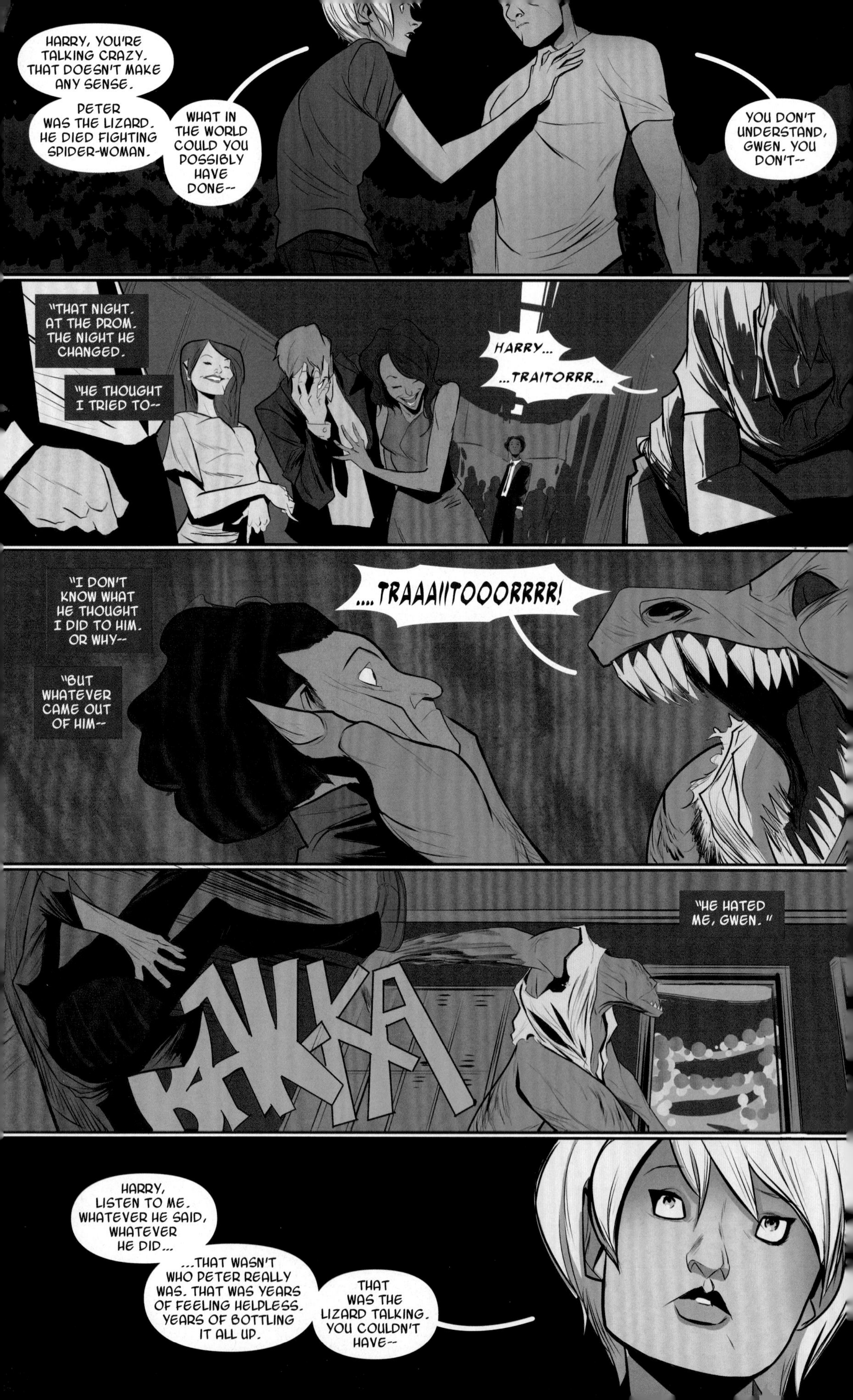
HARRY, YOU'RE TALKING CRAZY. THAT DOESN'T MAKE ANY SENSE.
PETER WAS THE LIZARD. HE DIED FIGHTING SPIDER-WOMAN.
WHAT IN THE WORLD COULD YOU POSSIBLY HAVE DONE--
YOU DON'T UNDERSTAND, GWEN. YOU DON'T--
"THAT NIGHT. AT THE PROM. THE NIGHT HE CHANGED.
"HE THOUGHT I TRIED TO--
HARRY...
...TRAITORRR...
"I DON'T KNOW WHAT HE THOUGHT I DID TO HIM. OR WHY--
"BUT WHATEVER CAME OUT OF HIM--
....TRAAAIITOOORRRR!
"HE HATED ME, GWEN."
KAKKA
HARRY, LISTEN TO ME. WHATEVER HE SAID, WHATEVER HE DID...
...THAT WASN'T WHO PETER REALLY WAS. THAT WAS YEARS OF FEELING HELPLESS. YEARS OF BOTTLING IT ALL UP.
THAT WAS THE LIZARD TALKING. YOU COULDN'T HAVE--

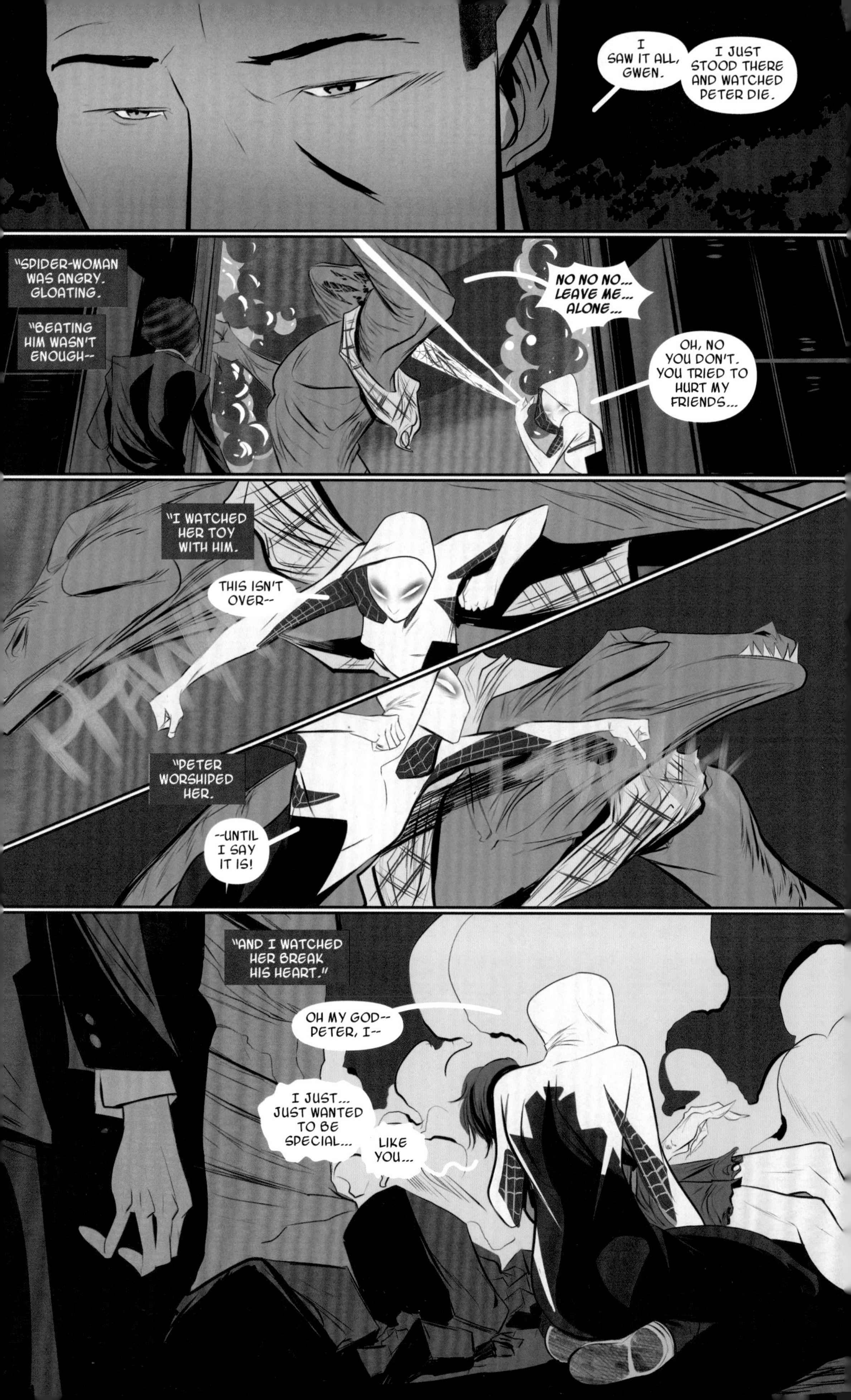
I SAW IT ALL, GWEN.
I JUST STOOD THERE AND WATCHED PETER DIE.
"SPIDER-WOMAN WAS ANGRY. GLOATING.
"BEATING HIM WASN'T ENOUGH--
NO NO NO... LEAVE ME... ALONE...
OH, NO YOU DON'T. YOU TRIED TO HURT MY FRIENDS...
"I WATCHED HER TOY WITH HIM.
THIS ISN'T OVER--
"PETER WORSHIPED HER.
--UNTIL I SAY IT IS!
"AND I WATCHED HER BREAK HIS HEART."
OH MY GOD-- PETER, I--
I JUST... JUST WANTED TO BE SPECIAL...
LIKE YOU...

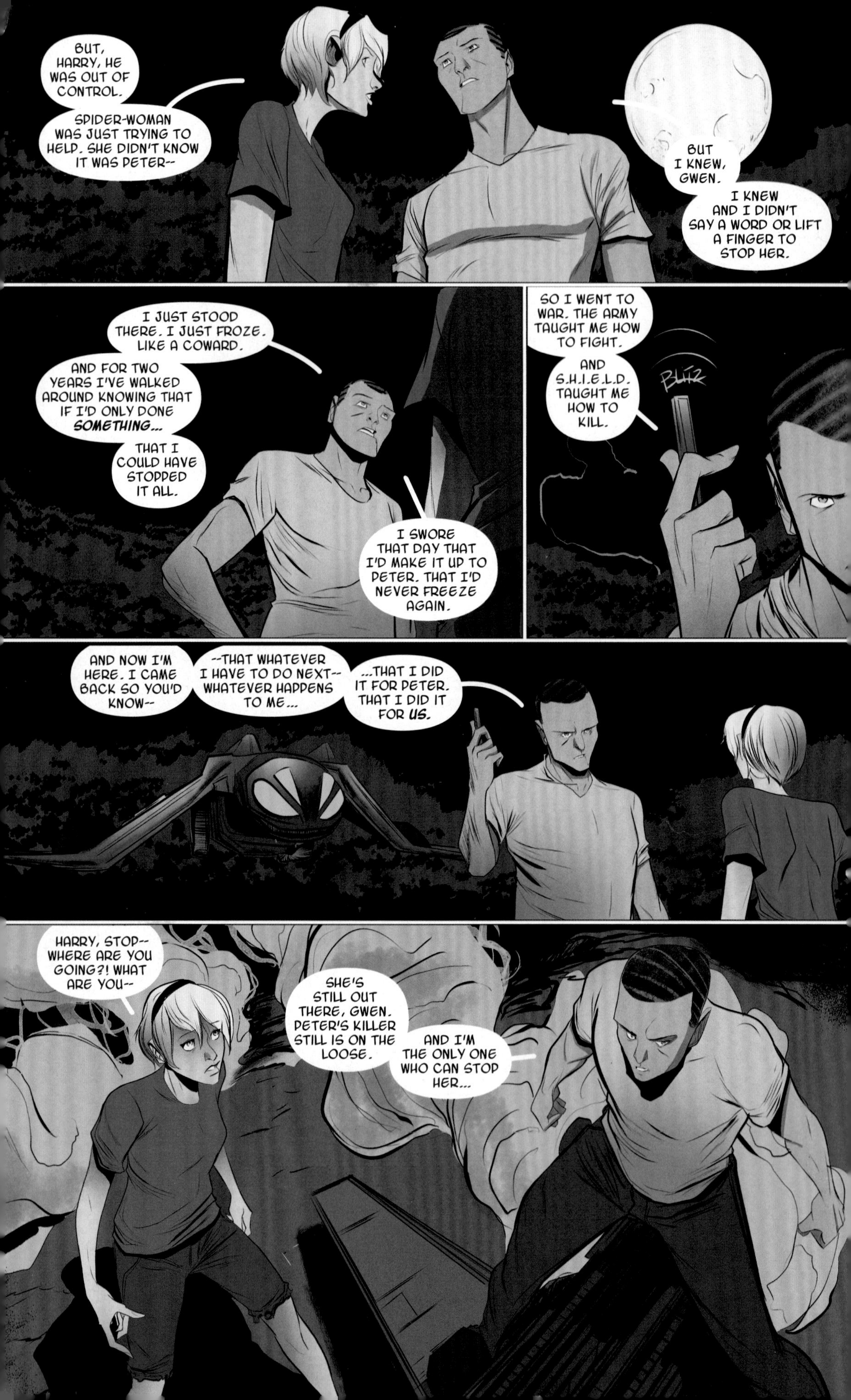
BUT, HARRY, HE WAS OUT OF CONTROL.
SPIDER-WOMAN WAS JUST TRYING TO HELP. SHE DIDN'T KNOW IT WAS PETER--
BUT I KNEW, GWEN.
I KNEW AND I DIDN'T SAY A WORD OR LIFT A FINGER TO STOP HER.
I JUST STOOD THERE. I JUST FROZE. LIKE A COWARD.
AND FOR TWO YEARS I'VE WALKED AROUND KNOWING THAT IF I'D ONLY DONE SOMETHING...
THAT I COULD HAVE STOPPED IT ALL.
I SWORE THAT DAY THAT I'D MAKE IT UP TO PETER. THAT I'D NEVER FREEZE AGAIN.
SO I WENT TO WAR. THE ARMY TAUGHT ME HOW TO FIGHT.
AND S.H.I.E.L.D. TAUGHT ME HOW TO KILL.
BLIZ
AND NOW I'M HERE. I CAME BACK SO YOU'D KNOW--
--THAT WHATEVER I HAVE TO DO NEXT-- WHATEVER HAPPENS TO ME...
...THAT I DID IT FOR PETER. THAT I DID IT FOR US.
HARRY, STOP-- WHERE ARE YOU GOING?! WHAT ARE YOU--
SHE'S STILL OUT THERE, GWEN. PETER'S KILLER STILL IS ON THE LOOSE.
AND I'M THE ONLY ONE WHO CAN STOP HER...

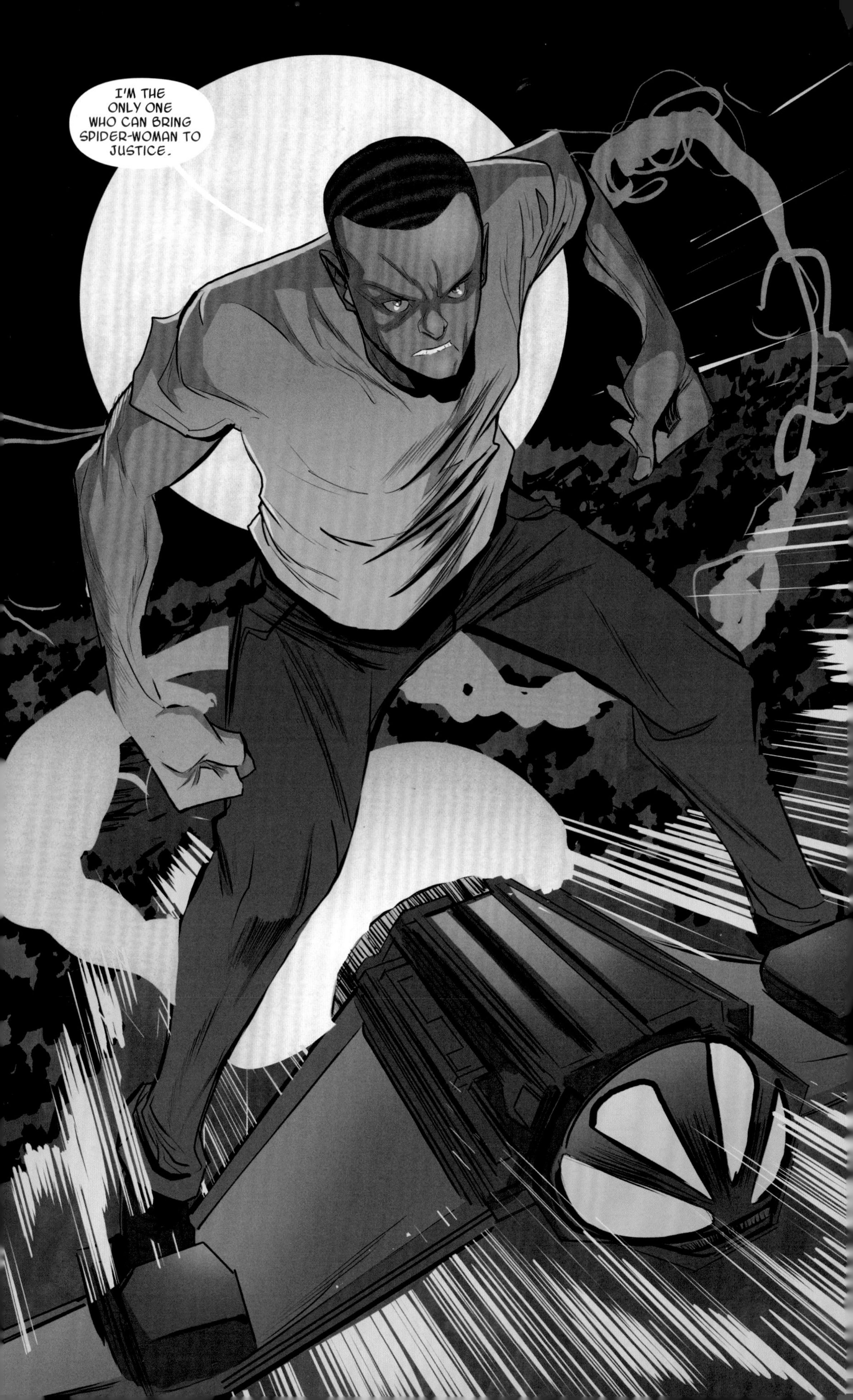
I'M THE ONLY ONE WHO CAN BRING SPIDER-WOMAN TO JUSTICE.

ENTER THE *GREEN GOBLIN!*

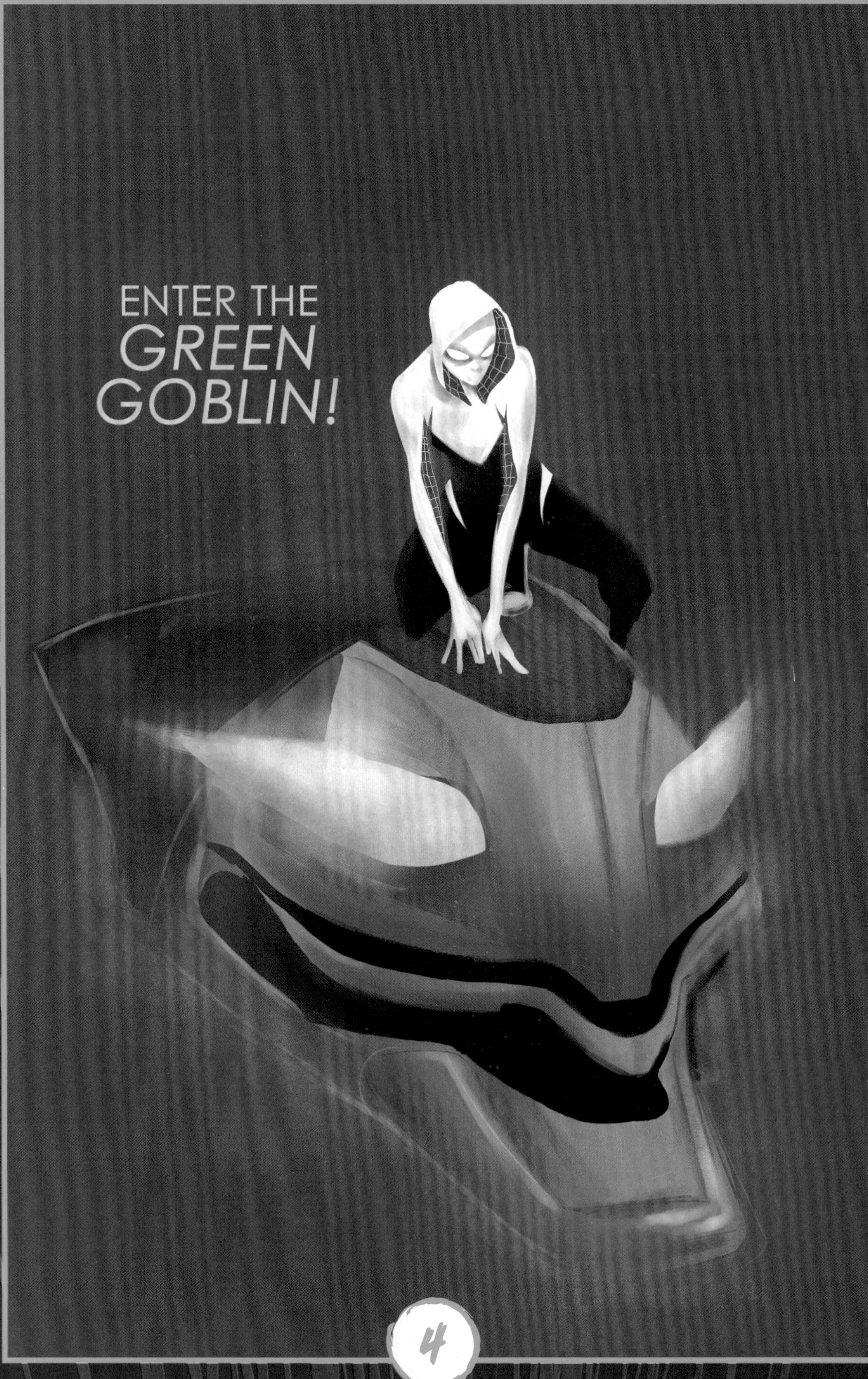

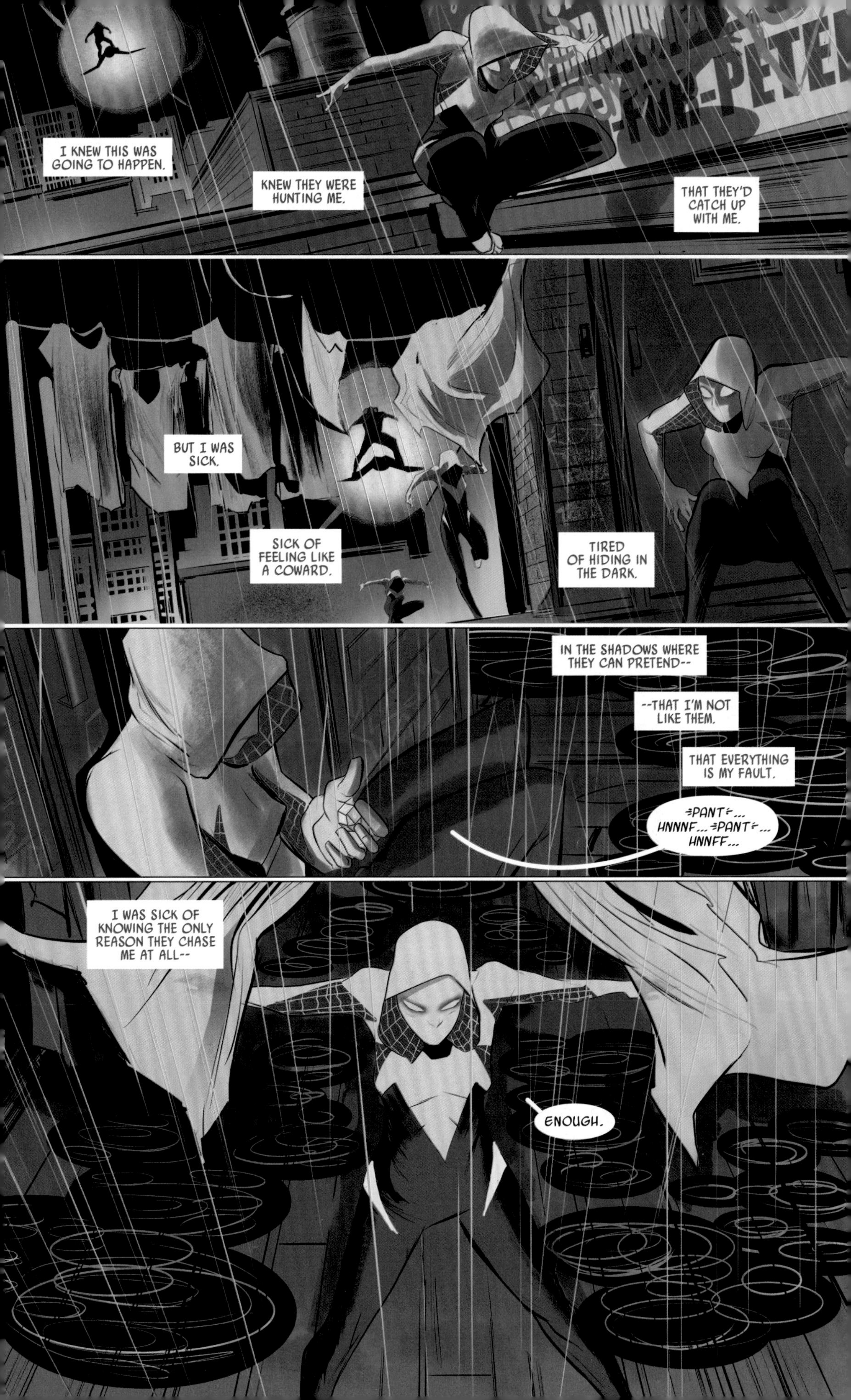
I KNEW THIS WAS GOING TO HAPPEN.
KNEW THEY WERE HUNTING ME.
THAT THEY'D CATCH UP WITH ME.
BUT I WAS SICK.
SICK OF FEELING LIKE A COWARD.
TIRED OF HIDING IN THE DARK.
IN THE SHADOWS WHERE THEY CAN PRETEND--
--THAT I'M NOT LIKE THEM.
THAT EVERYTHING IS MY FAULT.
=PANT=... HNNNF... =PANT=... HNNFF...
I WAS SICK OF KNOWING THE ONLY REASON THEY CHASE ME AT ALL--
ENOUGH.

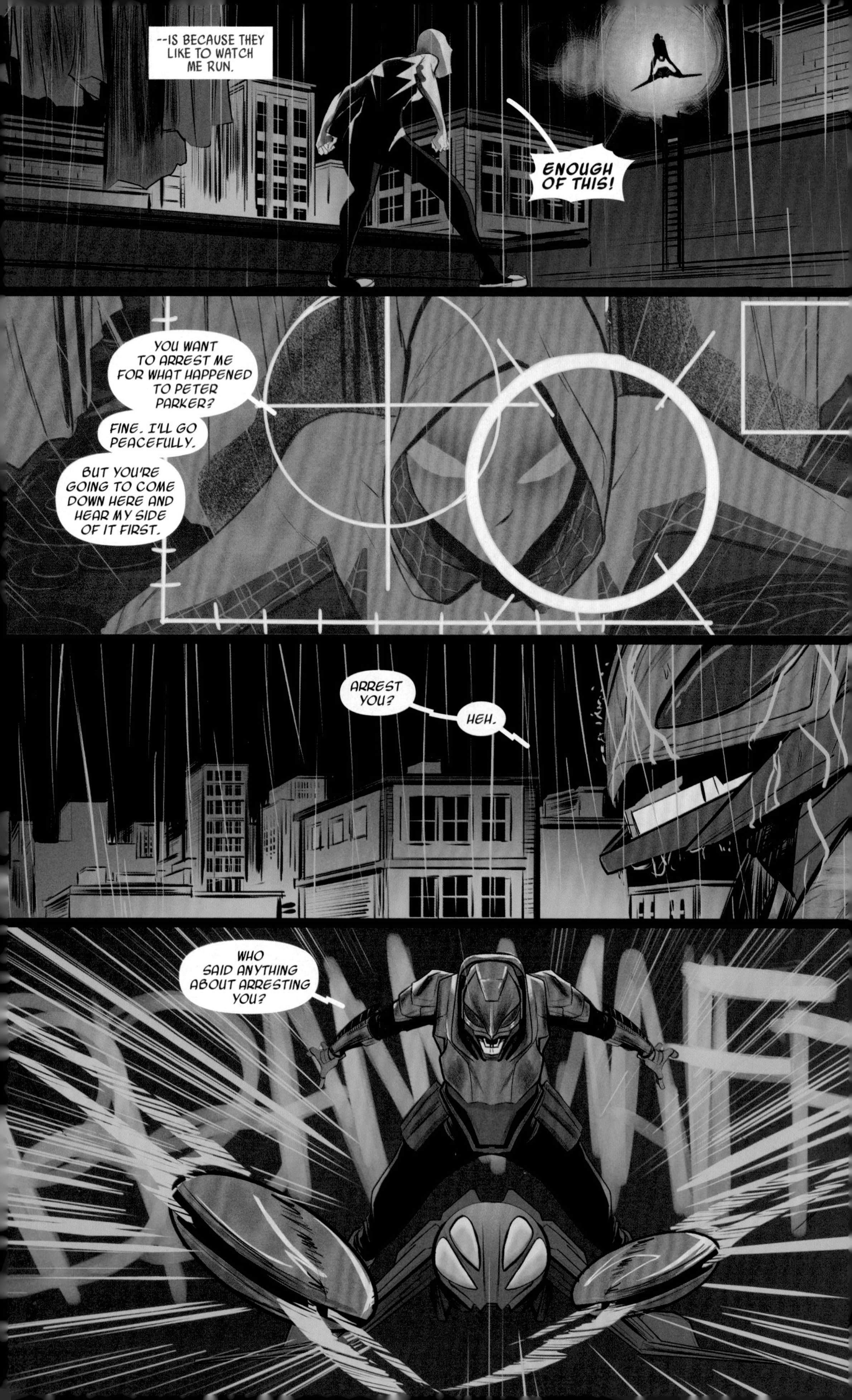
--IS BECAUSE THEY LIKE TO WATCH ME RUN.
ENOUGH OF THIS!
YOU WANT TO ARREST ME FOR WHAT HAPPENED TO PETER PARKER?
FINE. I'LL GO PEACEFULLY.
BUT YOU'RE GOING TO COME DOWN HERE AND HEAR MY SIDE OF IT FIRST.
ARREST YOU?
HEH.
WHO SAID ANYTHING ABOUT ARRESTING YOU?

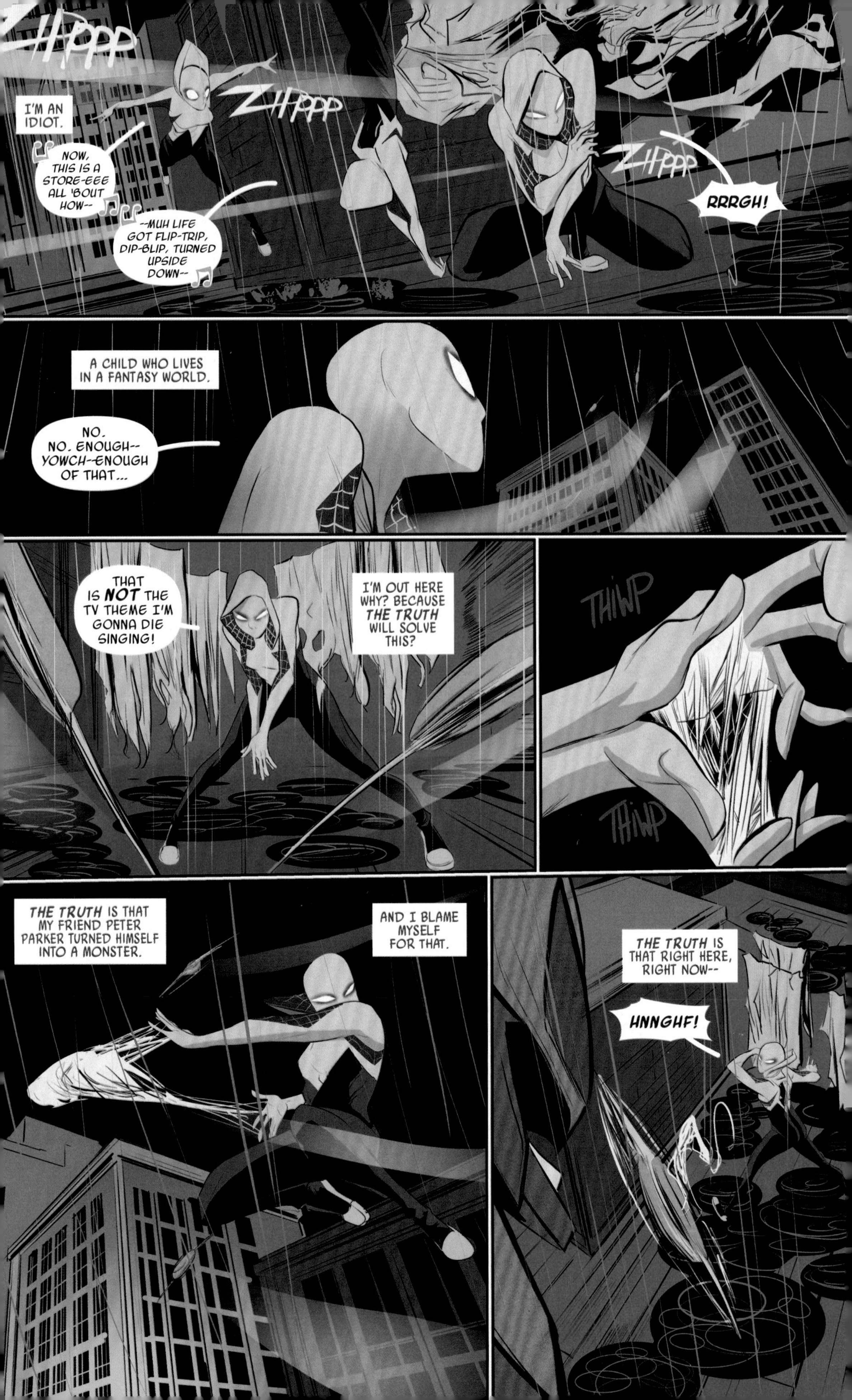
ZIPPP
I'M AN IDIOT.
NOW, THIS IS A STORE-EEE ALL 'BOUT HOW--
ZIPPP
--MUH LIFE GOT FLIP-TRIP, DIP-BLIP, TURNED UPSIDE DOWN--
ZIPPP
RRRGH!
A CHILD WHO LIVES IN A FANTASY WORLD.
NO. NO. ENOUGH-- YOWCH--ENOUGH OF THAT...
THAT IS NOT THE TV THEME I'M GONNA DIE SINGING!
I'M OUT HERE WHY? BECAUSE THE TRUTH WILL SOLVE THIS?
THIWP
THIWP
THE TRUTH IS THAT MY FRIEND PETER PARKER TURNED HIMSELF INTO A MONSTER.
AND I BLAME MYSELF FOR THAT.
THE TRUTH IS THAT RIGHT HERE, RIGHT NOW--
UNNGHF!

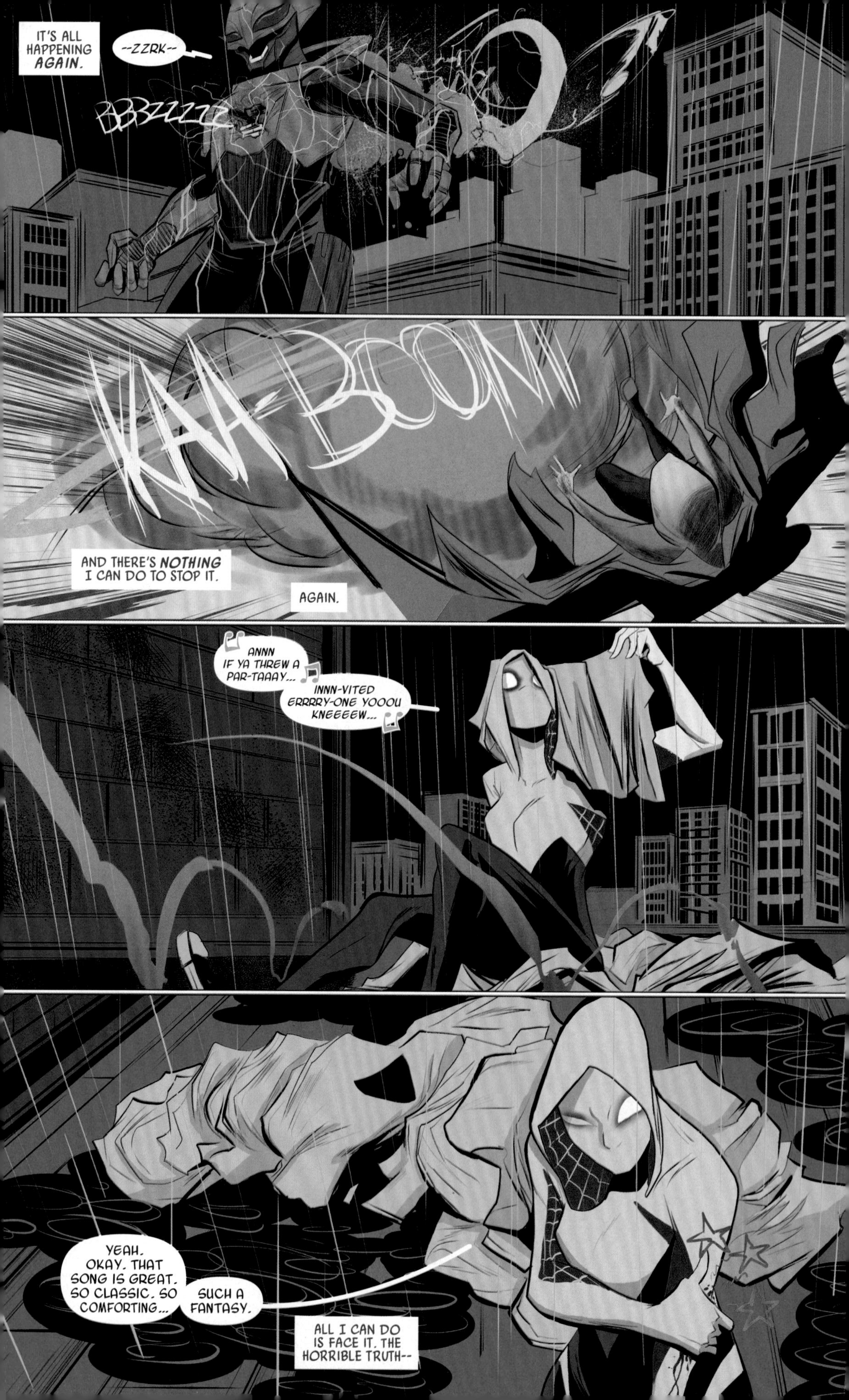
IT'S ALL HAPPENING AGAIN.
--ZZRK--
BBBZZZZZZ
KA-BOOM!
AND THERE'S NOTHING I CAN DO TO STOP IT.
AGAIN.
ANNN IF YA THREW A PAR-TAAAY...
INNN-VITED ERRRRY-ONE YOOOU KNEEEEW...
YEAH. OKAY. THAT SONG IS GREAT. SO CLASSIC. SO COMFORTING...
SUCH A FANTASY.
ALL I CAN DO IS FACE IT. THE HORRIBLE TRUTH--

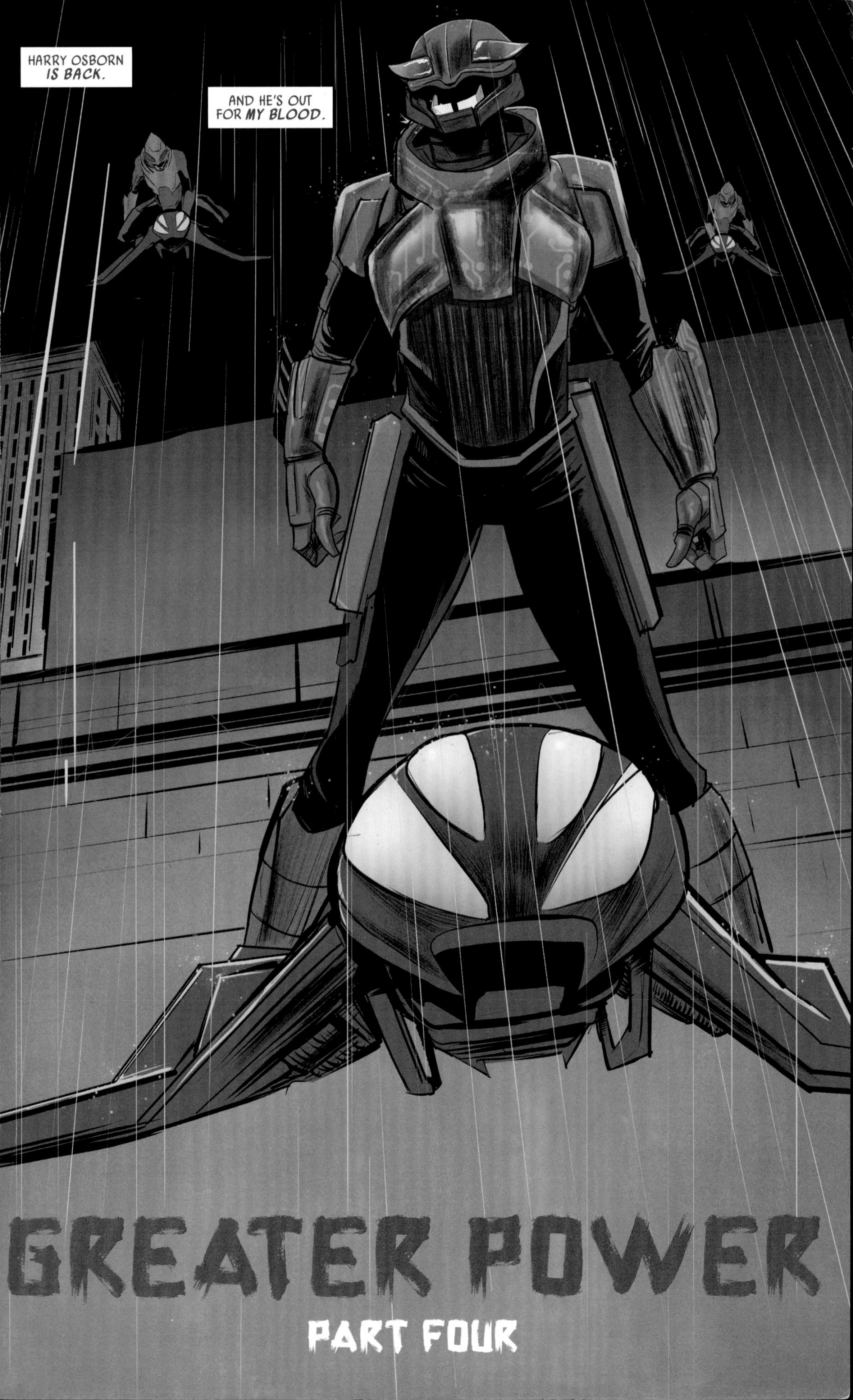
HARRY OSBORN IS BACK.
AND HE'S OUT FOR MY BLOOD.
GREATER POWER
PART FOUR

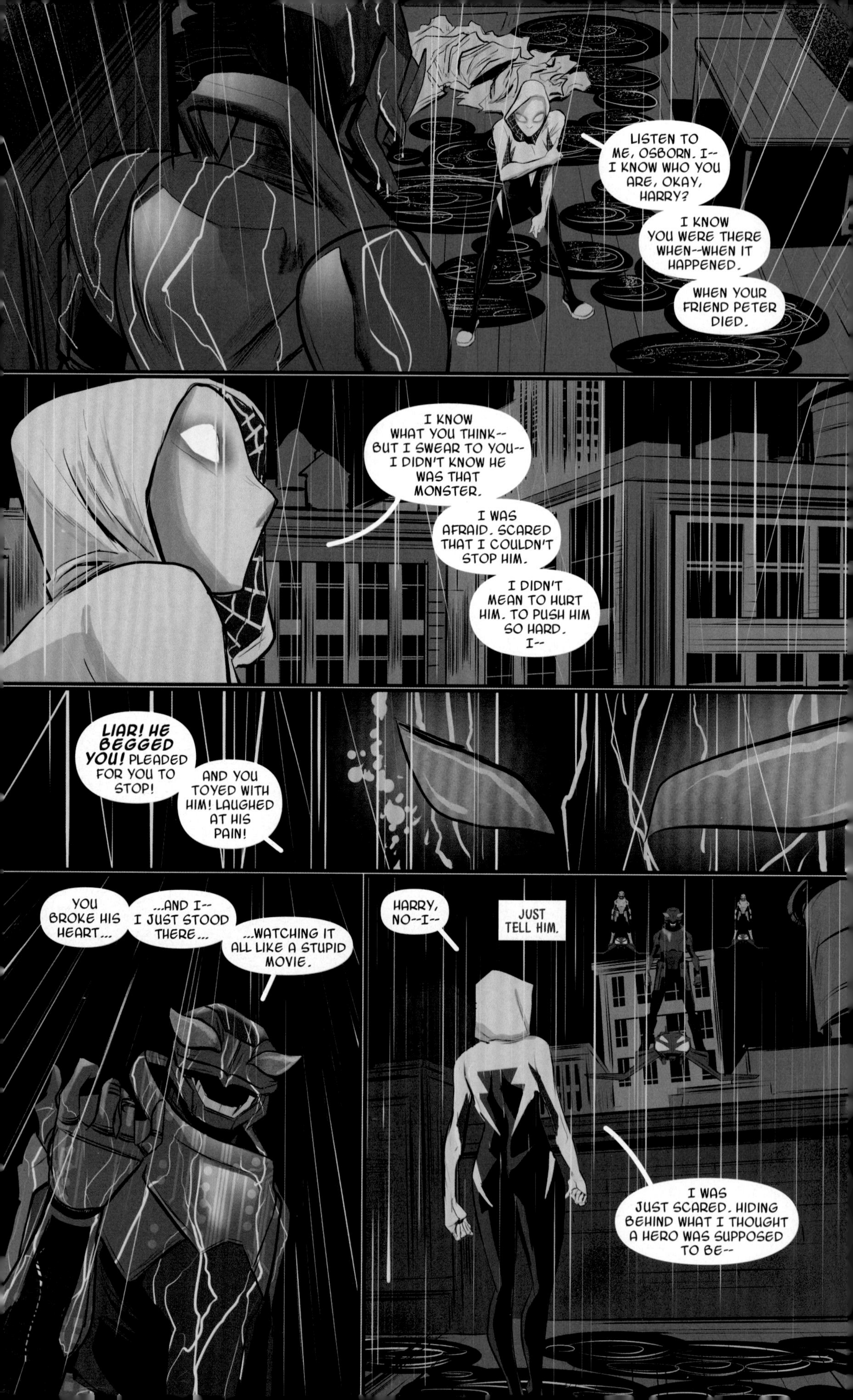
LISTEN TO ME, OSBORN. I-- I KNOW WHO YOU ARE, OKAY, HARRY?
I KNOW YOU WERE THERE WHEN--WHEN IT HAPPENED.
WHEN YOUR FRIEND PETER DIED.
I KNOW WHAT YOU THINK-- BUT I SWEAR TO YOU-- I DIDN'T KNOW HE WAS THAT MONSTER.
I WAS AFRAID. SCARED THAT I COULDN'T STOP HIM.
I DIDN'T MEAN TO HURT HIM. TO PUSH HIM SO HARD. I--
LIAR! HE BEGGED YOU! PLEADED FOR YOU TO STOP!
AND YOU TOYED WITH HIM! LAUGHED AT HIS PAIN!
YOU BROKE HIS HEART...
...AND I-- I JUST STOOD THERE...
...WATCHING IT ALL LIKE A STUPID MOVIE.
HARRY, NO--I--
JUST TELL HIM.
I WAS JUST SCARED. HIDING BEHIND WHAT I THOUGHT A HERO WAS SUPPOSED TO BE--

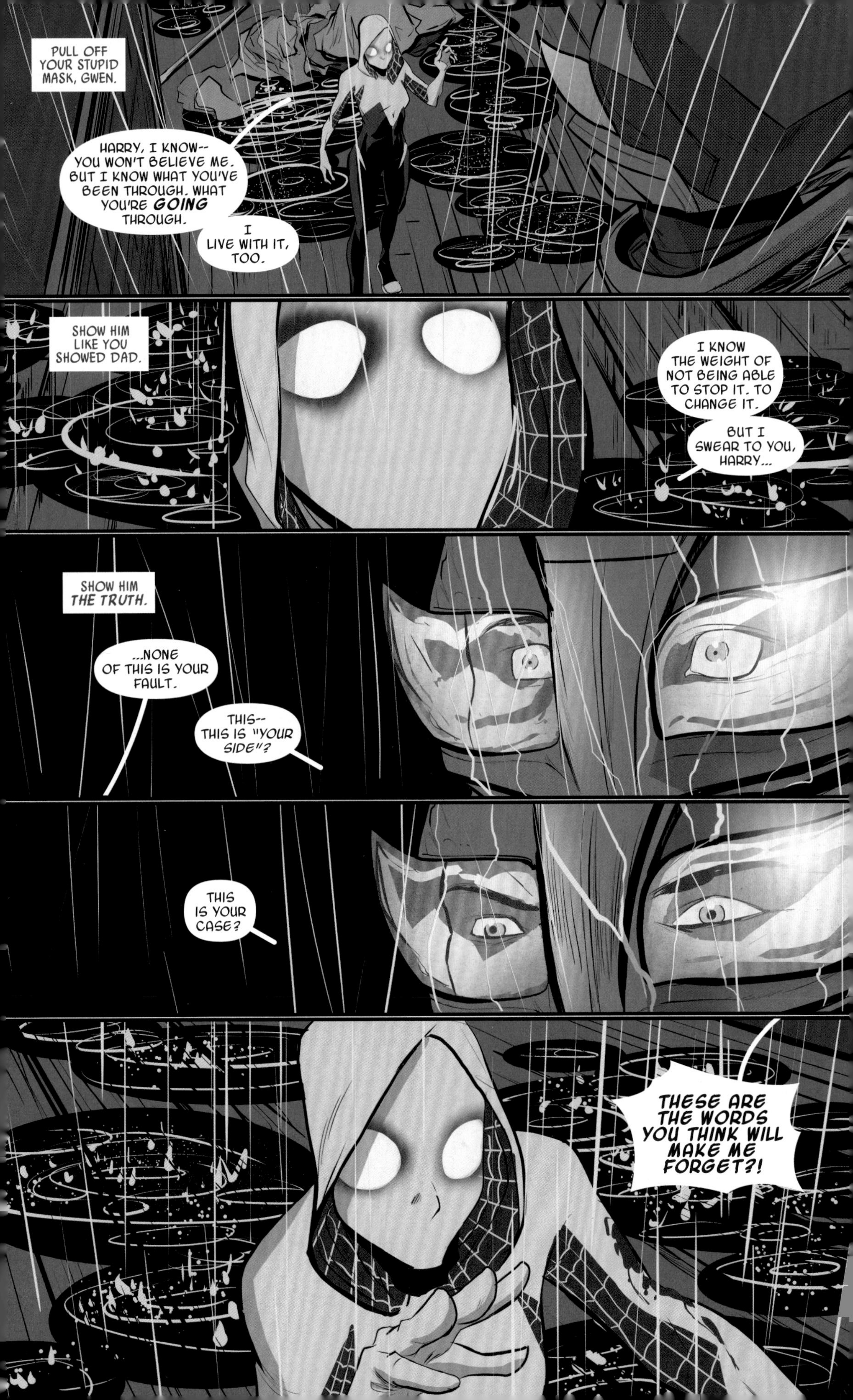
PULL OFF YOUR STUPID MASK, GWEN.
HARRY, I KNOW-- YOU WON'T BELIEVE ME. BUT I KNOW WHAT YOU'VE BEEN THROUGH. WHAT YOU'RE GOING THROUGH.
I LIVE WITH IT, TOO.
SHOW HIM LIKE YOU SHOWED DAD.
I KNOW THE WEIGHT OF NOT BEING ABLE TO STOP IT. TO CHANGE IT.
BUT I SWEAR TO YOU, HARRY...
SHOW HIM THE TRUTH.
...NONE OF THIS IS YOUR FAULT.
THIS-- THIS IS "YOUR SIDE"?
THIS IS YOUR CASE?
THESE ARE THE WORDS YOU THINK WILL MAKE ME FORGET?!

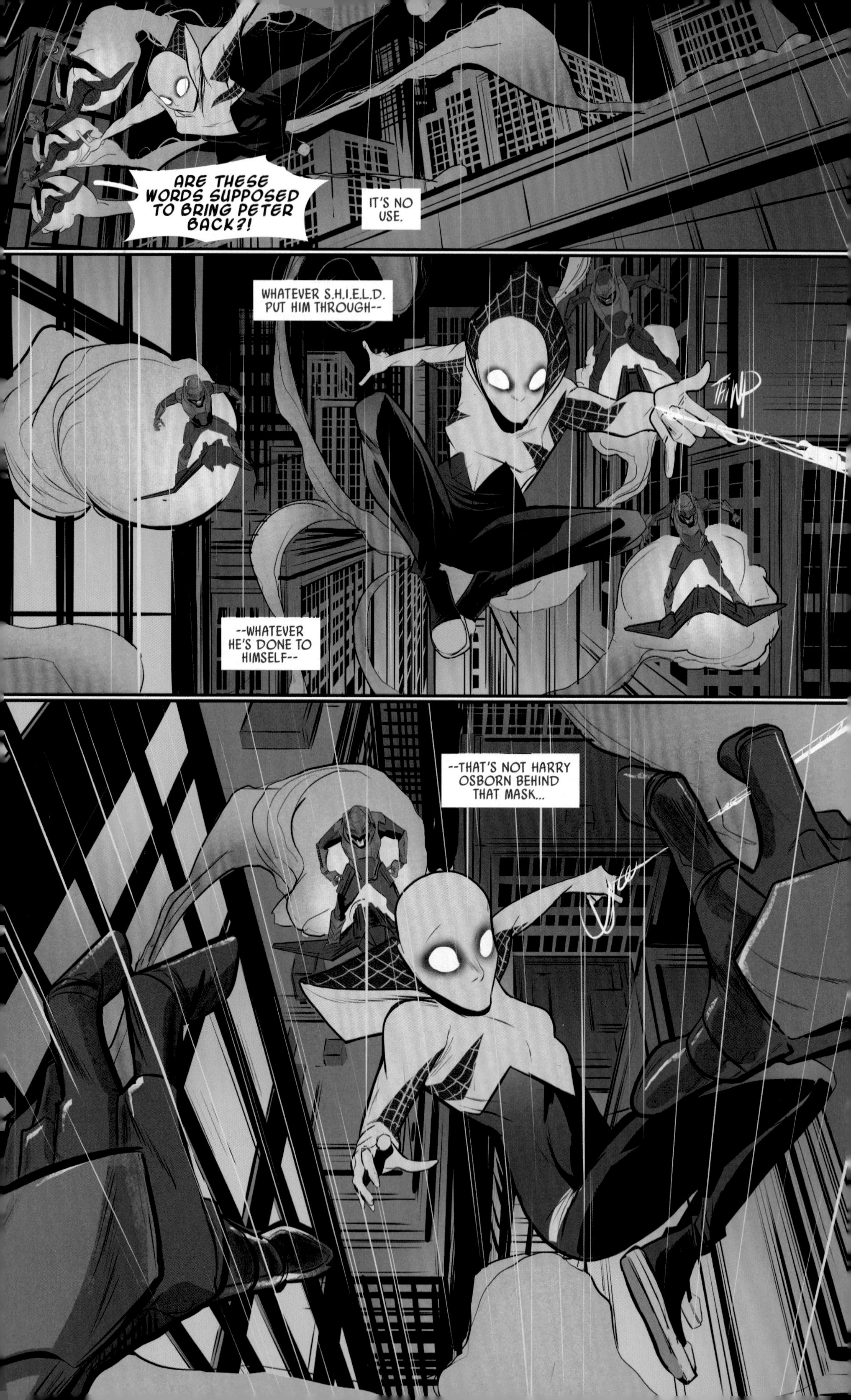
ARE THESE WORDS SUPPOSED TO BRING PETER BACK?!
IT'S NO USE.
WHATEVER S.H.I.E.L.D. PUT HIM THROUGH--
THWIP
--WHATEVER HE'S DONE TO HIMSELF--
--THAT'S NOT HARRY OSBORN BEHIND THAT MASK...

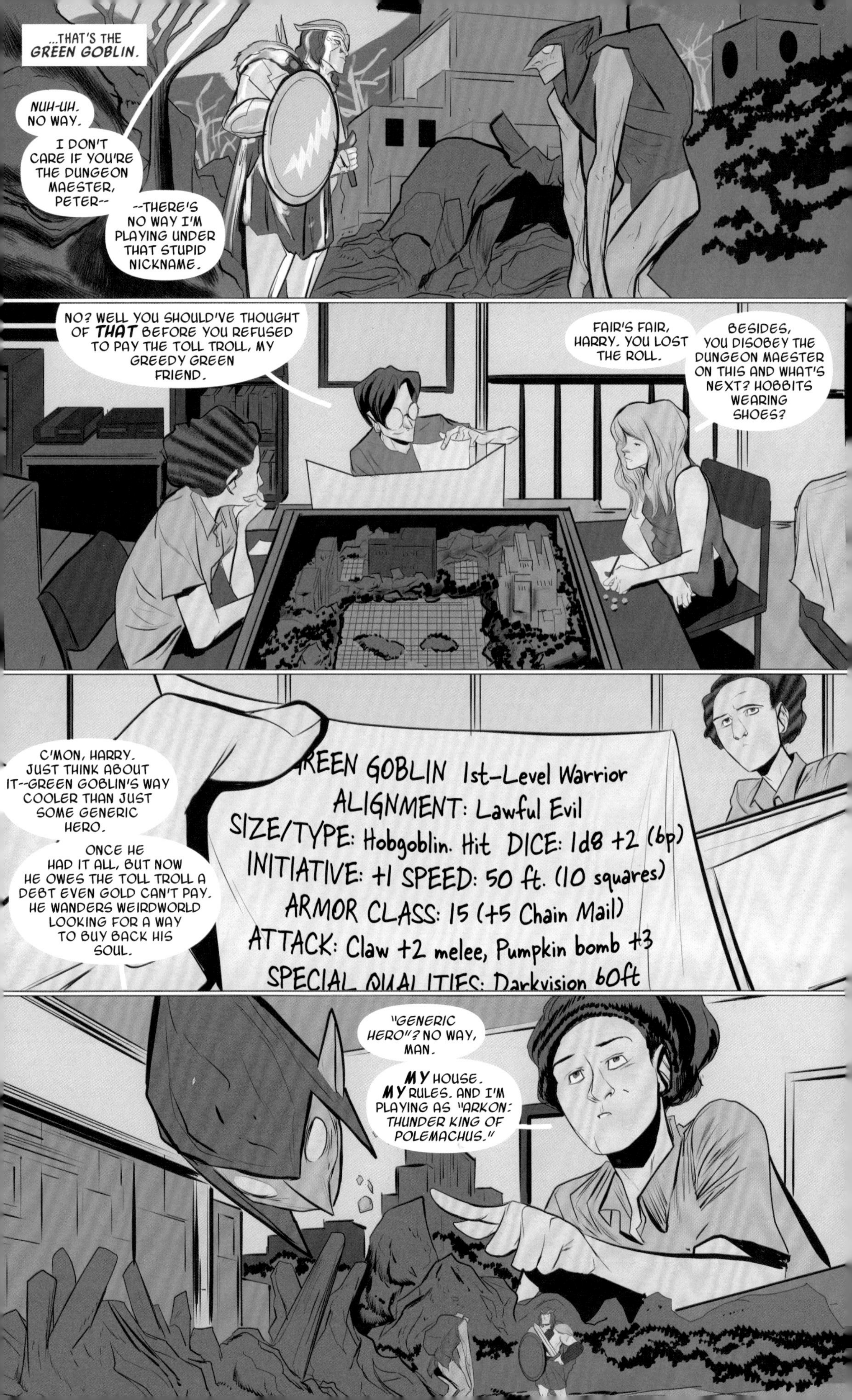
...THAT'S THE GREEN GOBLIN.
NUH-UH. NO WAY.
I DON'T CARE IF YOU'RE THE DUNGEON MAESTER, PETER--
--THERE'S NO WAY I'M PLAYING UNDER THAT STUPID NICKNAME.
NO? WELL YOU SHOULD'VE THOUGHT OF THAT BEFORE YOU REFUSED TO PAY THE TOLL TROLL, MY GREEDY GREEN FRIEND.
FAIR'S FAIR, HARRY. YOU LOST THE ROLL.
BESIDES, YOU DISOBEY THE DUNGEON MAESTER ON THIS AND WHAT'S NEXT? HOBBITS WEARING SHOES?
C'MON, HARRY. JUST THINK ABOUT IT--GREEN GOBLIN'S WAY COOLER THAN JUST SOME GENERIC HERO.
ONCE HE HAD IT ALL, BUT NOW HE OWES THE TOLL TROLL A DEBT EVEN GOLD CAN'T PAY. HE WANDERS WEIRDWORLD LOOKING FOR A WAY TO BUY BACK HIS SOUL.
REEN GOBLIN 1st-Level Warrior
ALIGNMENT: Lawful Evil
SIZE/TYPE: Hobgoblin. Hit DICE: 1d8 +2 (6p)
INITIATIVE: +1 SPEED: 50 ft. (10 squares)
ARMOR CLASS: 15 (+5 Chain Mail)
ATTACK: Claw +2 melee, Pumpkin bomb +3
"GENERIC HERO"? NO WAY, MAN.
MY HOUSE. MY RULES. AND I'M PLAYING AS "ARKON: THUNDER KING OF POLEMACHUS."

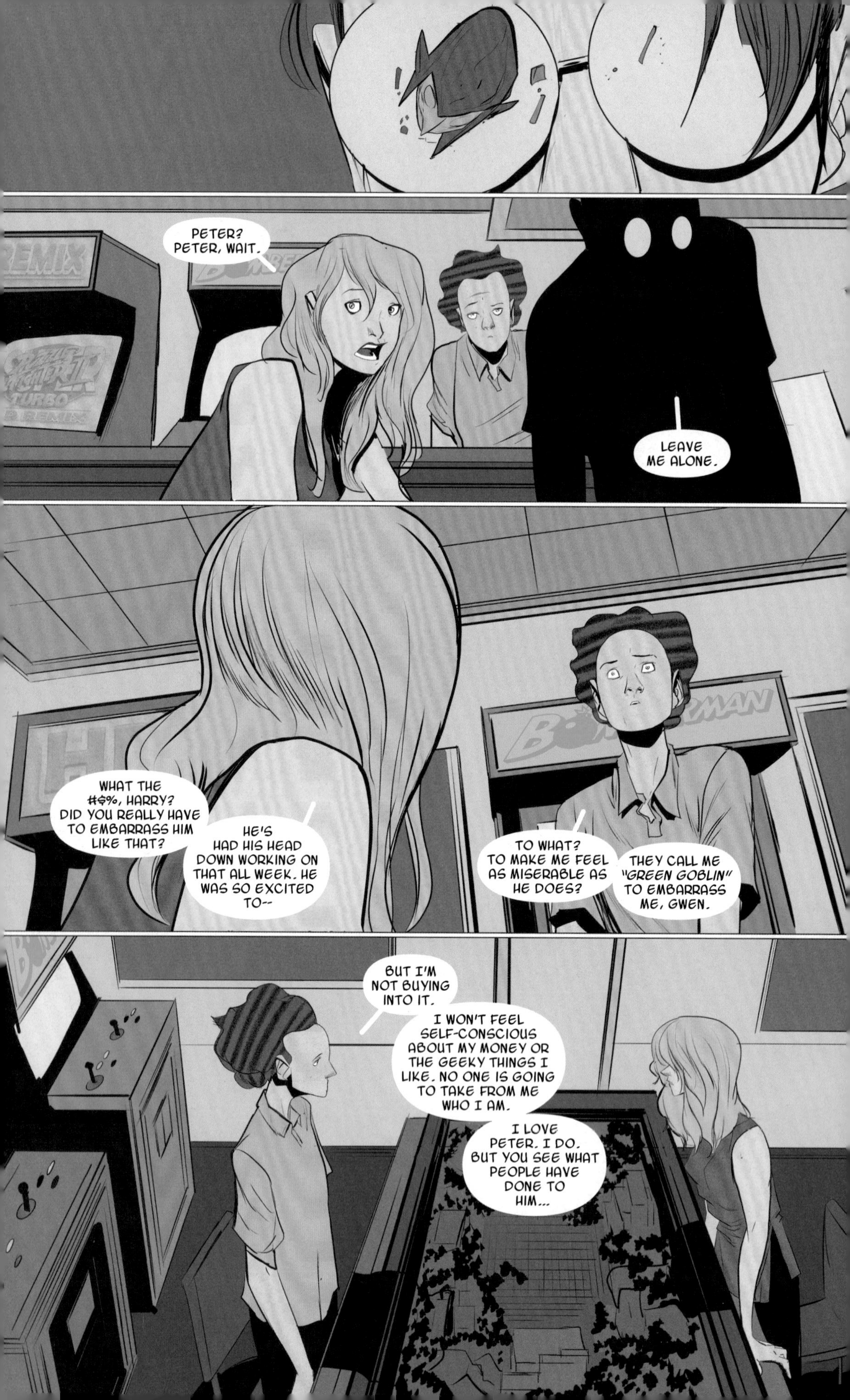

REMIX
PETER? PETER, WAIT.
STREET FIGHTER II TURBO HD REMIX
LEAVE ME ALONE.
WHAT THE #$%, HARRY? DID YOU REALLY HAVE TO EMBARRASS HIM LIKE THAT?
HE'S HAD HIS HEAD DOWN WORKING ON THAT ALL WEEK. HE WAS SO EXCITED TO--
TO WHAT? TO MAKE ME FEEL AS MISERABLE AS HE DOES?
THEY CALL ME "GREEN GOBLIN" TO EMBARRASS ME, GWEN.
BUT I'M NOT BUYING INTO IT.
I WON'T FEEL SELF-CONSCIOUS ABOUT MY MONEY OR THE GEEKY THINGS I LIKE. NO ONE IS GOING TO TAKE FROM ME WHO I AM.
I LOVE PETER. I DO. BUT YOU SEE WHAT PEOPLE HAVE DONE TO HIM...

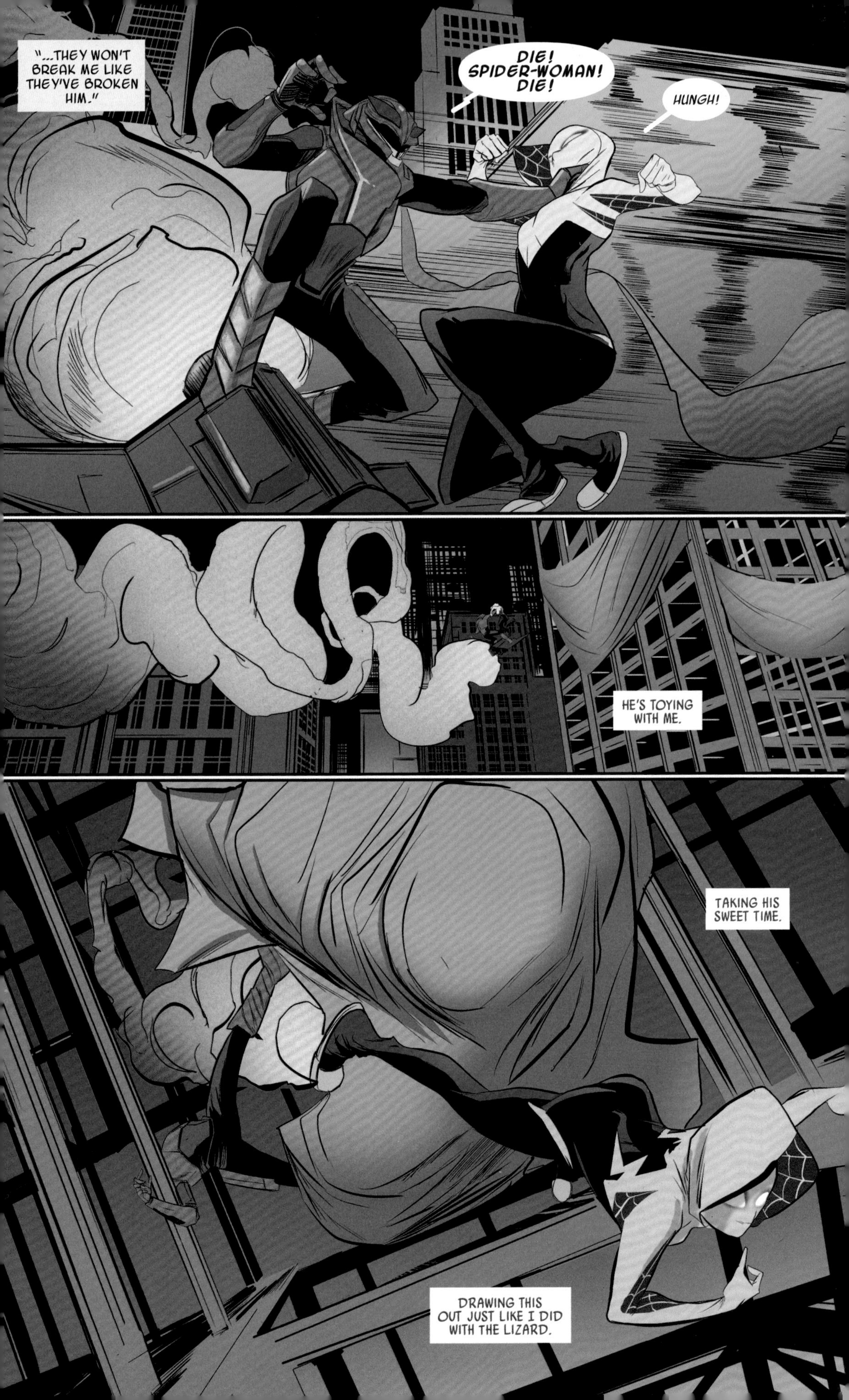
"...THEY WON'T BREAK ME LIKE THEY'VE BROKEN HIM."
DIE! SPIDER-WOMAN! DIE!
HUNGH!
HE'S TOYING WITH ME.
TAKING HIS SWEET TIME.
DRAWING THIS OUT JUST LIKE I DID WITH THE LIZARD.

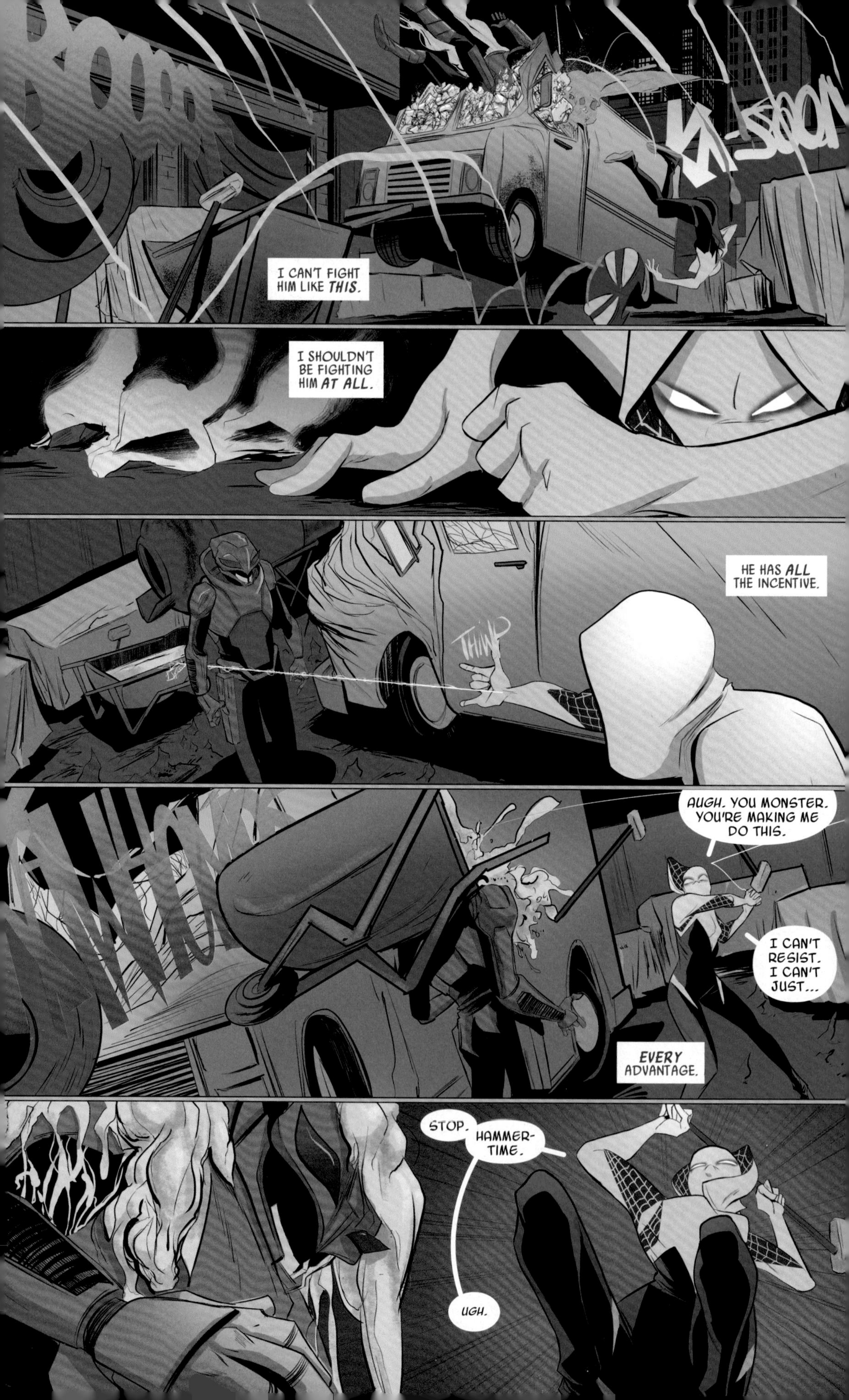

BOOOM
KA-SPOOM
I CAN'T FIGHT HIM LIKE THIS.
I SHOULDN'T BE FIGHTING HIM AT ALL.
HE HAS ALL THE INCENTIVE.
THWIP
AUGH. YOU MONSTER. YOU'RE MAKING ME DO THIS.
I CAN'T RESIST. I CAN'T JUST...
EVERY ADVANTAGE.
STOP.
HAMMER-TIME.
UGH.

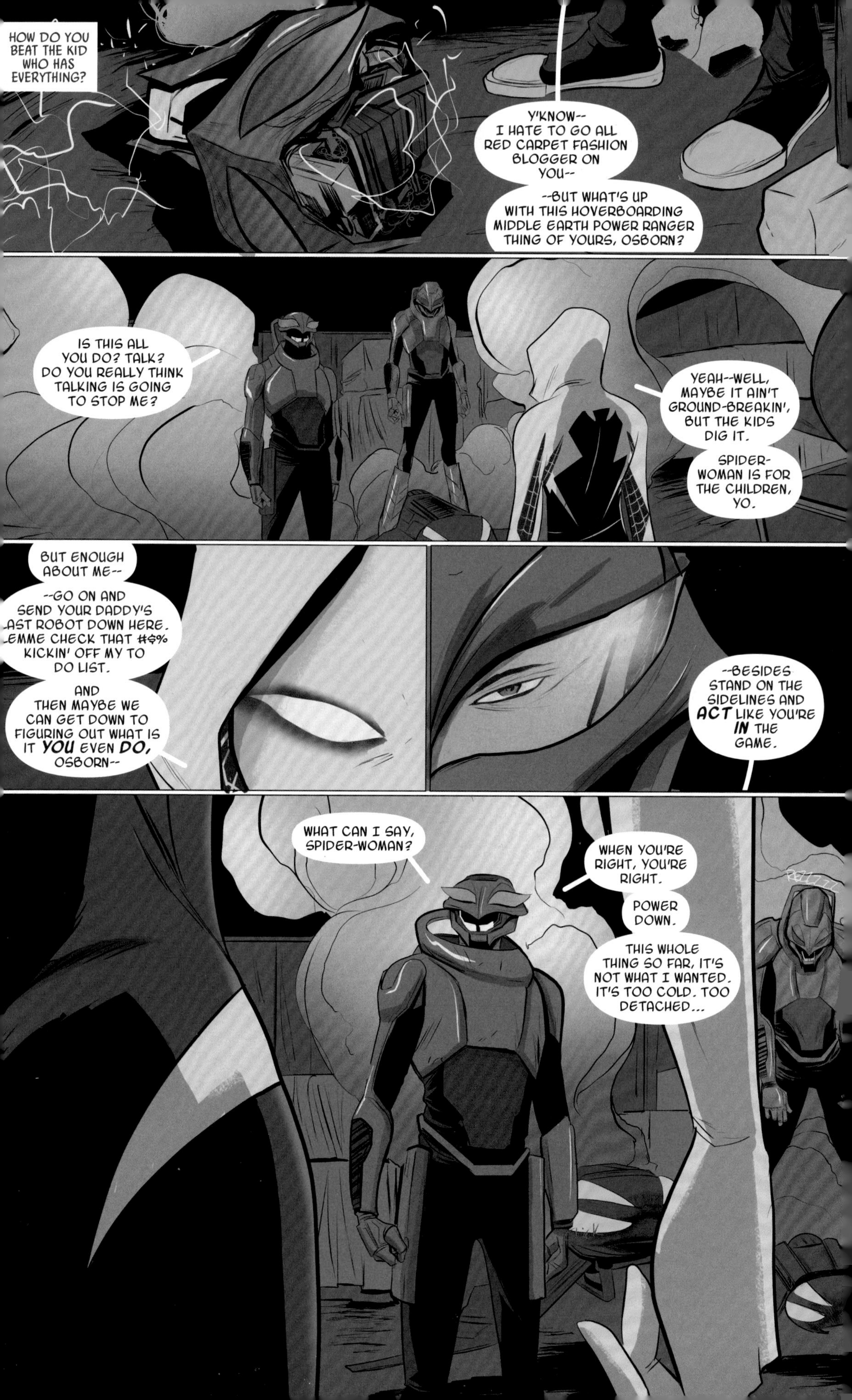

HOW DO YOU BEAT THE KID WHO HAS EVERYTHING?
Y'KNOW-- I HATE TO GO ALL RED CARPET FASHION BLOGGER ON YOU--
--BUT WHAT'S UP WITH THIS HOVERBOARDING MIDDLE EARTH POWER RANGER THING OF YOURS, OSBORN?
IS THIS ALL YOU DO? TALK? DO YOU REALLY THINK TALKING IS GOING TO STOP ME?
YEAH--WELL, MAYBE IT AIN'T GROUND-BREAKIN', BUT THE KIDS DIG IT.
SPIDER-WOMAN IS FOR THE CHILDREN, YO.
BUT ENOUGH ABOUT ME--
--GO ON AND SEND YOUR DADDY'S LAST ROBOT DOWN HERE. LEMME CHECK THAT #$% KICKIN' OFF MY TO DO LIST.
AND THEN MAYBE WE CAN GET DOWN TO FIGURING OUT WHAT IS IT **YOU** EVEN **DO,** OSBORN--
--BESIDES STAND ON THE SIDELINES AND **ACT** LIKE YOU'RE **IN** THE GAME.
WHAT CAN I SAY, SPIDER-WOMAN?
WHEN YOU'RE RIGHT, YOU'RE RIGHT.
POWER DOWN.
THIS WHOLE THING SO FAR, IT'S NOT WHAT I WANTED. IT'S TOO COLD. TOO DETACHED...

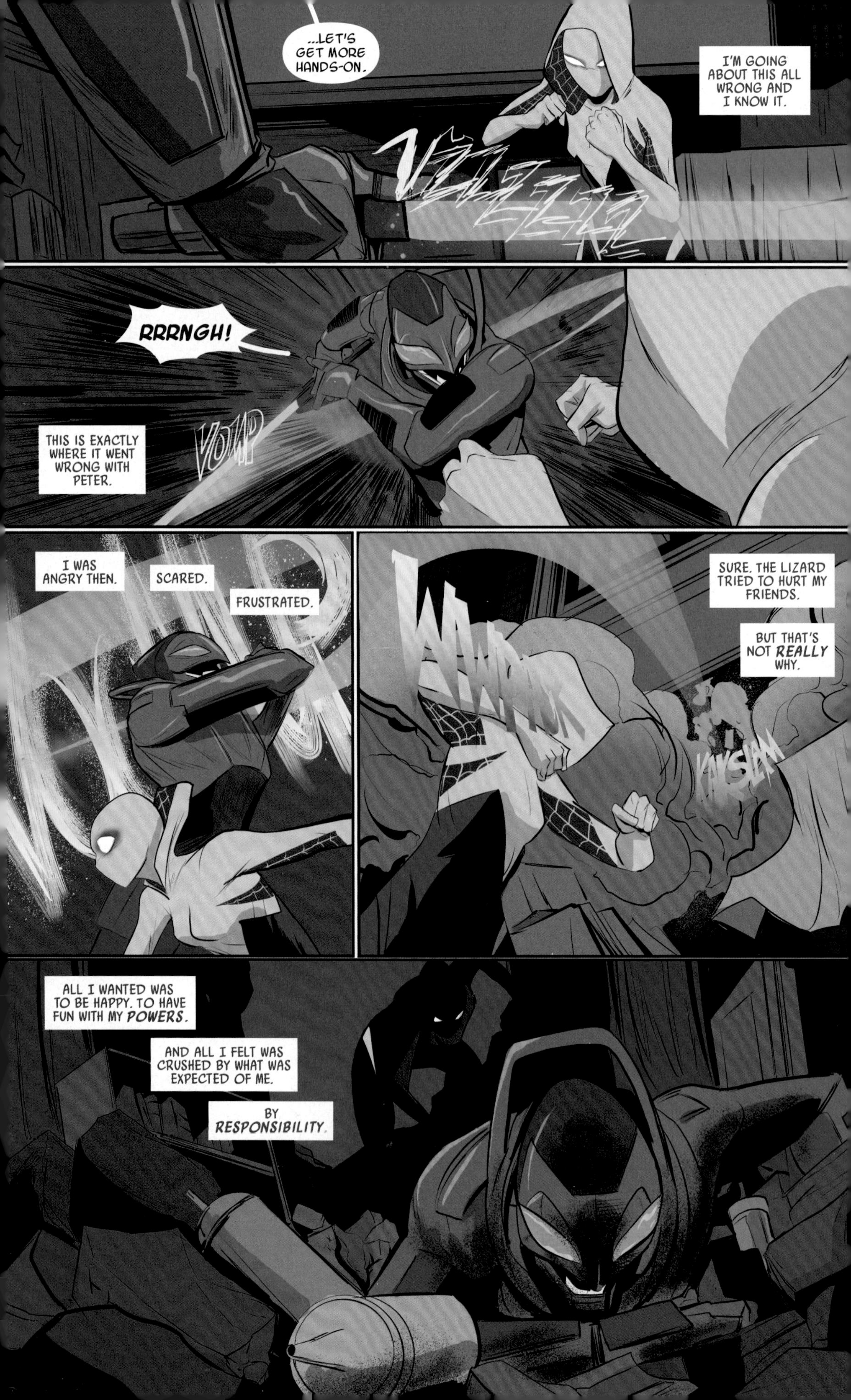

...LET'S GET MORE HANDS-ON.
I'M GOING ABOUT THIS ALL WRONG AND I KNOW IT.
RRRNGH!
THIS IS EXACTLY WHERE IT WENT WRONG WITH PETER.
VOMP
I WAS ANGRY THEN.
SCARED.
FRUSTRATED.
SURE, THE LIZARD TRIED TO HURT MY FRIENDS.
BUT THAT'S NOT *REALLY* WHY.
ALL I WANTED WAS TO BE HAPPY. TO HAVE FUN WITH MY *POWERS*.
AND ALL I FELT WAS CRUSHED BY WHAT WAS EXPECTED OF ME.
BY *RESPONSIBILITY*.

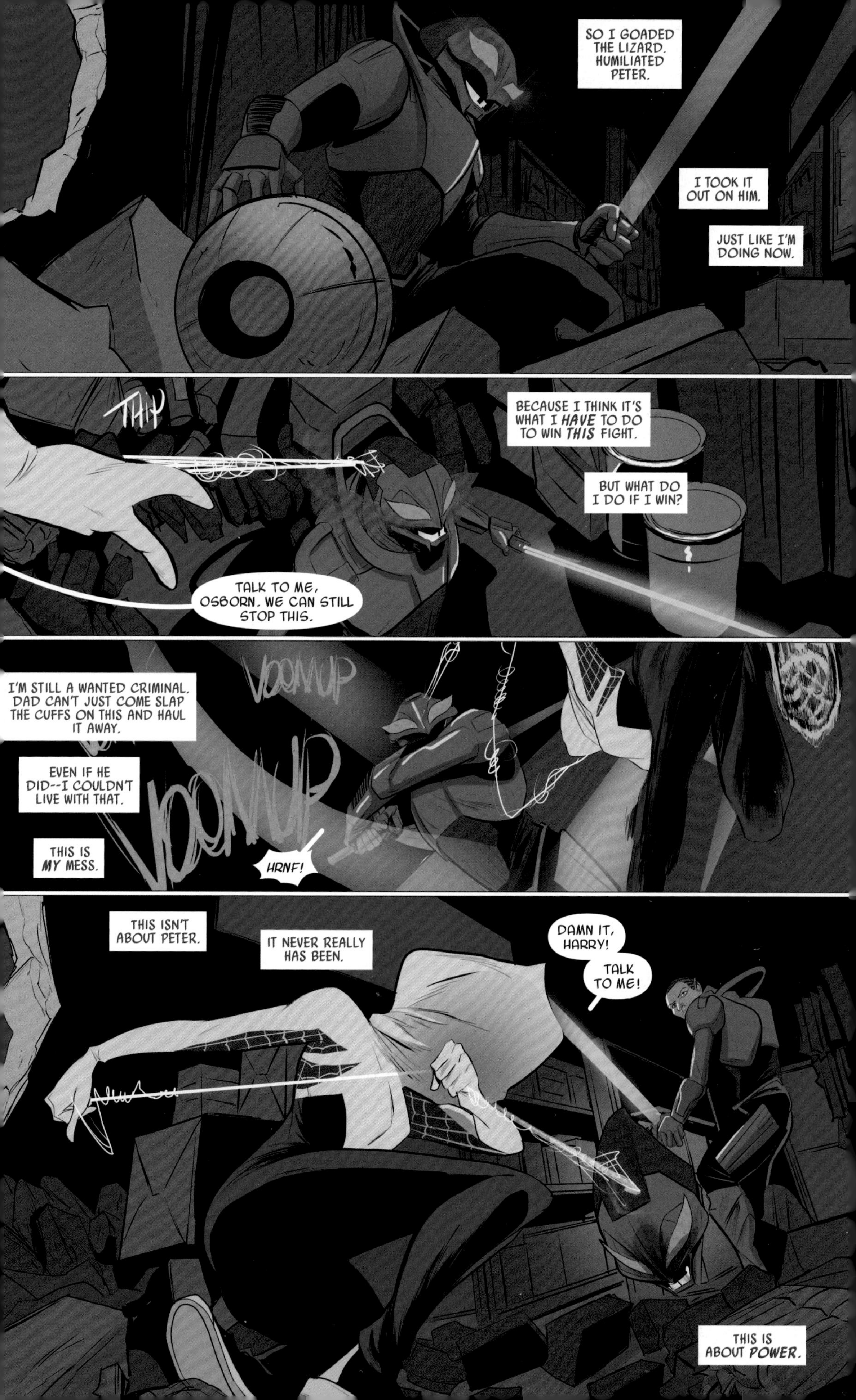
SO I GOADED THE LIZARD. HUMILIATED PETER.
I TOOK IT OUT ON HIM.
JUST LIKE I'M DOING NOW.
THIP
BECAUSE I THINK IT'S WHAT I *HAVE* TO DO TO WIN *THIS* FIGHT.
BUT WHAT DO I DO IF I WIN?
TALK TO ME, OSBORN. WE CAN STILL STOP THIS.
VOOMUP
I'M STILL A WANTED CRIMINAL. DAD CAN'T JUST COME SLAP THE CUFFS ON THIS AND HAUL IT AWAY.
VOOMUP
EVEN IF HE DID--I COULDN'T LIVE WITH THAT.
THIS IS *MY* MESS.
HRNF!
THIS ISN'T ABOUT PETER.
IT NEVER REALLY HAS BEEN.
DAMN IT, HARRY!
TALK TO ME!
THIS IS ABOUT *POWER*.

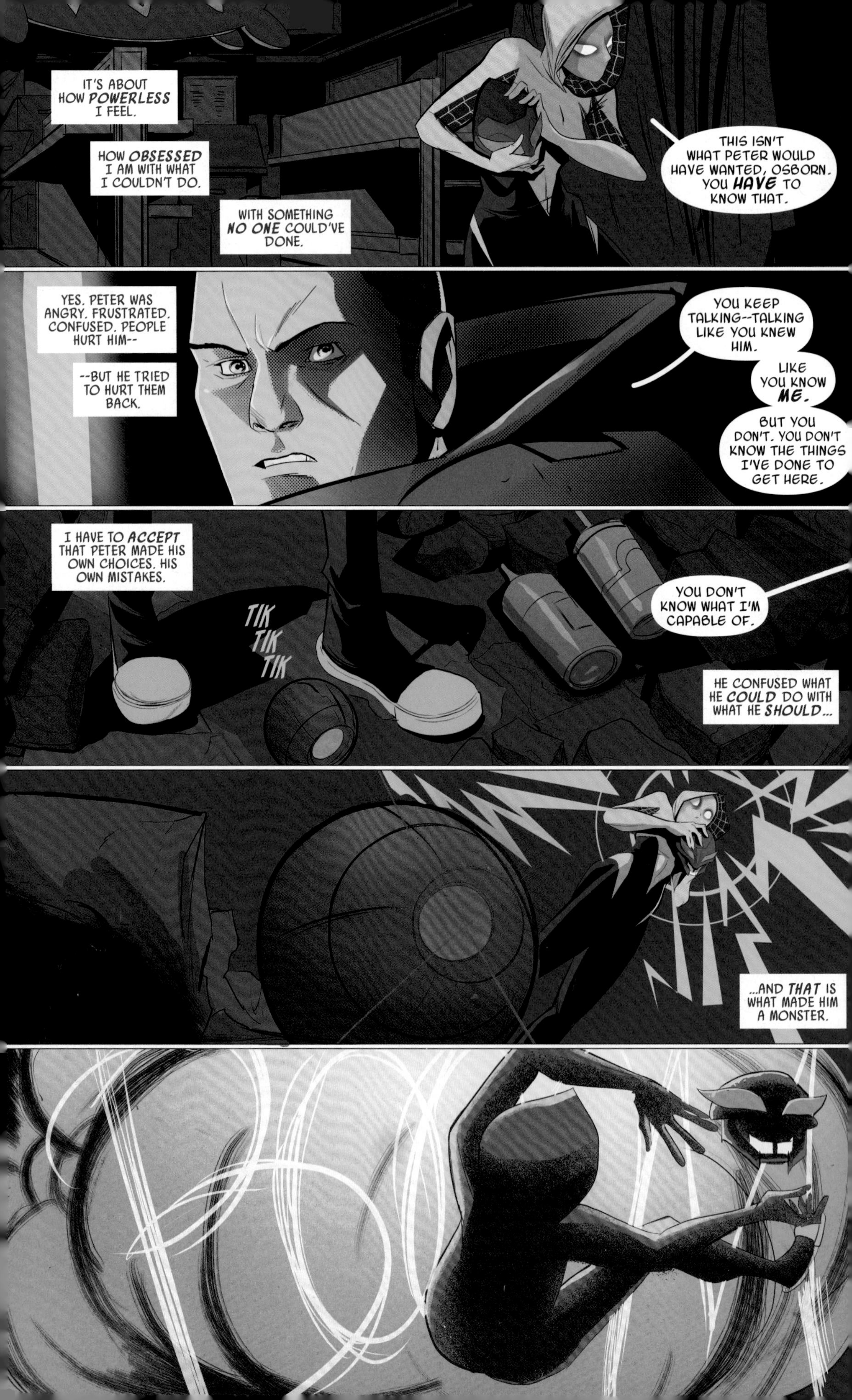
IT'S ABOUT HOW POWERLESS I FEEL.
HOW OBSESSED I AM WITH WHAT I COULDN'T DO.
WITH SOMETHING NO ONE COULD'VE DONE.
THIS ISN'T WHAT PETER WOULD HAVE WANTED, OSBORN. YOU HAVE TO KNOW THAT.
YES. PETER WAS ANGRY. FRUSTRATED. CONFUSED. PEOPLE HURT HIM--
--BUT HE TRIED TO HURT THEM BACK.
YOU KEEP TALKING--TALKING LIKE YOU KNEW HIM.
LIKE YOU KNOW ME.
BUT YOU DON'T. YOU DON'T KNOW THE THINGS I'VE DONE TO GET HERE.
I HAVE TO ACCEPT THAT PETER MADE HIS OWN CHOICES. HIS OWN MISTAKES.
TIK TIK TIK
YOU DON'T KNOW WHAT I'M CAPABLE OF.
HE CONFUSED WHAT HE COULD DO WITH WHAT HE SHOULD...
...AND THAT IS WHAT MADE HIM A MONSTER.

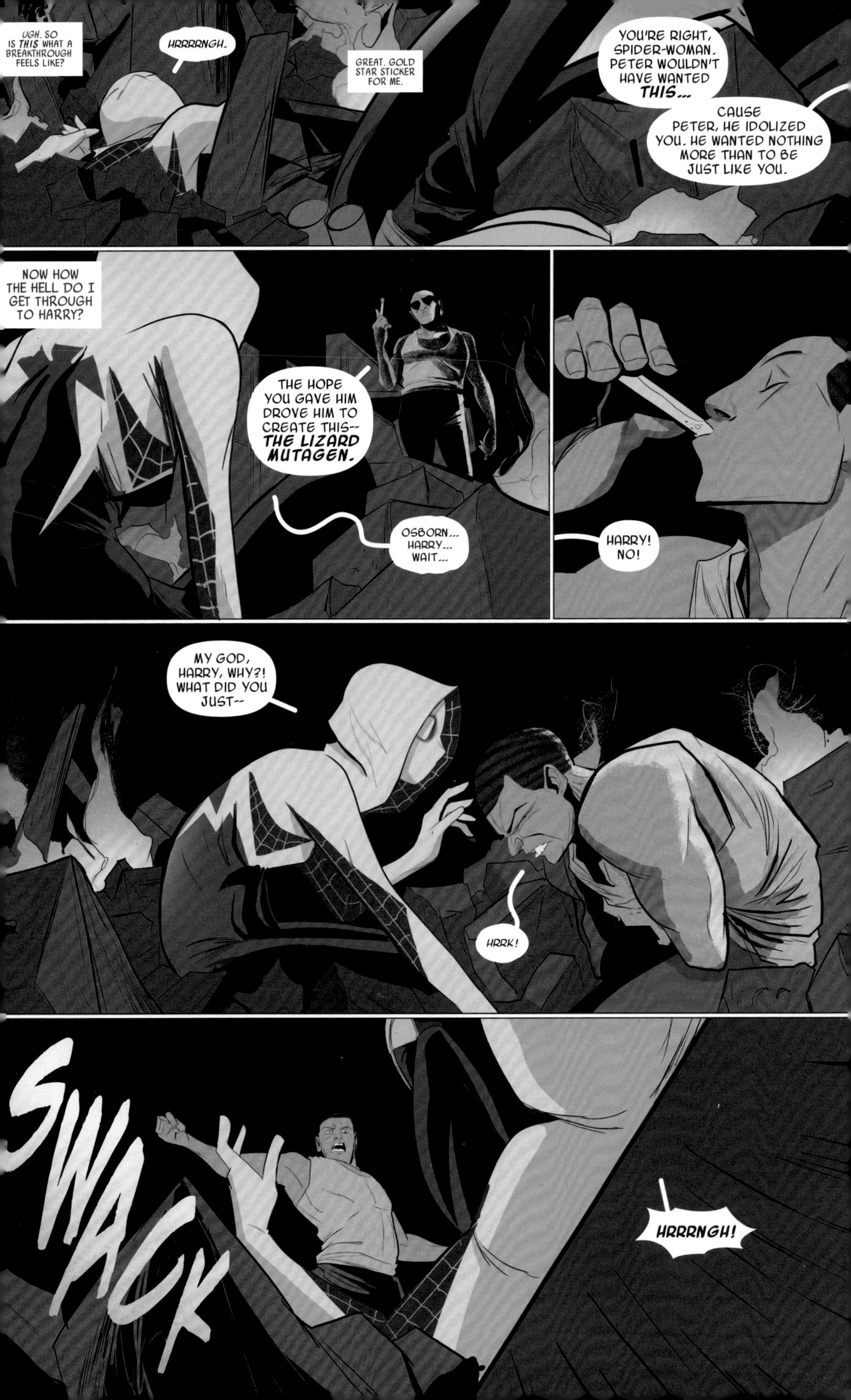
UGH. SO IS THIS WHAT A BREAKTHROUGH FEELS LIKE?
HRRRRNGH.
GREAT. GOLD STAR STICKER FOR ME.
YOU'RE RIGHT, SPIDER-WOMAN. PETER WOULDN'T HAVE WANTED THIS...
CAUSE PETER, HE IDOLIZED YOU. HE WANTED NOTHING MORE THAN TO BE JUST LIKE YOU.
NOW HOW THE HELL DO I GET THROUGH TO HARRY?
THE HOPE YOU GAVE HIM DROVE HIM TO CREATE THIS-- THE LIZARD MUTAGEN.
OSBORN... HARRY... WAIT...
HARRY! NO!
MY GOD, HARRY, WHY?! WHAT DID YOU JUST--
HRRK!
SWACK
HRRRNGH!

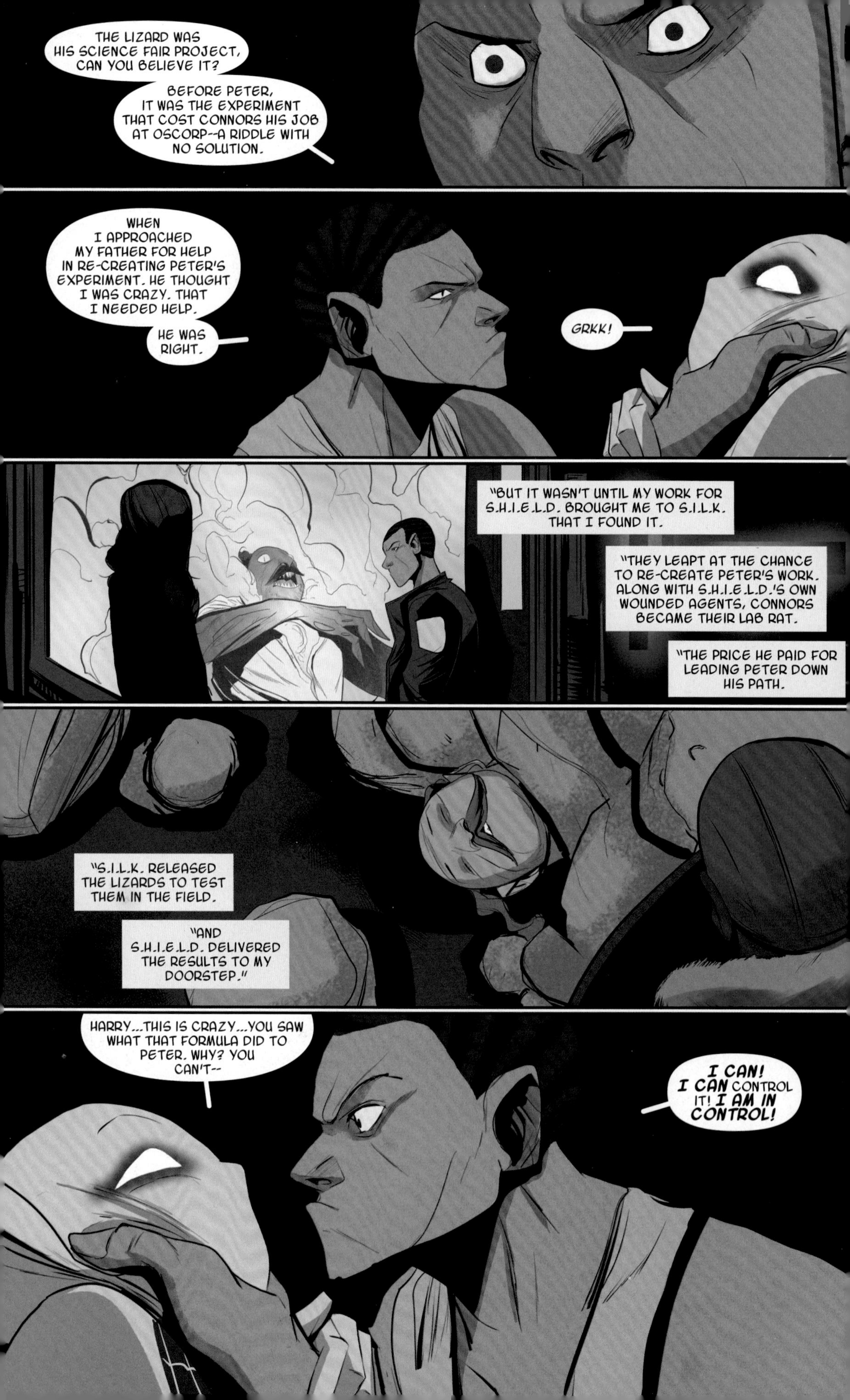
THE LIZARD WAS HIS SCIENCE FAIR PROJECT, CAN YOU BELIEVE IT?
BEFORE PETER, IT WAS THE EXPERIMENT THAT COST CONNORS HIS JOB AT OSCORP--A RIDDLE WITH NO SOLUTION.
WHEN I APPROACHED MY FATHER FOR HELP IN RE-CREATING PETER'S EXPERIMENT. HE THOUGHT I WAS CRAZY. THAT I NEEDED HELP.
HE WAS RIGHT.
GRKK!
"BUT IT WASN'T UNTIL MY WORK FOR S.H.I.E.L.D. BROUGHT ME TO S.I.L.K. THAT I FOUND IT.
"THEY LEAPT AT THE CHANCE TO RE-CREATE PETER'S WORK. ALONG WITH S.H.I.E.L.D.'S OWN WOUNDED AGENTS, CONNORS BECAME THEIR LAB RAT.
"THE PRICE HE PAID FOR LEADING PETER DOWN HIS PATH.
"S.I.L.K. RELEASED THE LIZARDS TO TEST THEM IN THE FIELD.
"AND S.H.I.E.L.D. DELIVERED THE RESULTS TO MY DOORSTEP."
HARRY...THIS IS CRAZY...YOU SAW WHAT THAT FORMULA DID TO PETER. WHY? YOU CAN'T--
I CAN! I CAN CONTROL IT! I AM IN CONTROL!

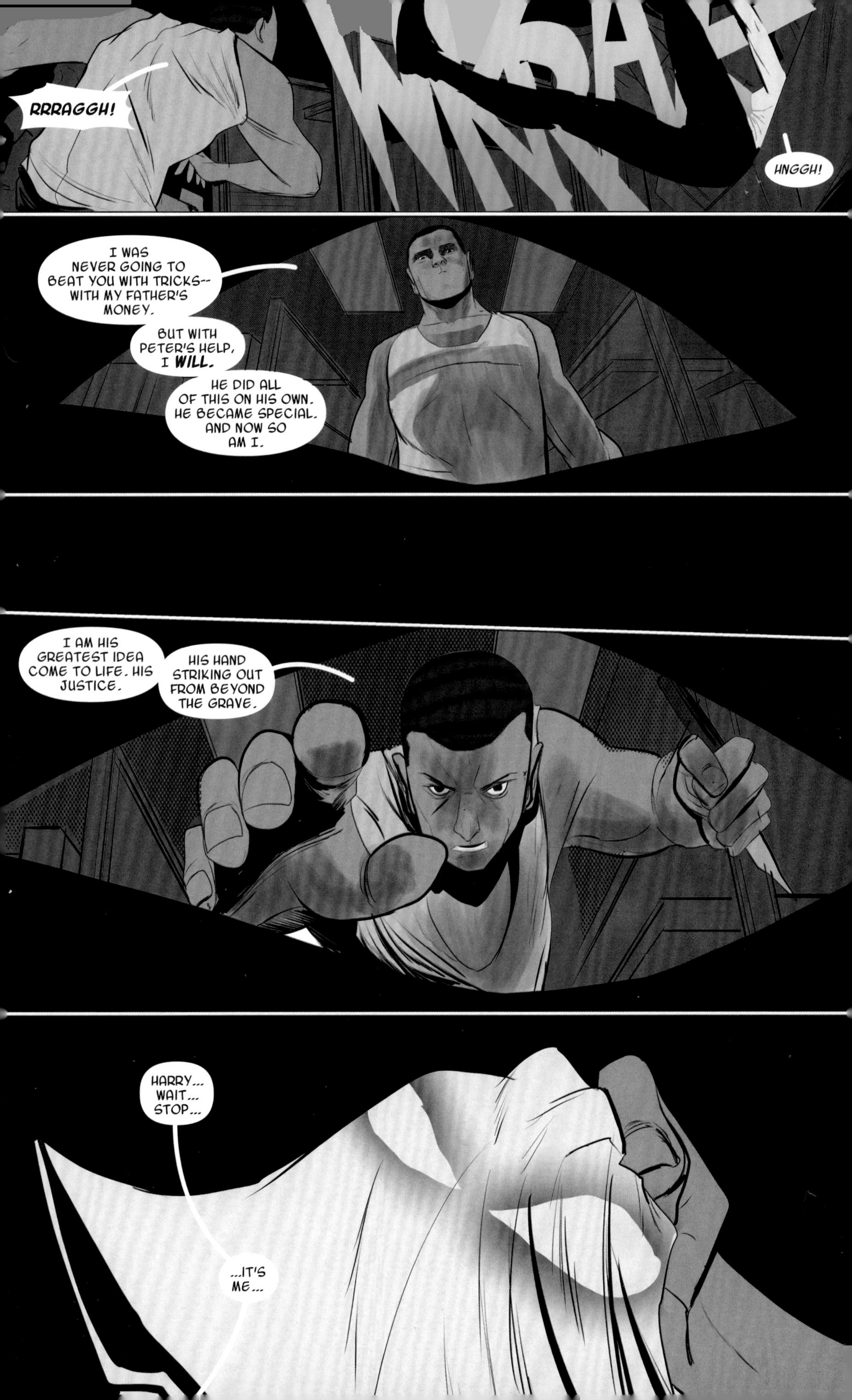

RRRAGGH!
HNGGH!
I WAS NEVER GOING TO BEAT YOU WITH TRICKS-- WITH MY FATHER'S MONEY.
BUT WITH PETER'S HELP, I **WILL.**
HE DID ALL OF THIS ON HIS OWN. HE BECAME SPECIAL. AND NOW SO AM I.
I AM HIS GREATEST IDEA COME TO LIFE. HIS JUSTICE.
HIS HAND STRIKING OUT FROM BEYOND THE GRAVE.
HARRY... WAIT... STOP...
...IT'S ME...

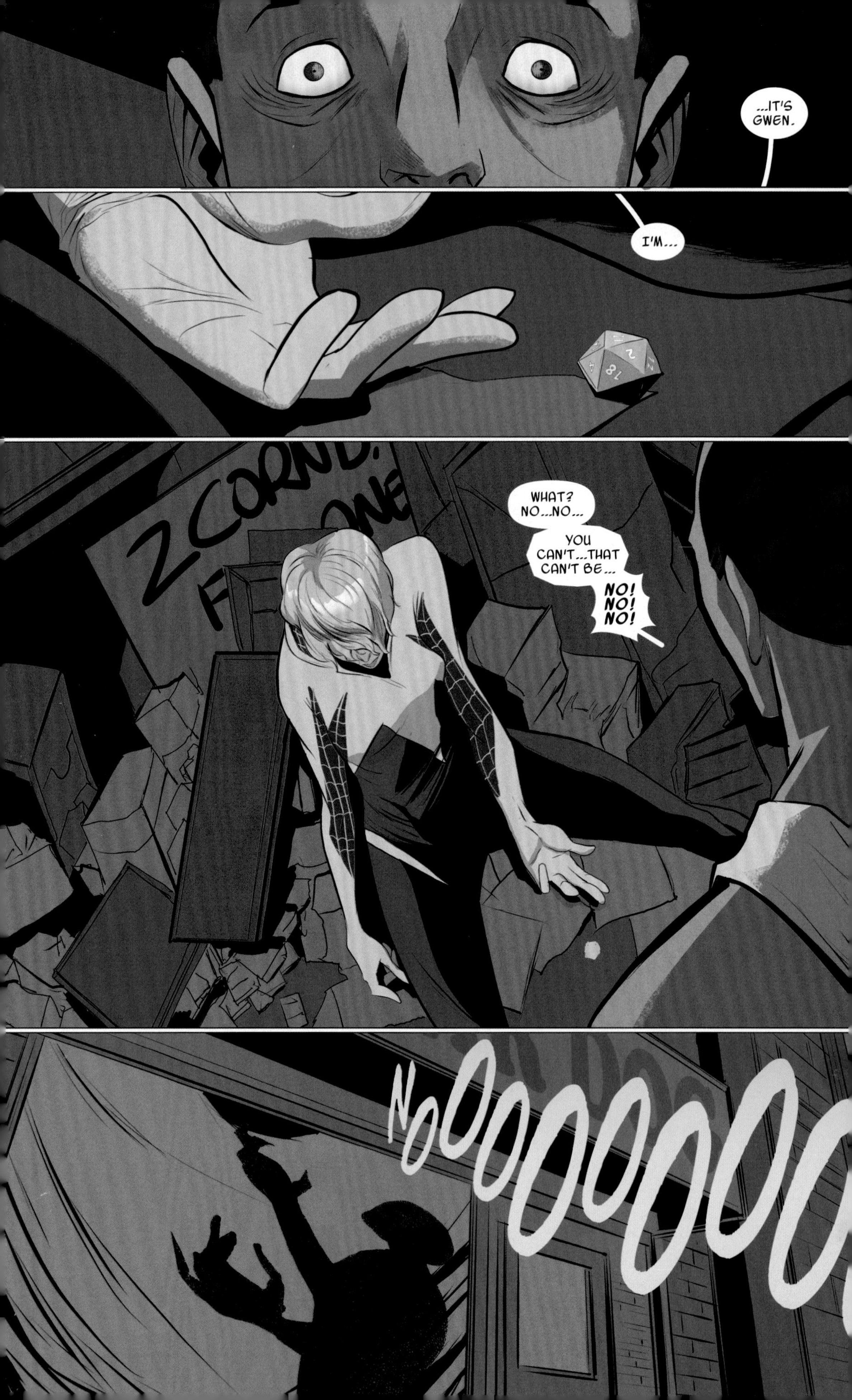
...IT'S GWEN.
I'M...
ZCORNDO
WHAT? NO...NO...
YOU CAN'T...THAT CAN'T BE...
NO! NO! NO!
NOOOOOOOOO

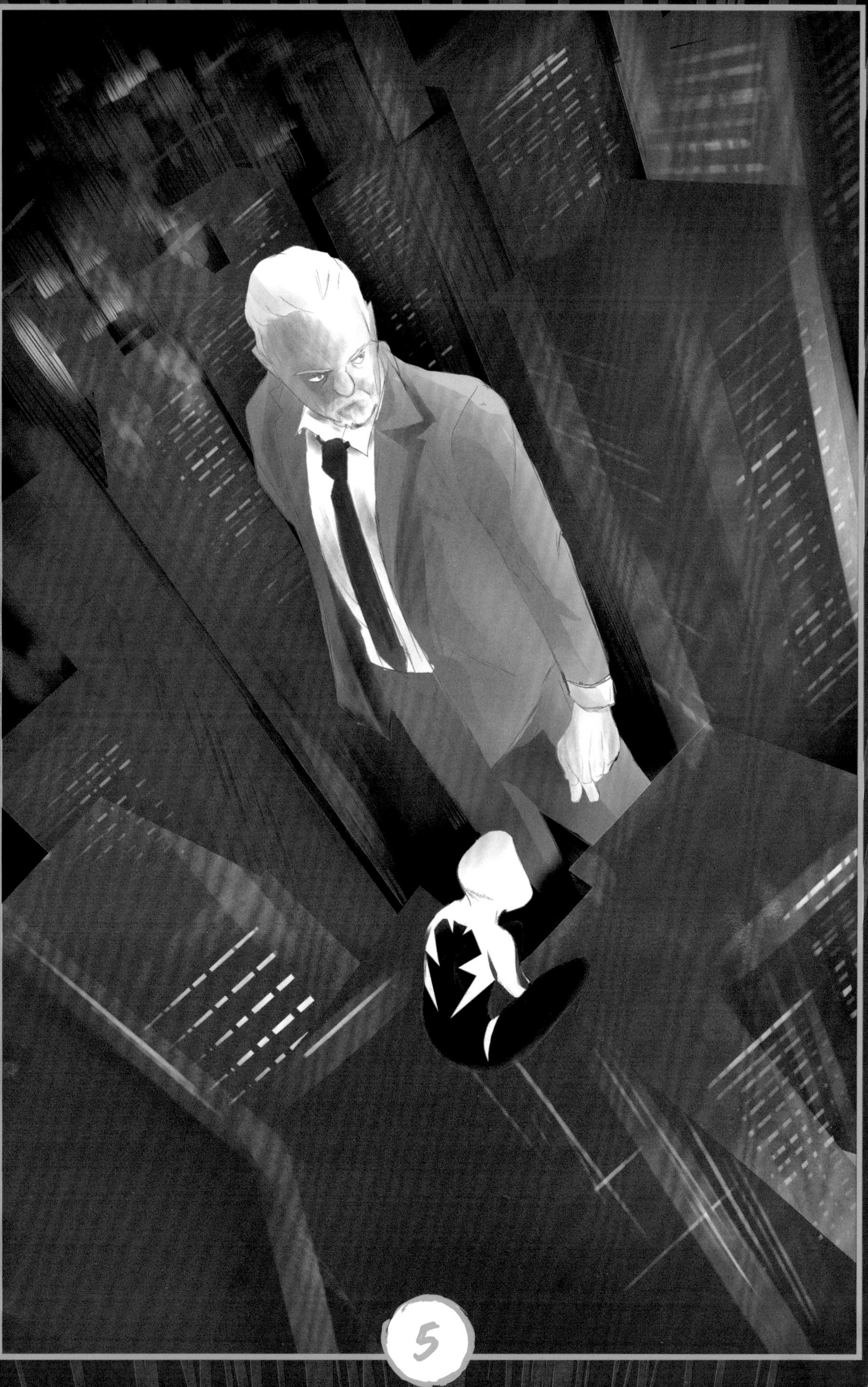
5

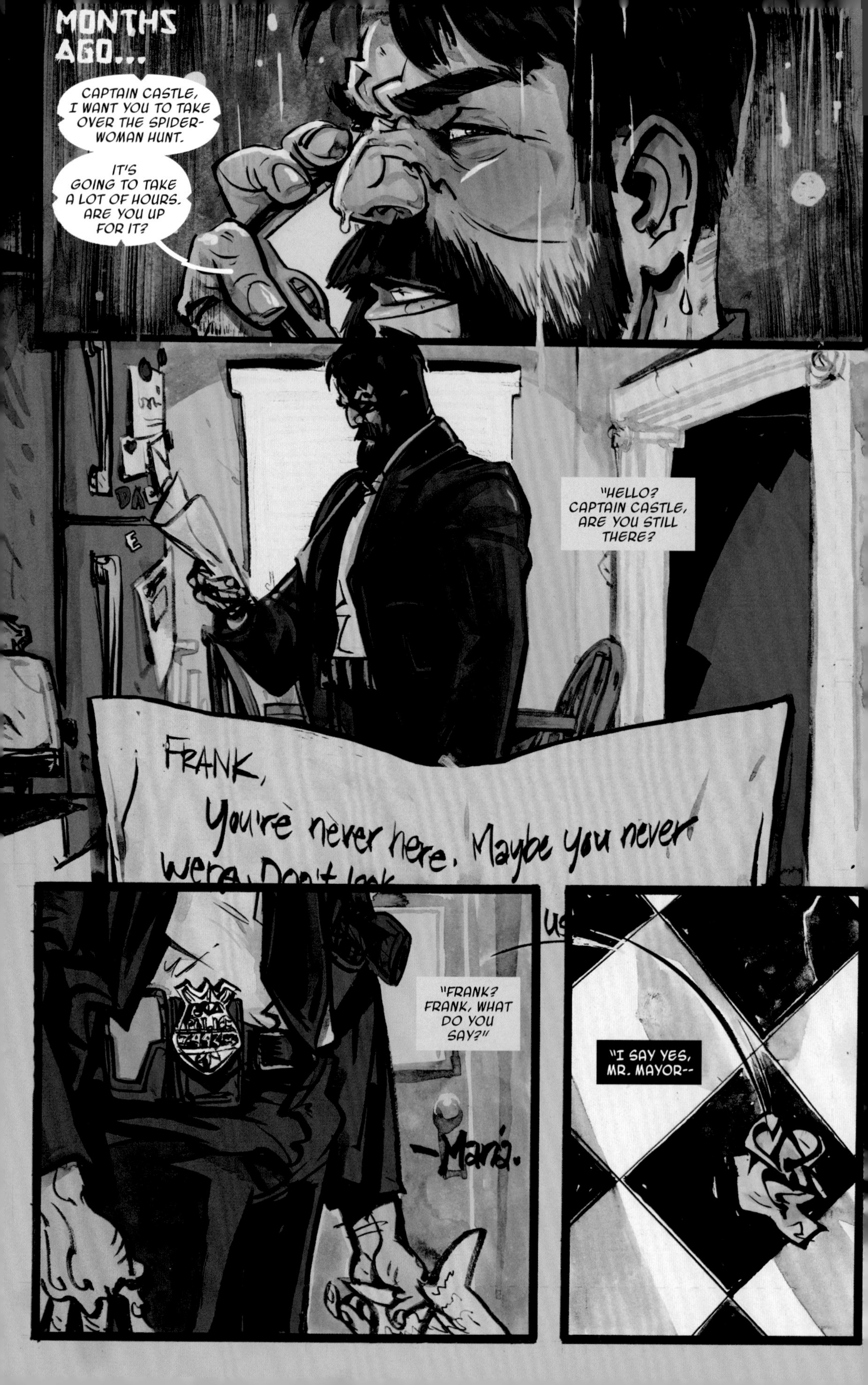
MONTHS AGO...
CAPTAIN CASTLE, I WANT YOU TO TAKE OVER THE SPIDER-WOMAN HUNT.
IT'S GOING TO TAKE A LOT OF HOURS. ARE YOU UP FOR IT?
"HELLO? CAPTAIN CASTLE, ARE YOU STILL THERE?
FRANK,
You're never here. Maybe you never
"FRANK? FRANK, WHAT DO YOU SAY?"
-María.
"I SAY YES, MR. MAYOR--

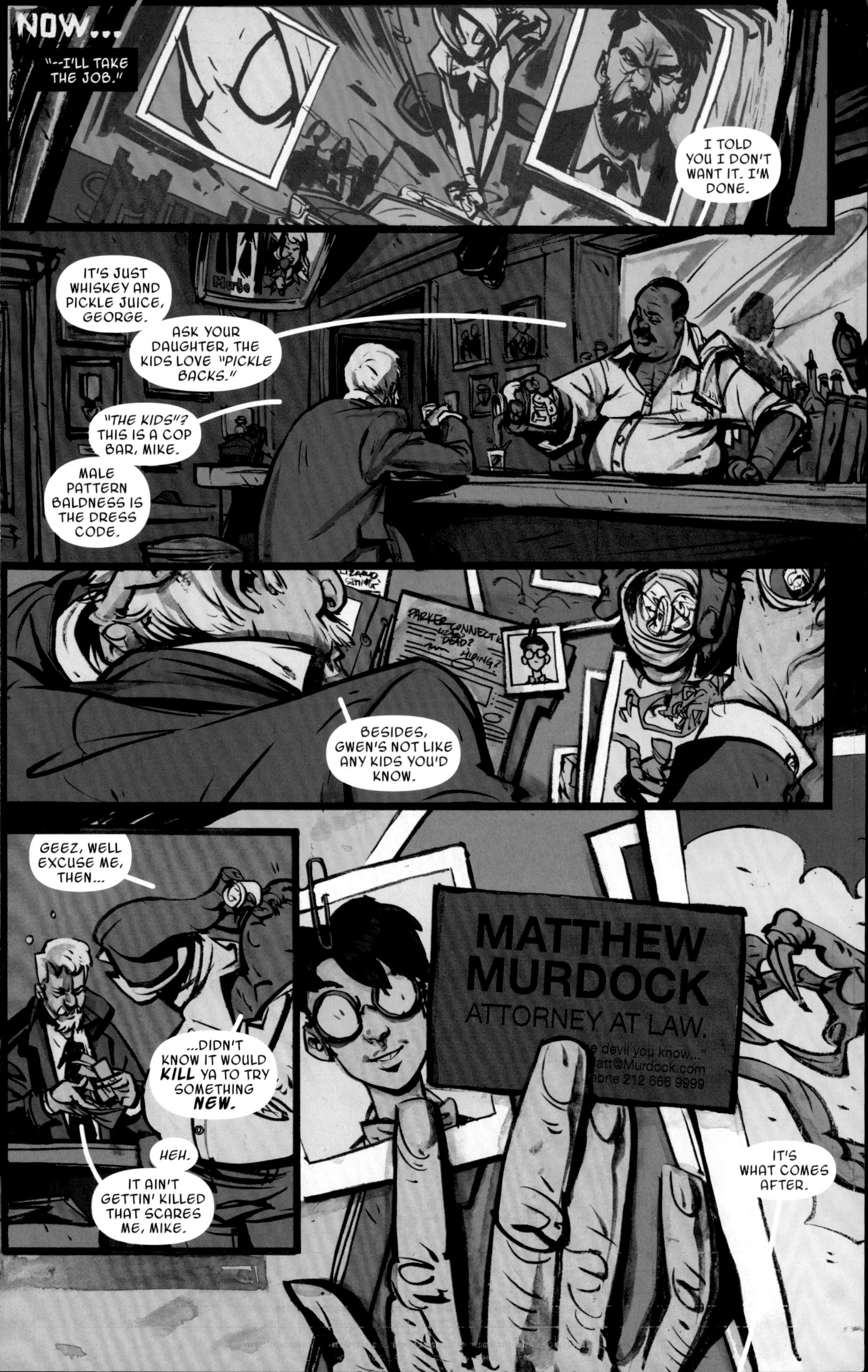
NOW...
"--I'LL TAKE THE JOB."
I TOLD YOU I DON'T WANT IT. I'M DONE.
IT'S JUST WHISKEY AND PICKLE JUICE, GEORGE.
ASK YOUR DAUGHTER, THE KIDS LOVE "PICKLE BACKS."
"THE KIDS"? THIS IS A COP BAR, MIKE.
MALE PATTERN BALDNESS IS THE DRESS CODE.
BESIDES, GWEN'S NOT LIKE ANY KIDS YOU'D KNOW.
GEEZ, WELL EXCUSE ME, THEN...
...DIDN'T KNOW IT WOULD KILL YA TO TRY SOMETHING NEW.
HEH.
IT AIN'T GETTIN' KILLED THAT SCARES ME, MIKE.
MATTHEW MURDOCK
ATTORNEY AT LAW.
IT'S WHAT COMES AFTER.

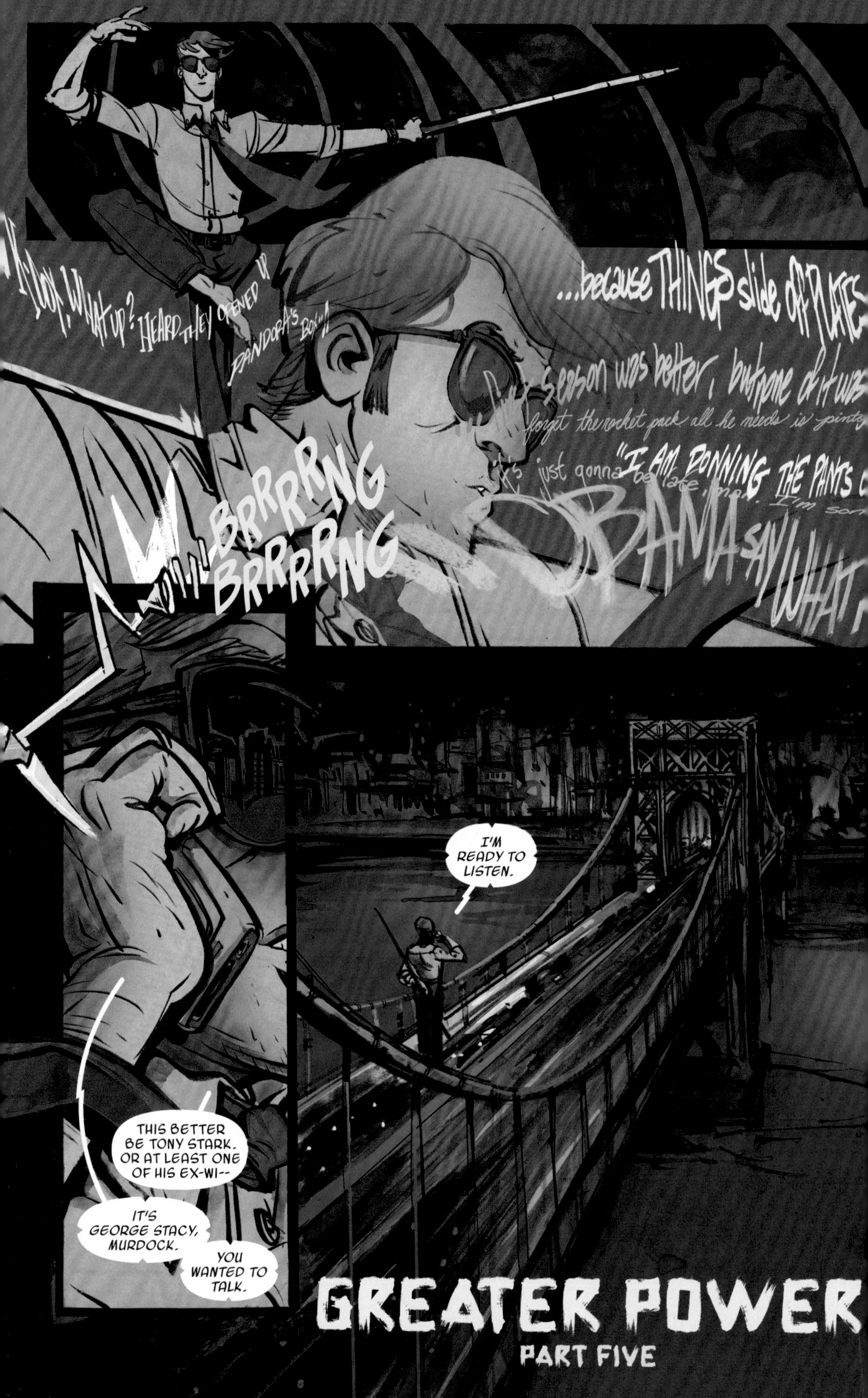
WHAT UP? HEARD THEY OPENED UP PANDORA'S BOX!
...because THINGS slide off PLATES
season was better, but none of it was
forget the rocket pack all he needs is pinto
just gonna be late
"I AM DONNING THE PANTS
BAMA
SAY WHAT
BRRRRNG BRRRRNG
THIS BETTER BE TONY STARK. OR AT LEAST ONE OF HIS EX-WI--
IT'S GEORGE STACY, MURDOCK.
YOU WANTED TO TALK.
I'M READY TO LISTEN.

GREATER POWER

PART FIVE

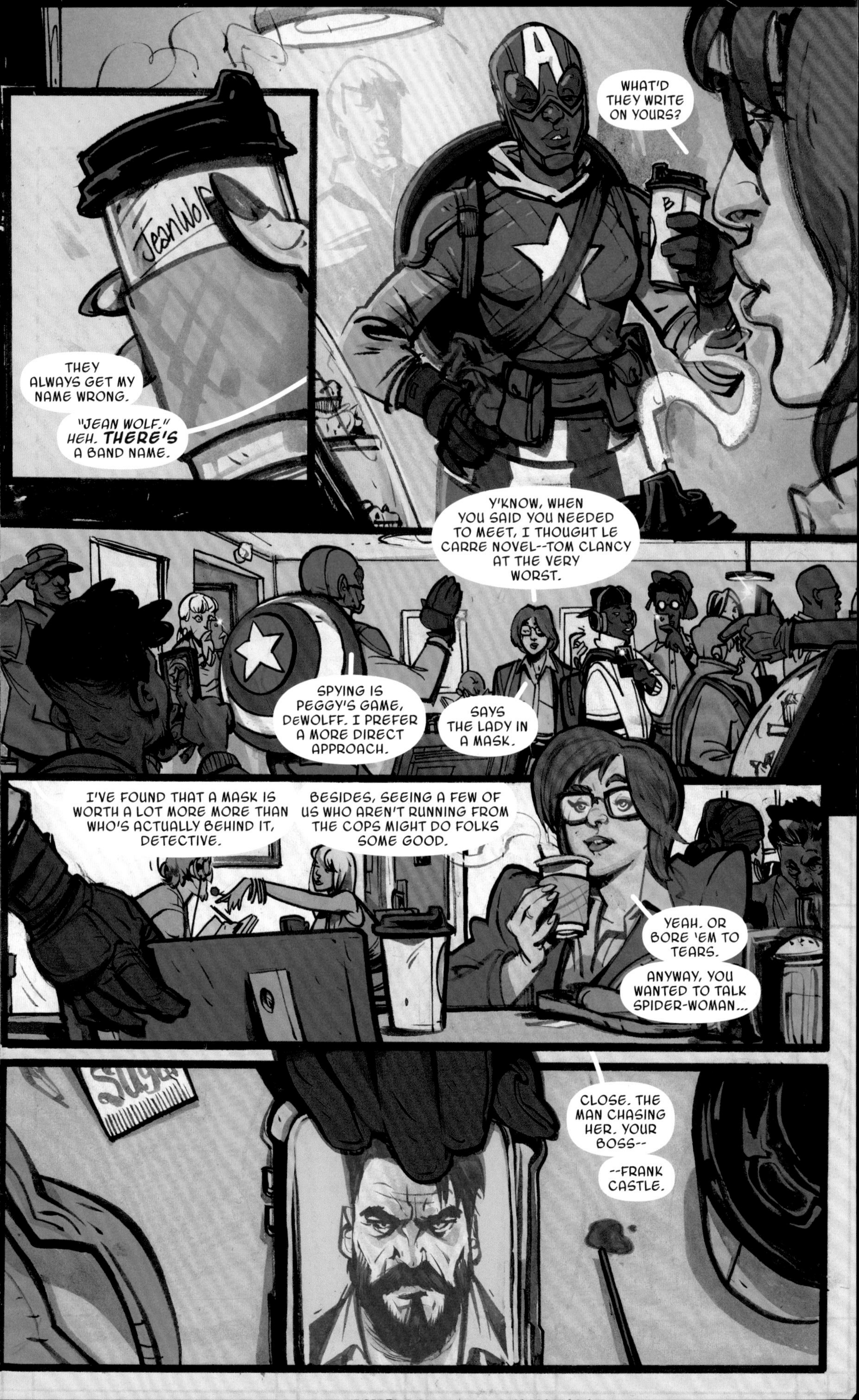
Jean Wolf
THEY ALWAYS GET MY NAME WRONG.
"JEAN WOLF." HEH. **THERE'S** A BAND NAME.
WHAT'D THEY WRITE ON YOURS?
B
Y'KNOW, WHEN YOU SAID YOU NEEDED TO MEET, I THOUGHT LE CARRE NOVEL--TOM CLANCY AT THE VERY WORST.
SPYING IS PEGGY'S GAME, DEWOLFF. I PREFER A MORE DIRECT APPROACH.
SAYS THE LADY IN A MASK.
I'VE FOUND THAT A MASK IS WORTH A LOT MORE MORE THAN WHO'S ACTUALLY BEHIND IT, DETECTIVE.
BESIDES, SEEING A FEW OF US WHO AREN'T RUNNING FROM THE COPS MIGHT DO FOLKS SOME GOOD.
YEAH. OR BORE 'EM TO TEARS.
ANYWAY, YOU WANTED TO TALK SPIDER-WOMAN...
CLOSE. THE MAN CHASING HER. YOUR BOSS--
--FRANK CASTLE.

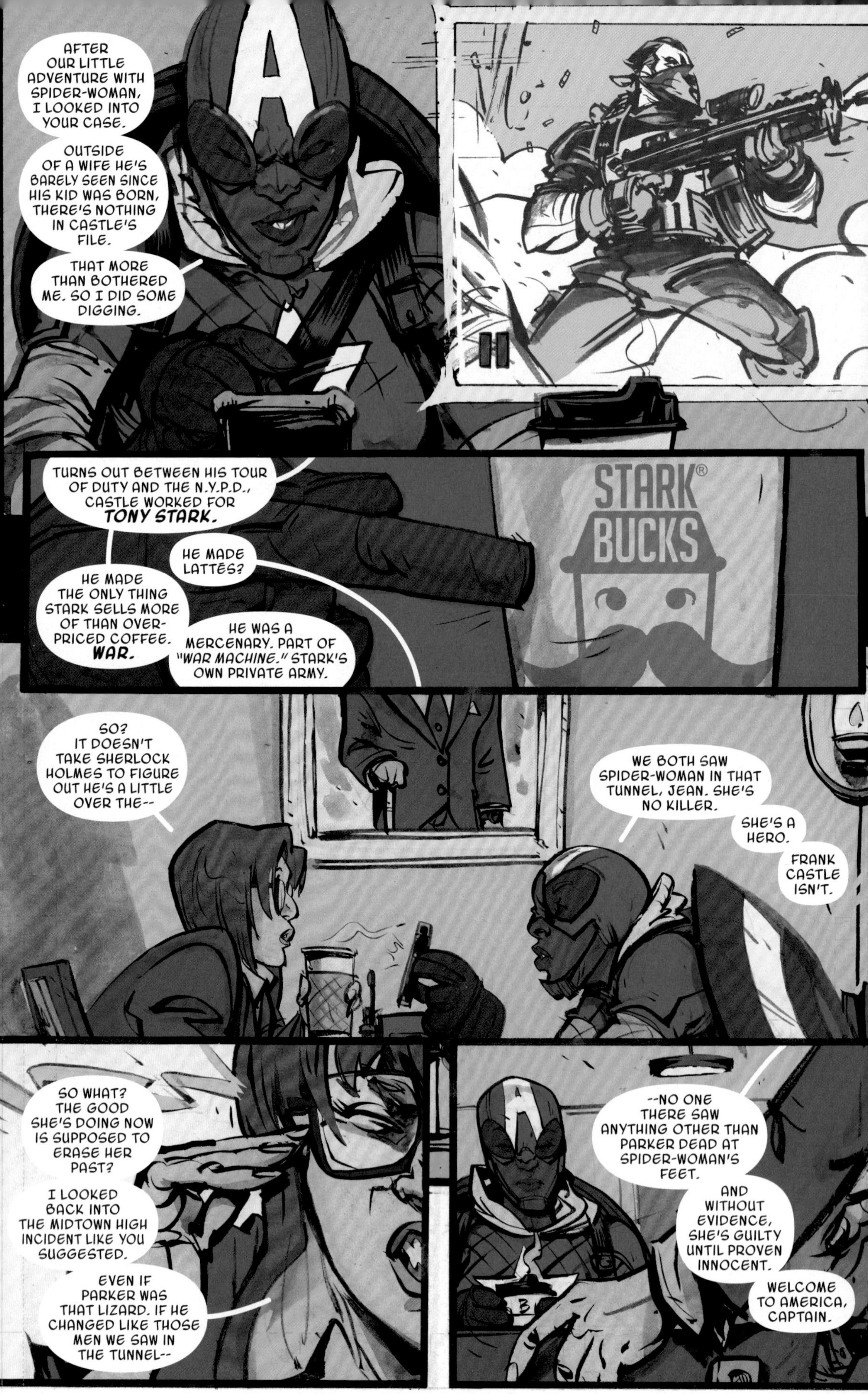
AFTER OUR LITTLE ADVENTURE WITH SPIDER-WOMAN, I LOOKED INTO YOUR CASE.
OUTSIDE OF A WIFE HE'S BARELY SEEN SINCE HIS KID WAS BORN, THERE'S NOTHING IN CASTLE'S FILE.
THAT MORE THAN BOTHERED ME. SO I DID SOME DIGGING.
TURNS OUT BETWEEN HIS TOUR OF DUTY AND THE N.Y.P.D., CASTLE WORKED FOR TONY STARK.
HE MADE THE ONLY THING STARK SELLS MORE OF THAN OVER-PRICED COFFEE. WAR.
HE MADE LATTÉS?
HE WAS A MERCENARY. PART OF "WAR MACHINE." STARK'S OWN PRIVATE ARMY.
STARK® BUCKS
SO? IT DOESN'T TAKE SHERLOCK HOLMES TO FIGURE OUT HE'S A LITTLE OVER THE--
WE BOTH SAW SPIDER-WOMAN IN THAT TUNNEL, JEAN. SHE'S NO KILLER.
SHE'S A HERO.
FRANK CASTLE ISN'T.
SO WHAT? THE GOOD SHE'S DOING NOW IS SUPPOSED TO ERASE HER PAST?
I LOOKED BACK INTO THE MIDTOWN HIGH INCIDENT LIKE YOU SUGGESTED.
EVEN IF PARKER WAS THAT LIZARD. IF HE CHANGED LIKE THOSE MEN WE SAW IN THE TUNNEL--
--NO ONE THERE SAW ANYTHING OTHER THAN PARKER DEAD AT SPIDER-WOMAN'S FEET.
AND WITHOUT EVIDENCE, SHE'S GUILTY UNTIL PROVEN INNOCENT.
WELCOME TO AMERICA, CAPTAIN.

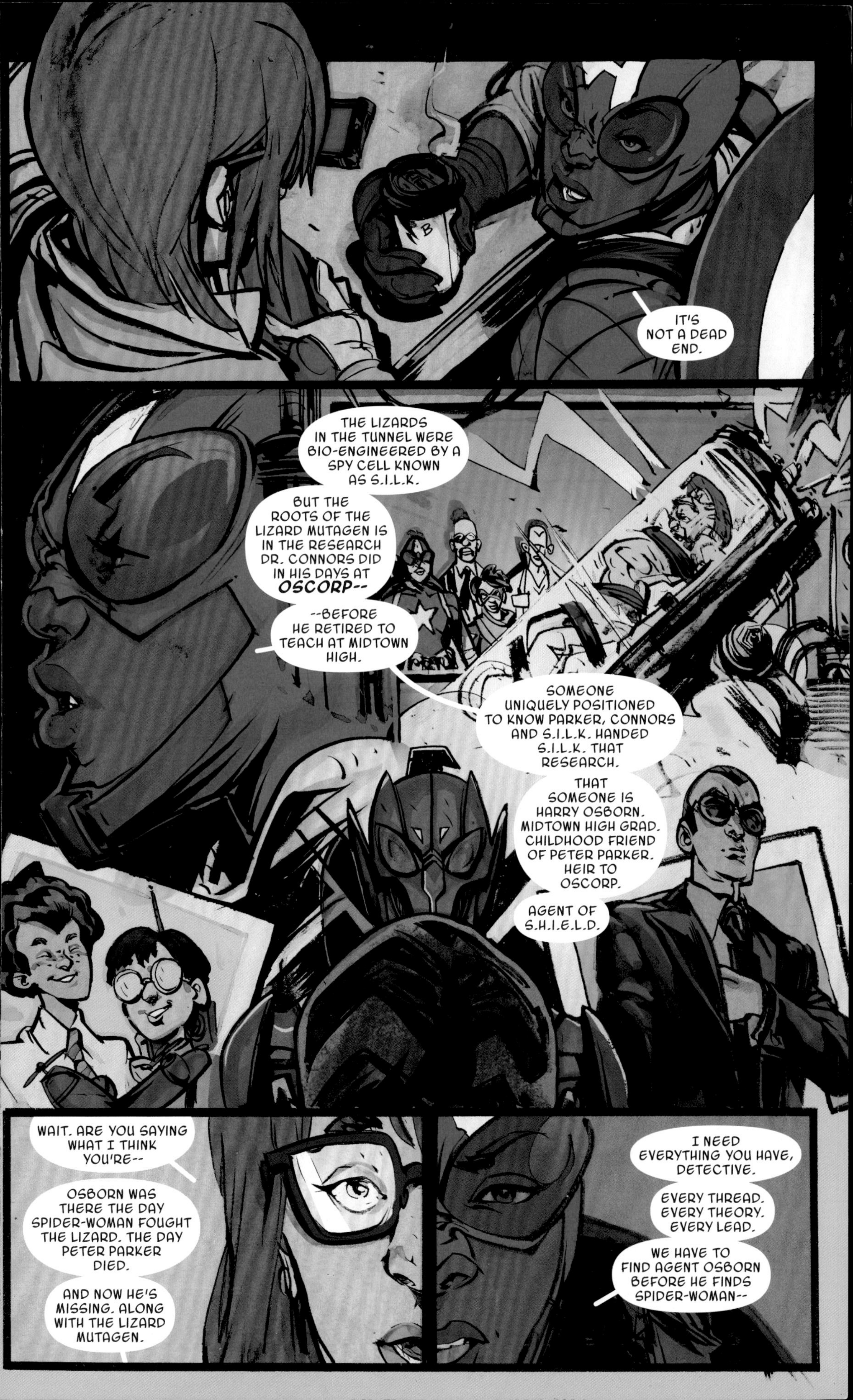

B
IT'S NOT A DEAD END.
THE LIZARDS IN THE TUNNEL WERE BIO-ENGINEERED BY A SPY CELL KNOWN AS S.I.L.K.
BUT THE ROOTS OF THE LIZARD MUTAGEN IS IN THE RESEARCH DR. CONNORS DID IN HIS DAYS AT OSCORP--
--BEFORE HE RETIRED TO TEACH AT MIDTOWN HIGH.
SOMEONE UNIQUELY POSITIONED TO KNOW PARKER, CONNORS AND S.I.L.K. HANDED S.I.L.K. THAT RESEARCH.
THAT SOMEONE IS HARRY OSBORN. MIDTOWN HIGH GRAD. CHILDHOOD FRIEND OF PETER PARKER. HEIR TO OSCORP.
AGENT OF S.H.I.E.L.D.
WAIT. ARE YOU SAYING WHAT I THINK YOU'RE--
OSBORN WAS THERE THE DAY SPIDER-WOMAN FOUGHT THE LIZARD. THE DAY PETER PARKER DIED.
AND NOW HE'S MISSING. ALONG WITH THE LIZARD MUTAGEN.
I NEED EVERYTHING YOU HAVE, DETECTIVE.
EVERY THREAD. EVERY THEORY. EVERY LEAD.
WE HAVE TO FIND AGENT OSBORN BEFORE HE FINDS SPIDER-WOMAN--

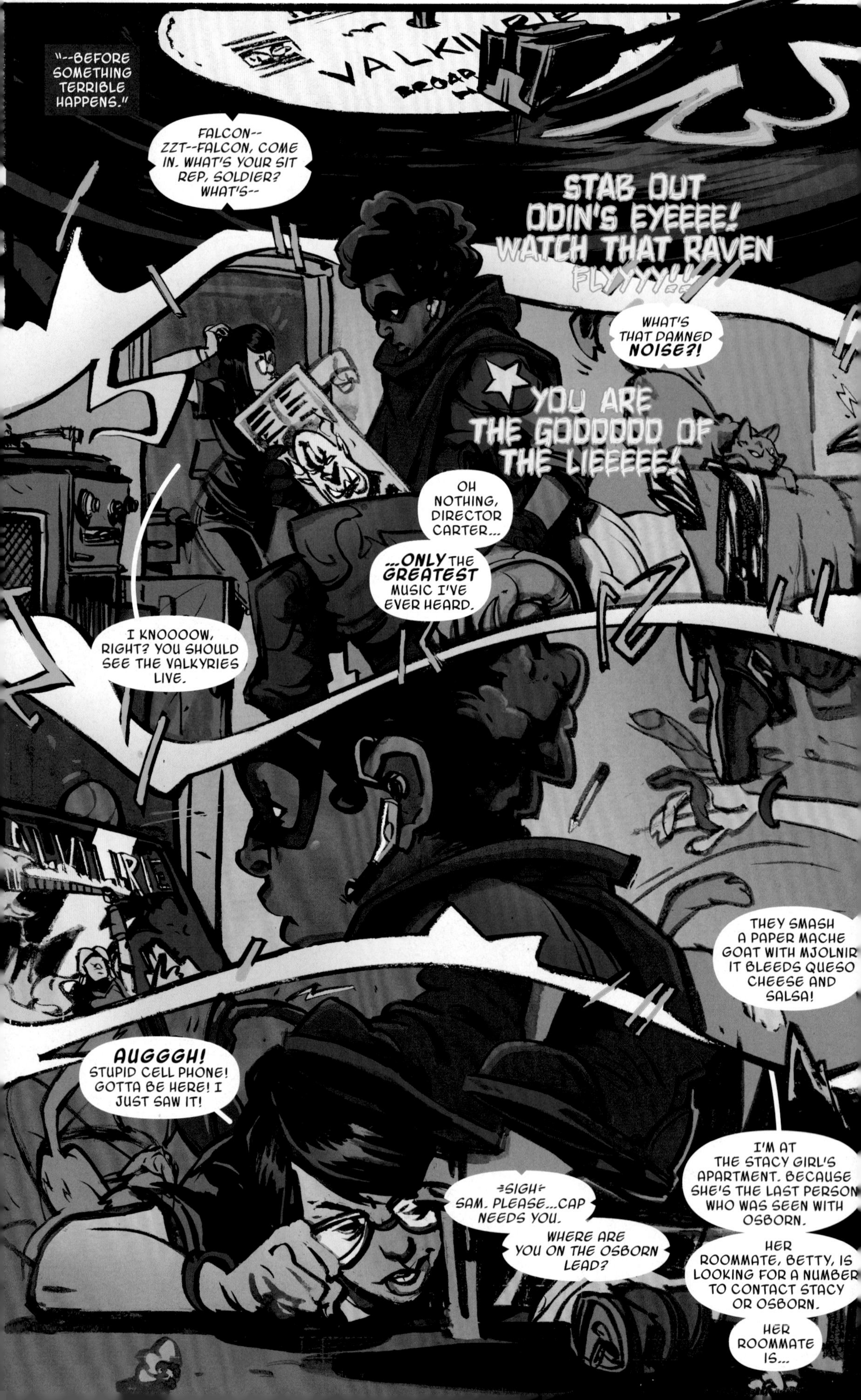

"--BEFORE SOMETHING TERRIBLE HAPPENS."
FALCON-- ZZT--FALCON, COME IN. WHAT'S YOUR SIT REP, SOLDIER? WHAT'S--
STAB OUT ODIN'S EYEEEE! WATCH THAT RAVEN FLYYYY!!!
WHAT'S THAT DAMNED NOISE?!
YOU ARE THE GODDDDD OF THE LIEEEEE!
OH NOTHING, DIRECTOR CARTER...
...ONLY THE GREATEST MUSIC I'VE EVER HEARD.
I KNOOOOW, RIGHT? YOU SHOULD SEE THE VALKYRIES LIVE.
THEY SMASH A PAPER MACHE GOAT WITH MJOLNIR IT BLEEDS QUESO CHEESE AND SALSA!
AUGGGH! STUPID CELL PHONE! GOTTA BE HERE! I JUST SAW IT!
=SIGH= SAM. PLEASE...CAP NEEDS YOU.
WHERE ARE YOU ON THE OSBORN LEAD?
I'M AT THE STACY GIRL'S APARTMENT. BECAUSE SHE'S THE LAST PERSON WHO WAS SEEN WITH OSBORN.
HER ROOMMATE, BETTY, IS LOOKING FOR A NUMBER TO CONTACT STACY OR OSBORN.
HER ROOMMATE IS...

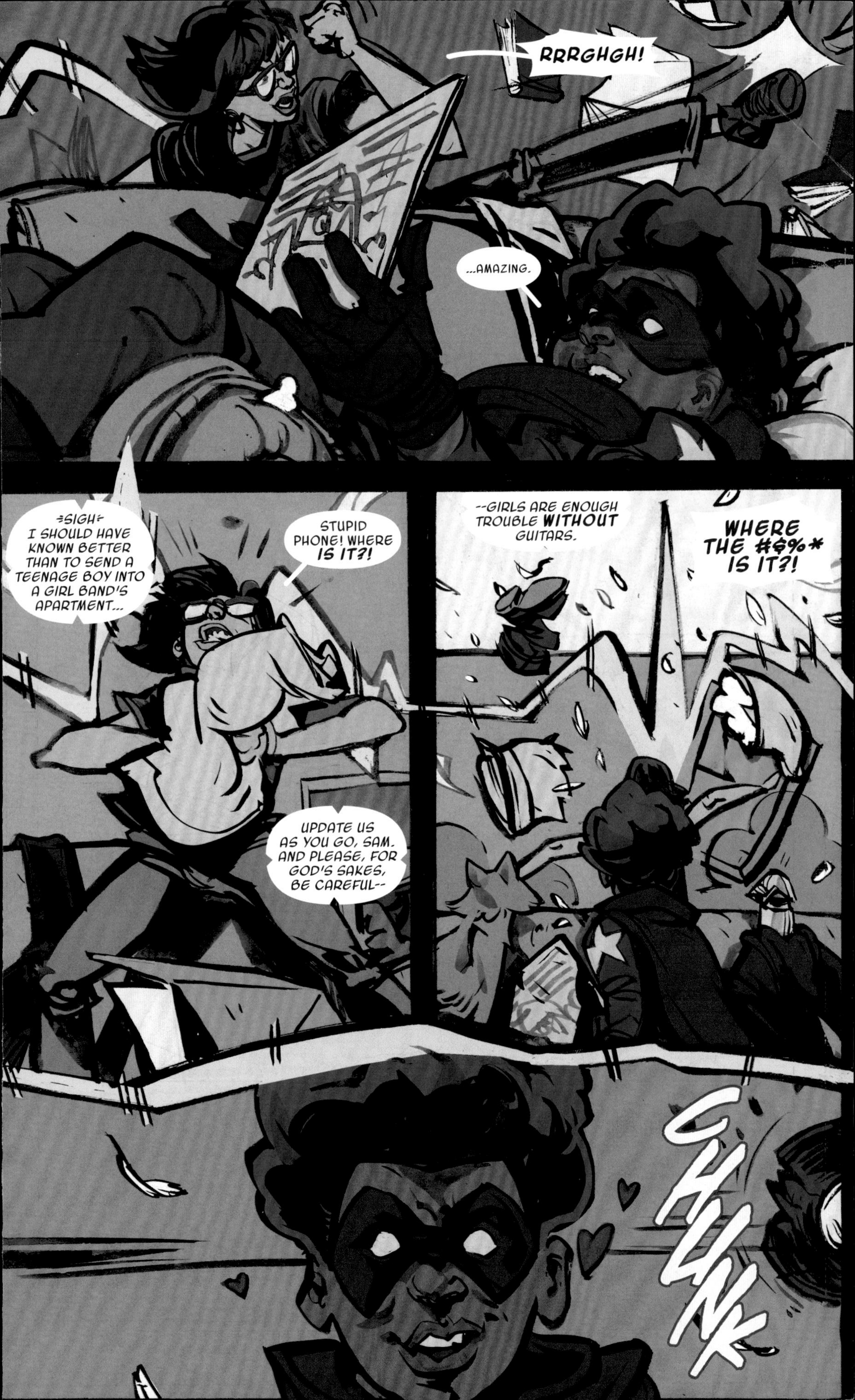
RRRGHGH!
...AMAZING.
=SIGH=
I SHOULD HAVE KNOWN BETTER THAN TO SEND A TEENAGE BOY INTO A GIRL BAND'S APARTMENT...
STUPID PHONE! WHERE IS IT?!
UPDATE US AS YOU GO, SAM. AND PLEASE, FOR GOD'S SAKES, BE CAREFUL--
--GIRLS ARE ENOUGH TROUBLE WITHOUT GUITARS.
WHERE THE #$%* IS IT?!
CHUNK

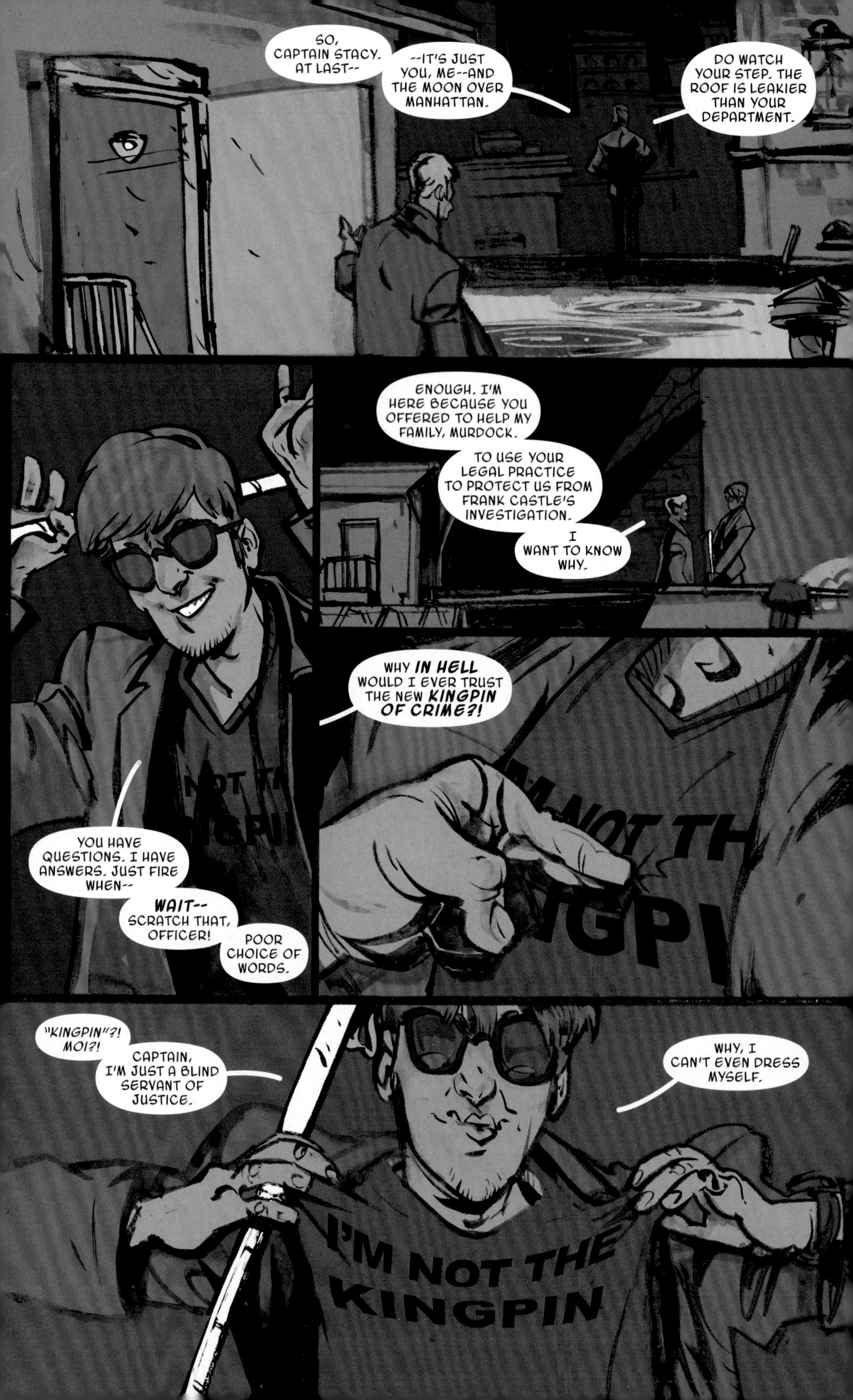
SO, CAPTAIN STACY. AT LAST--
--IT'S JUST YOU, ME--AND THE MOON OVER MANHATTAN.
DO WATCH YOUR STEP. THE ROOF IS LEAKIER THAN YOUR DEPARTMENT.
ENOUGH. I'M HERE BECAUSE YOU OFFERED TO HELP MY FAMILY, MURDOCK.
TO USE YOUR LEGAL PRACTICE TO PROTECT US FROM FRANK CASTLE'S INVESTIGATION.
I WANT TO KNOW WHY.
YOU HAVE QUESTIONS. I HAVE ANSWERS. JUST FIRE WHEN--
WAIT-- SCRATCH THAT, OFFICER!
POOR CHOICE OF WORDS.
WHY IN HELL WOULD I EVER TRUST THE NEW KINGPIN OF CRIME?!
"KINGPIN"?! MOI?!
CAPTAIN, I'M JUST A BLIND SERVANT OF JUSTICE.
WHY, I CAN'T EVEN DRESS MYSELF.
I'M NOT THE KINGPIN

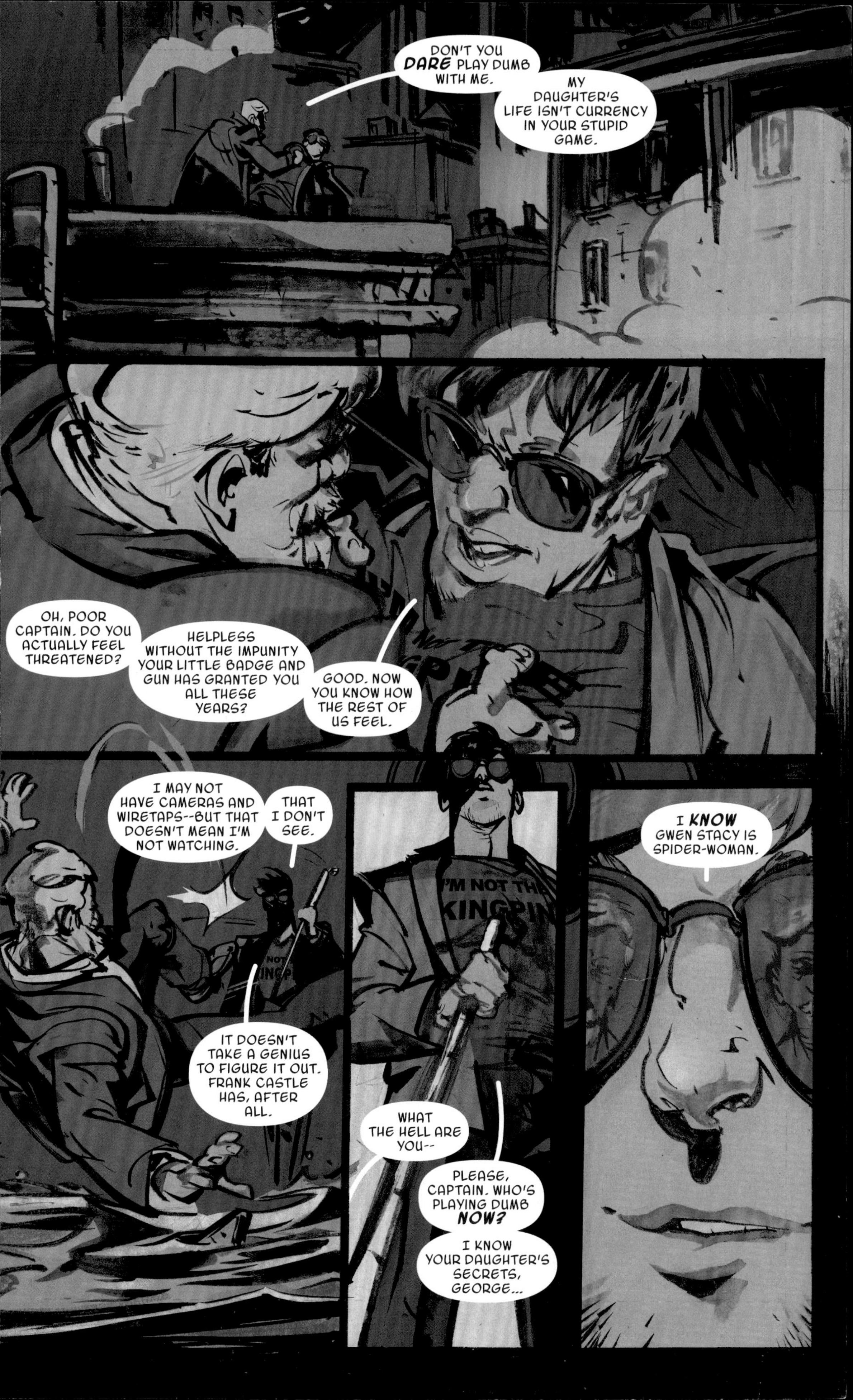
DON'T YOU **DARE** PLAY DUMB WITH ME.
MY DAUGHTER'S LIFE ISN'T CURRENCY IN YOUR STUPID GAME.
OH, POOR CAPTAIN. DO YOU ACTUALLY FEEL THREATENED?
HELPLESS WITHOUT THE IMPUNITY YOUR LITTLE BADGE AND GUN HAS GRANTED YOU ALL THESE YEARS?
GOOD. NOW YOU KNOW HOW THE REST OF US FEEL.
I MAY NOT HAVE CAMERAS AND WIRETAPS--BUT THAT DOESN'T MEAN I'M NOT WATCHING.
THAT I DON'T SEE.
IT DOESN'T TAKE A GENIUS TO FIGURE IT OUT. FRANK CASTLE HAS, AFTER ALL.
WHAT THE HELL ARE YOU--
PLEASE, CAPTAIN. WHO'S PLAYING DUMB **NOW?**
I KNOW YOUR DAUGHTER'S SECRETS, GEORGE...
I **KNOW** GWEN STACY IS SPIDER-WOMAN.

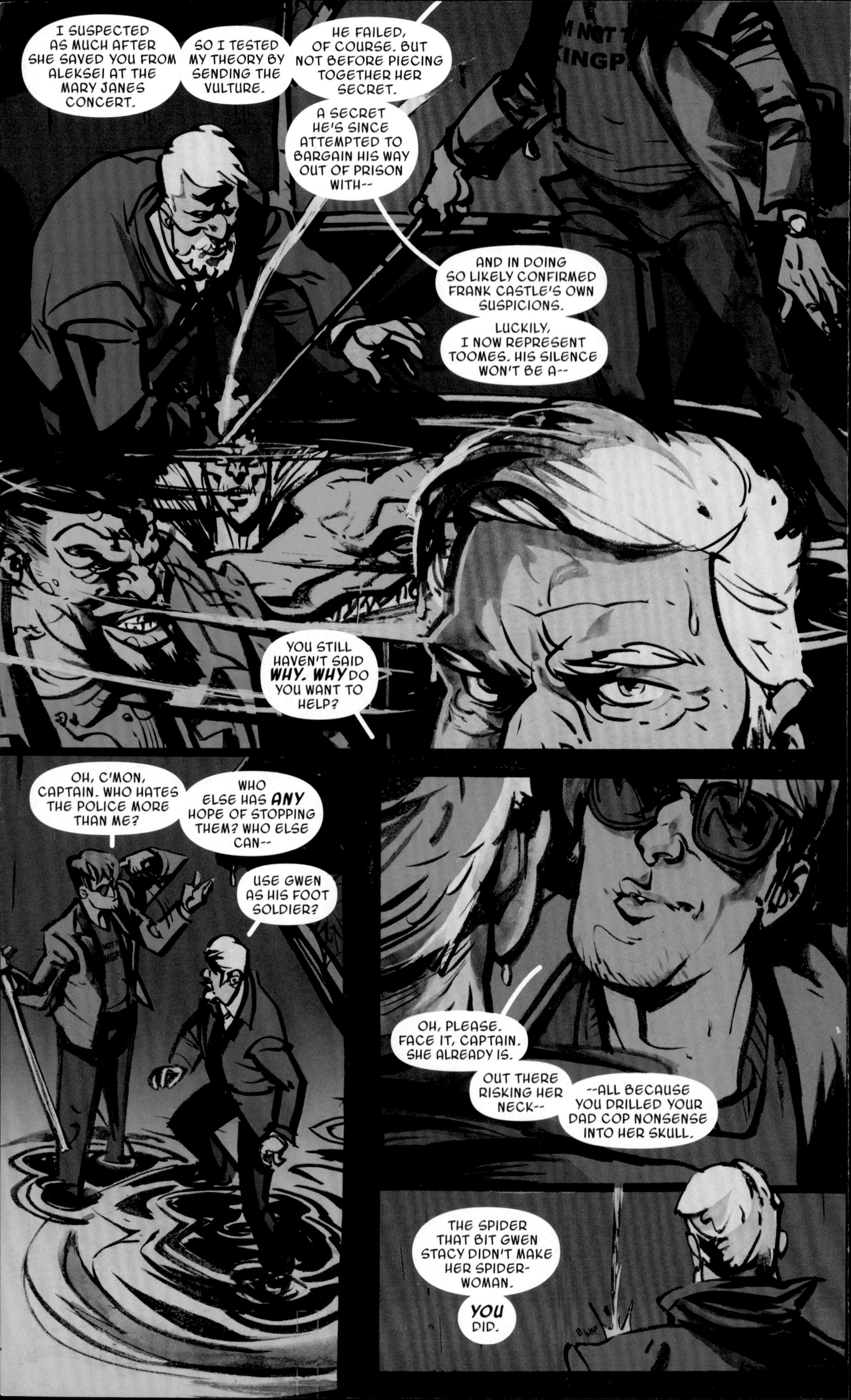
I SUSPECTED AS MUCH AFTER SHE SAVED YOU FROM ALEKSEI AT THE MARY JANES CONCERT.
SO I TESTED MY THEORY BY SENDING THE VULTURE.
HE FAILED, OF COURSE. BUT NOT BEFORE PIECING TOGETHER HER SECRET.
A SECRET HE'S SINCE ATTEMPTED TO BARGAIN HIS WAY OUT OF PRISON WITH--
AND IN DOING SO LIKELY CONFIRMED FRANK CASTLE'S OWN SUSPICIONS.
LUCKILY, I NOW REPRESENT TOOMES. HIS SILENCE WON'T BE A--
YOU STILL HAVEN'T SAID **WHY. WHY** DO YOU WANT TO HELP?
OH, C'MON, CAPTAIN. WHO HATES THE POLICE MORE THAN ME?
WHO ELSE HAS **ANY** HOPE OF STOPPING THEM? WHO ELSE CAN--
USE GWEN AS HIS FOOT SOLDIER?
OH, PLEASE. FACE IT, CAPTAIN. SHE ALREADY IS.
OUT THERE RISKING HER NECK--
--ALL BECAUSE YOU DRILLED YOUR DAD COP NONSENSE INTO HER SKULL.
THE SPIDER THAT BIT GWEN STACY DIDN'T MAKE HER SPIDER-WOMAN.
YOU DID.

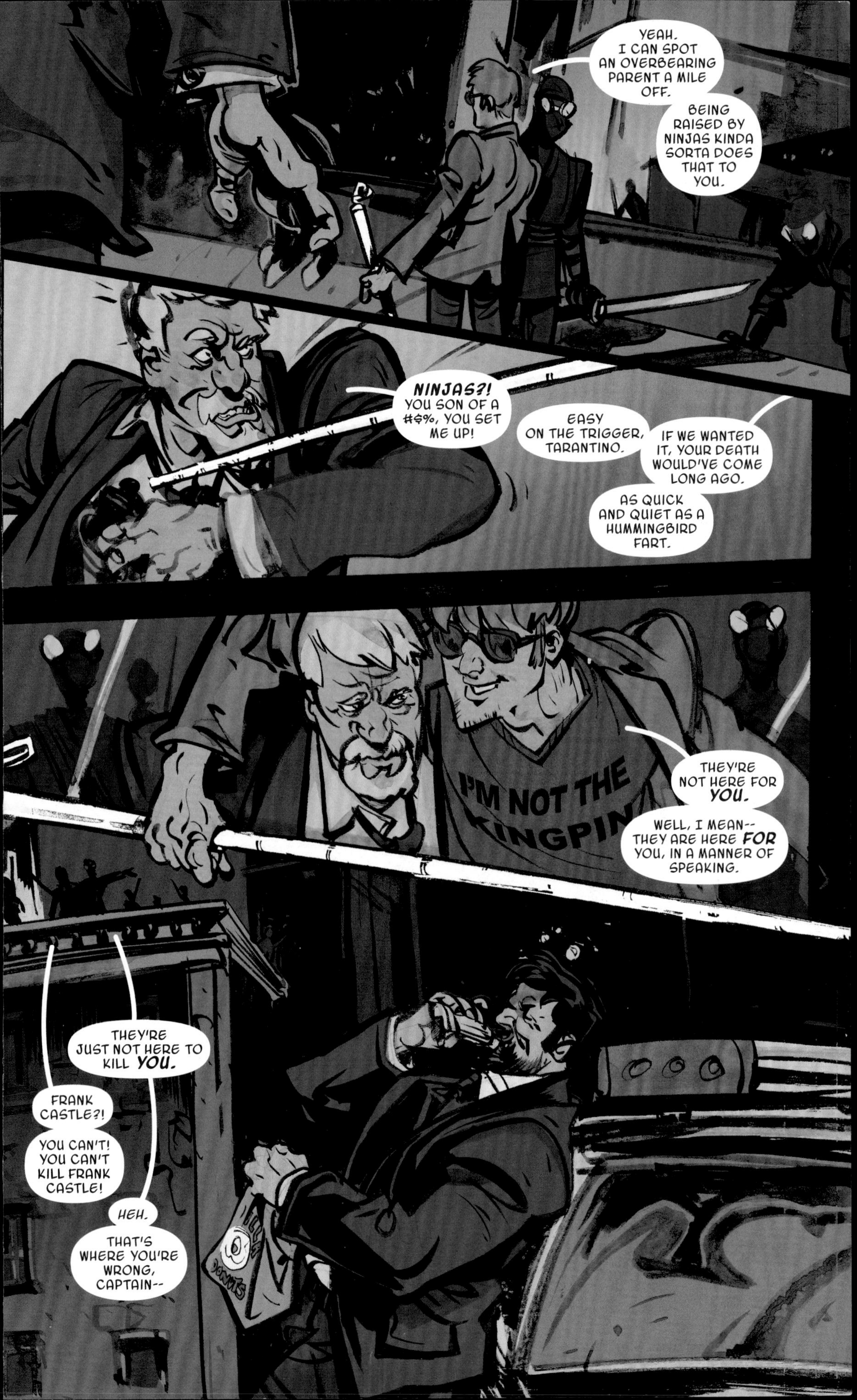
YEAH. I CAN SPOT AN OVERBEARING PARENT A MILE OFF.
BEING RAISED BY NINJAS KINDA SORTA DOES THAT TO YOU.
NINJAS?! YOU SON OF A #$%, YOU SET ME UP!
EASY ON THE TRIGGER, TARANTINO.
IF WE WANTED IT, YOUR DEATH WOULD'VE COME LONG AGO.
AS QUICK AND QUIET AS A HUMMINGBIRD FART.
I'M NOT THE KINGPIN
THEY'RE NOT HERE FOR YOU.
WELL, I MEAN-- THEY ARE HERE FOR YOU, IN A MANNER OF SPEAKING.
THEY'RE JUST NOT HERE TO KILL YOU.
FRANK CASTLE?!
YOU CAN'T! YOU CAN'T KILL FRANK CASTLE!
HEH.
THAT'S WHERE YOU'RE WRONG, CAPTAIN--

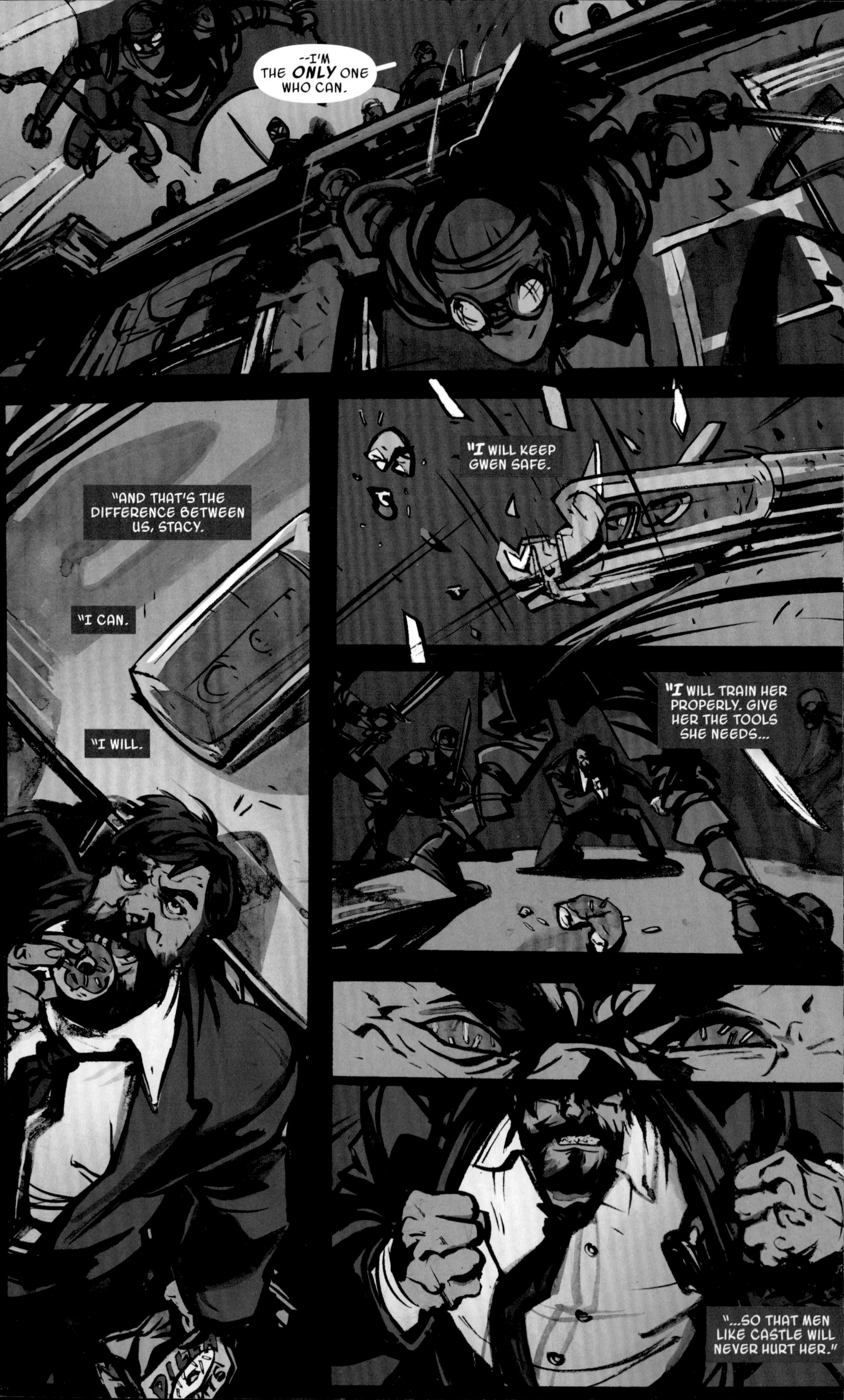
--I'M THE ONLY ONE WHO CAN.
"AND THAT'S THE DIFFERENCE BETWEEN US, STACY.
"I CAN.
"I WILL.
"I WILL KEEP GWEN SAFE.
"I WILL TRAIN HER PROPERLY. GIVE HER THE TOOLS SHE NEEDS...
"...SO THAT MEN LIKE CASTLE WILL NEVER HURT HER."

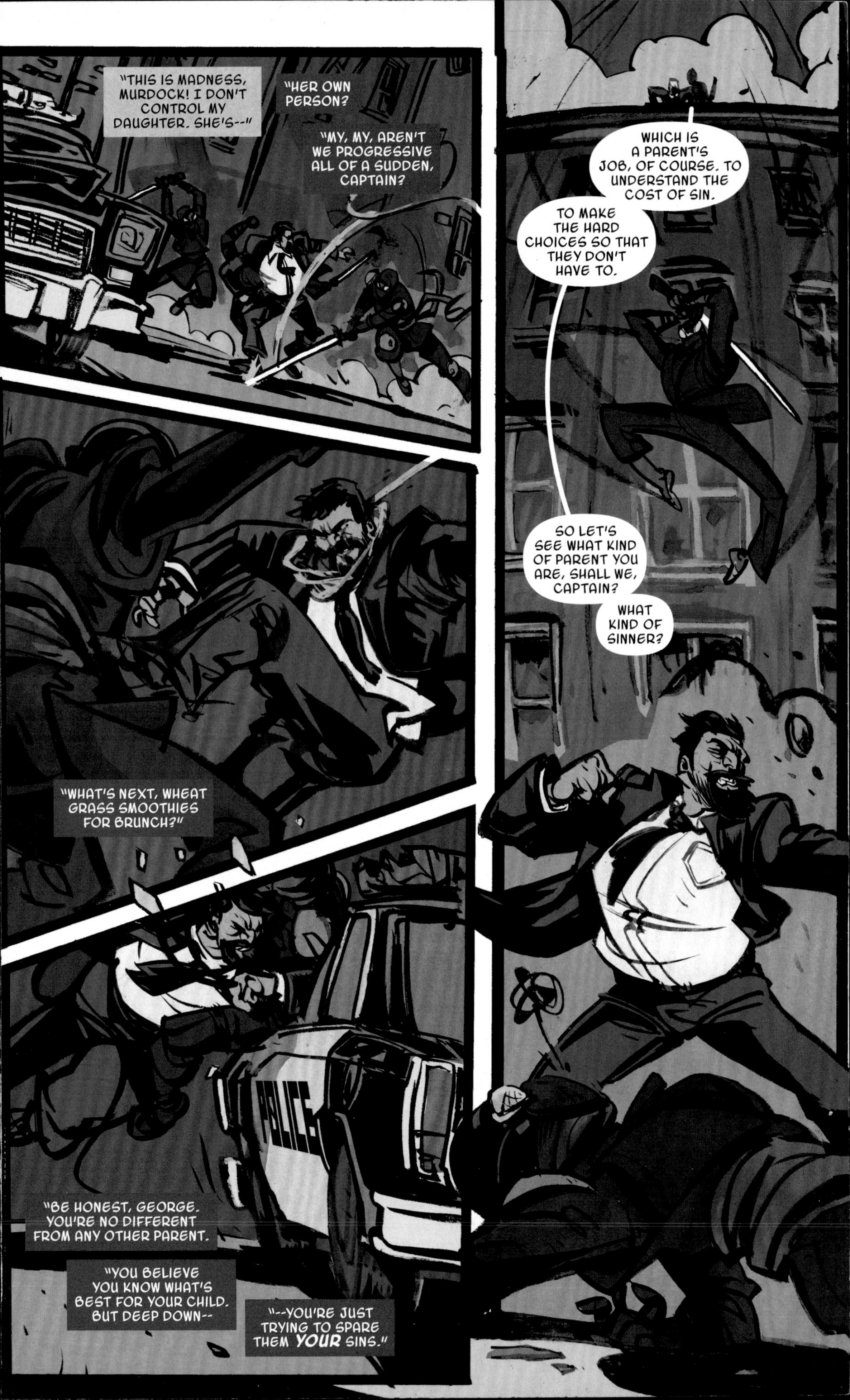
"THIS IS MADNESS, MURDOCK! I DON'T CONTROL MY DAUGHTER. SHE'S--"
"HER OWN PERSON?
"MY, MY, AREN'T WE PROGRESSIVE ALL OF A SUDDEN, CAPTAIN?
"WHAT'S NEXT, WHEAT GRASS SMOOTHIES FOR BRUNCH?"
POLICE
"BE HONEST, GEORGE. YOU'RE NO DIFFERENT FROM ANY OTHER PARENT.
"YOU BELIEVE YOU KNOW WHAT'S BEST FOR YOUR CHILD. BUT DEEP DOWN--
"--YOU'RE JUST TRYING TO SPARE THEM YOUR SINS."
WHICH IS A PARENT'S JOB, OF COURSE. TO UNDERSTAND THE COST OF SIN.
TO MAKE THE HARD CHOICES SO THAT THEY DON'T HAVE TO.
SO LET'S SEE WHAT KIND OF PARENT YOU ARE, SHALL WE, CAPTAIN?
WHAT KIND OF SINNER?

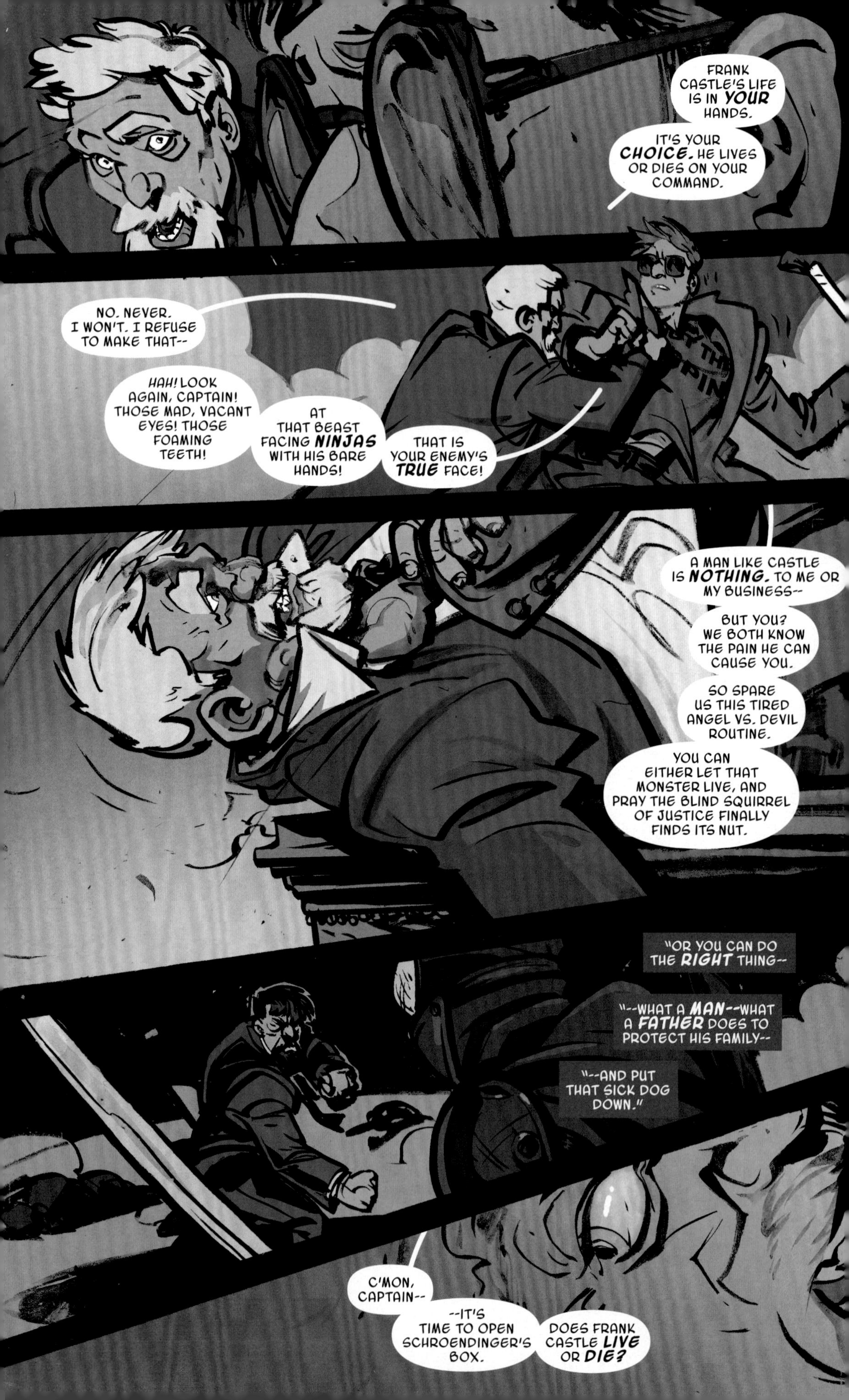
FRANK CASTLE'S LIFE IS IN YOUR HANDS.
IT'S YOUR CHOICE. HE LIVES OR DIES ON YOUR COMMAND.
NO. NEVER. I WON'T. I REFUSE TO MAKE THAT--
HAH! LOOK AGAIN, CAPTAIN! THOSE MAD, VACANT EYES! THOSE FOAMING TEETH!
AT THAT BEAST FACING NINJAS WITH HIS BARE HANDS!
THAT IS YOUR ENEMY'S TRUE FACE!
A MAN LIKE CASTLE IS NOTHING. TO ME OR MY BUSINESS--
BUT YOU? WE BOTH KNOW THE PAIN HE CAN CAUSE YOU.
SO SPARE US THIS TIRED ANGEL VS. DEVIL ROUTINE.
YOU CAN EITHER LET THAT MONSTER LIVE, AND PRAY THE BLIND SQUIRREL OF JUSTICE FINALLY FINDS ITS NUT.
"OR YOU CAN DO THE RIGHT THING--
"--WHAT A MAN--WHAT A FATHER DOES TO PROTECT HIS FAMILY--
"--AND PUT THAT SICK DOG DOWN."
C'MON, CAPTAIN--
--IT'S TIME TO OPEN SCHROENDINGER'S BOX.
DOES FRANK CASTLE LIVE OR DIE?

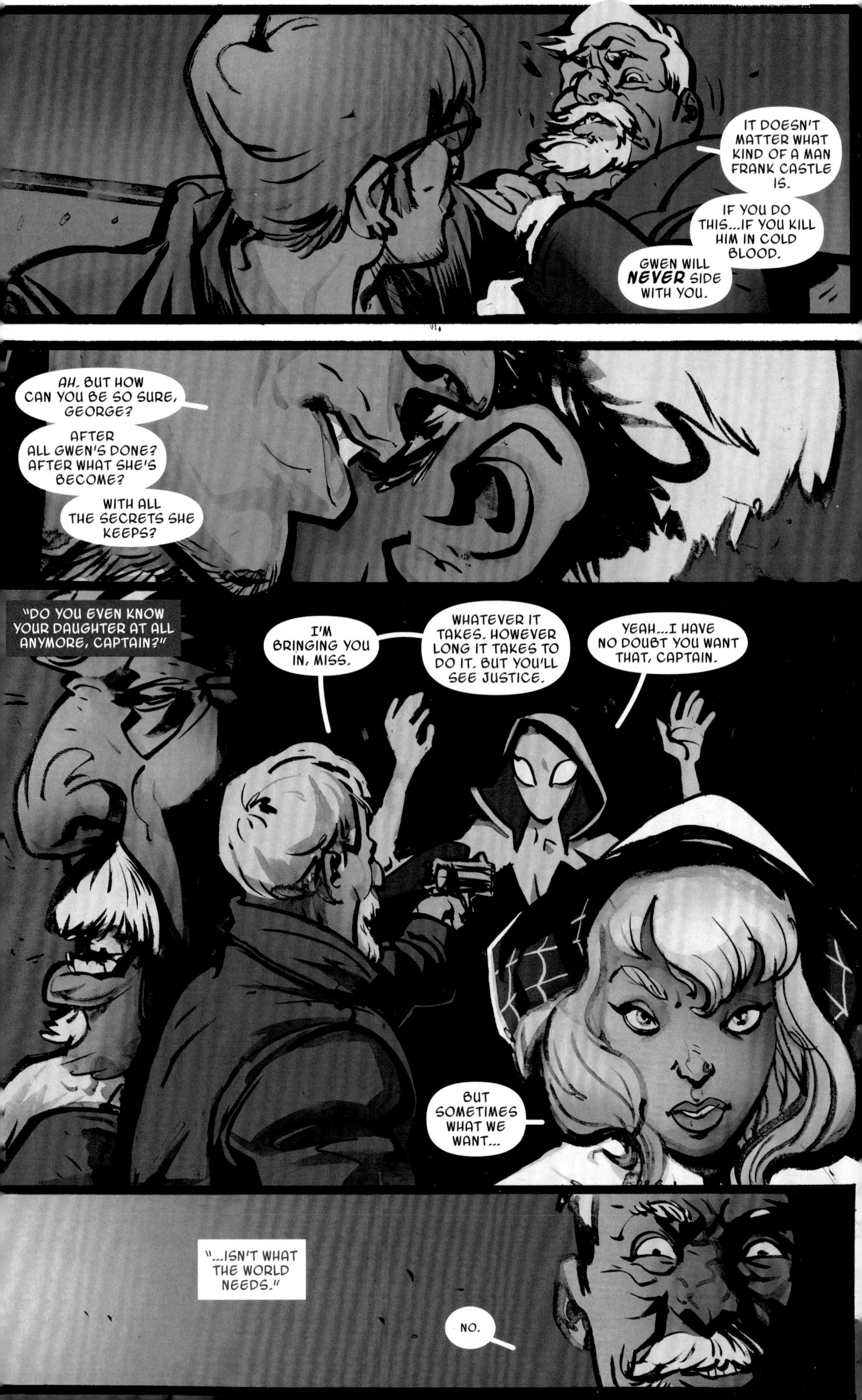
IT DOESN'T MATTER WHAT KIND OF A MAN FRANK CASTLE IS.
IF YOU DO THIS...IF YOU KILL HIM IN COLD BLOOD.
GWEN WILL NEVER SIDE WITH YOU.
AH. BUT HOW CAN YOU BE SO SURE, GEORGE?
AFTER ALL GWEN'S DONE? AFTER WHAT SHE'S BECOME?
WITH ALL THE SECRETS SHE KEEPS?
"DO YOU EVEN KNOW YOUR DAUGHTER AT ALL ANYMORE, CAPTAIN?"
I'M BRINGING YOU IN, MISS.
WHATEVER IT TAKES. HOWEVER LONG IT TAKES TO DO IT. BUT YOU'LL SEE JUSTICE.
YEAH...I HAVE NO DOUBT YOU WANT THAT, CAPTAIN.
BUT SOMETIMES WHAT WE WANT...
"...ISN'T WHAT THE WORLD NEEDS."
NO.

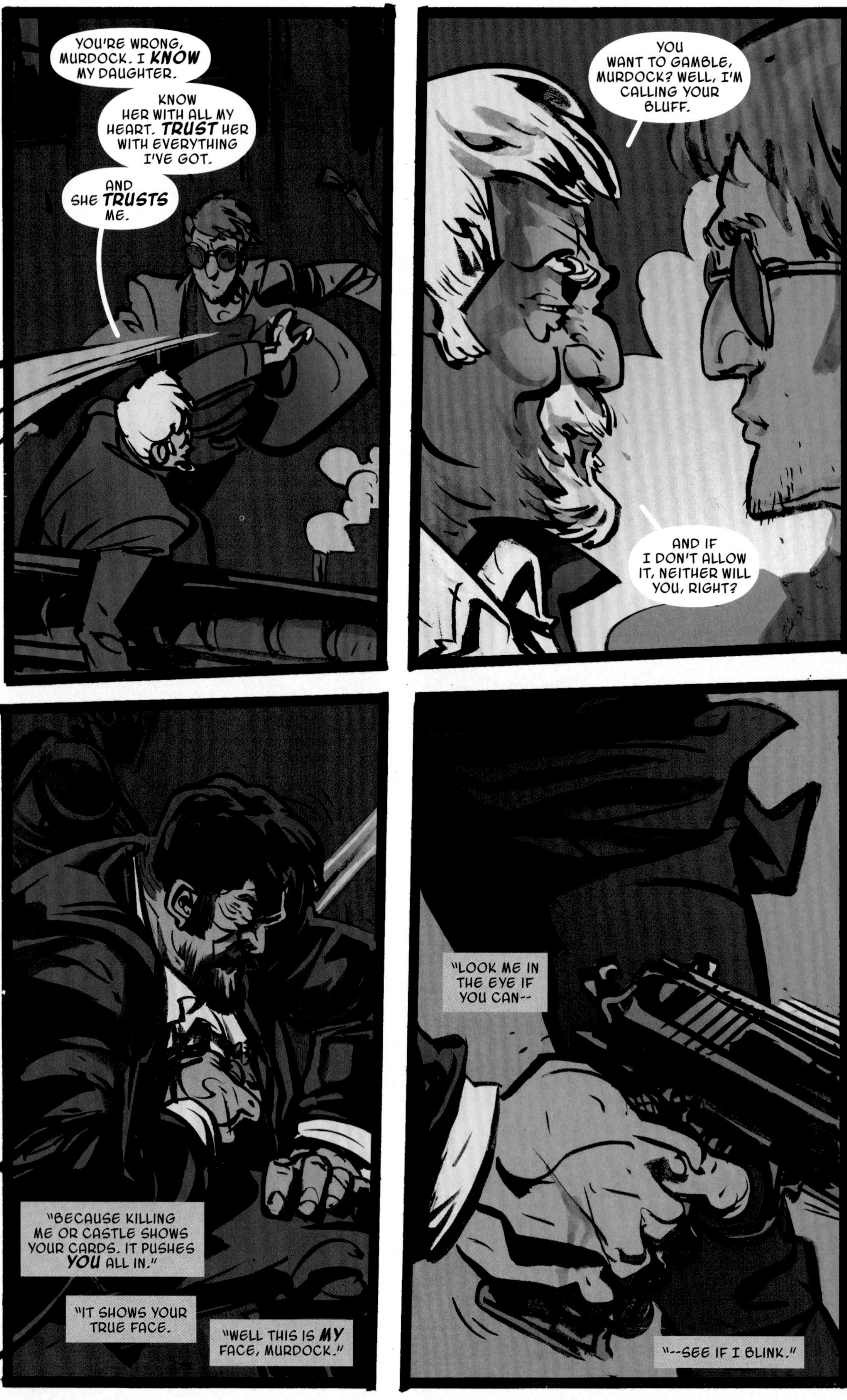
YOU'RE WRONG, MURDOCK. I KNOW MY DAUGHTER.
KNOW HER WITH ALL MY HEART. TRUST HER WITH EVERYTHING I'VE GOT.
AND SHE TRUSTS ME.
YOU WANT TO GAMBLE, MURDOCK? WELL, I'M CALLING YOUR BLUFF.
AND IF I DON'T ALLOW IT, NEITHER WILL YOU, RIGHT?
"BECAUSE KILLING ME OR CASTLE SHOWS YOUR CARDS. IT PUSHES YOU ALL IN."
"IT SHOWS YOUR TRUE FACE.
"WELL THIS IS MY FACE, MURDOCK."
"LOOK ME IN THE EYE IF YOU CAN--
"--SEE IF I BLINK."

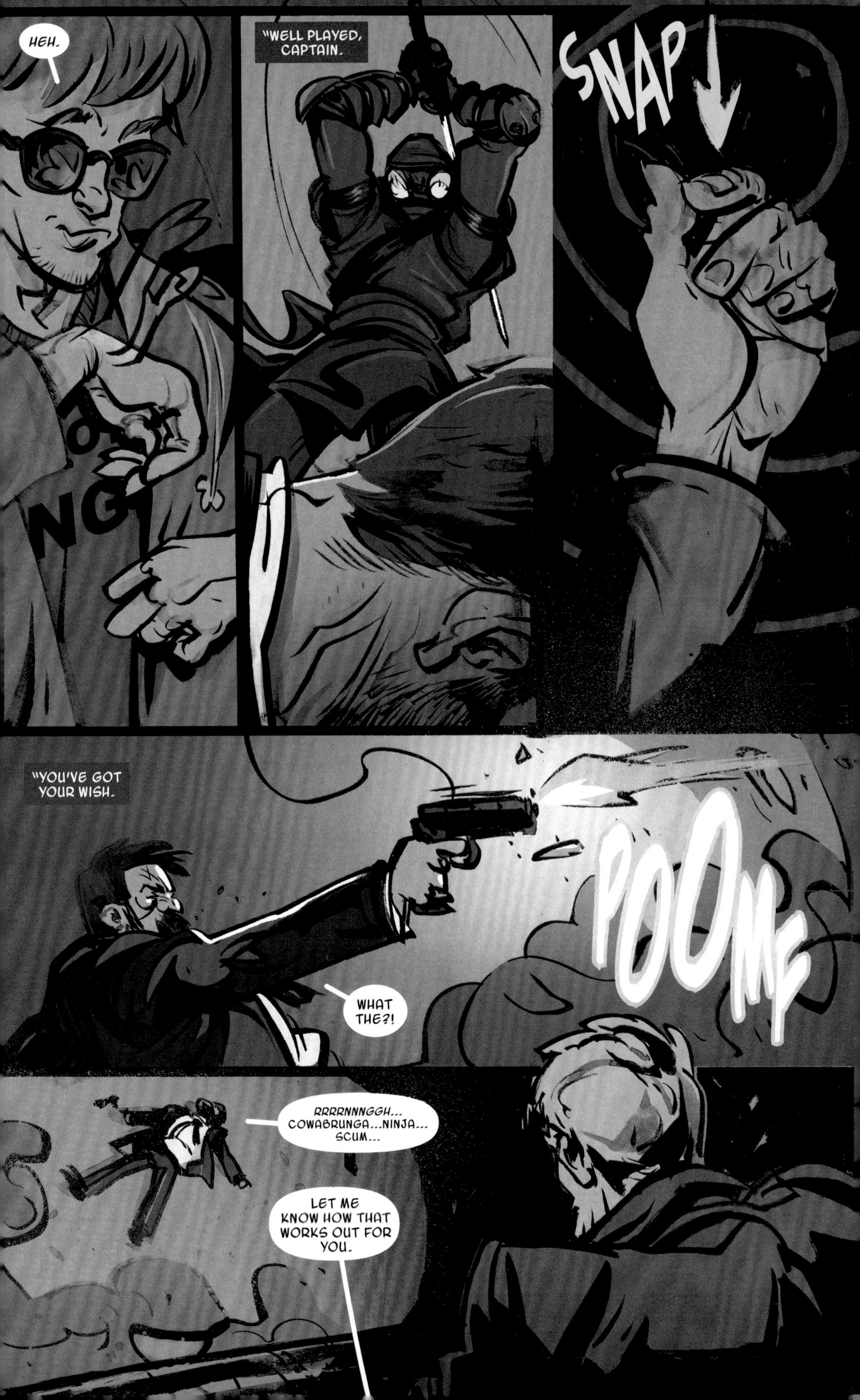
HEH.
"WELL PLAYED, CAPTAIN.
SNAP
"YOU'VE GOT YOUR WISH.
POOM
WHAT THE?!
RRRRNNNGGH... COWABRUNGA... NINJA... SCUM...
LET ME KNOW HOW THAT WORKS OUT FOR YOU.

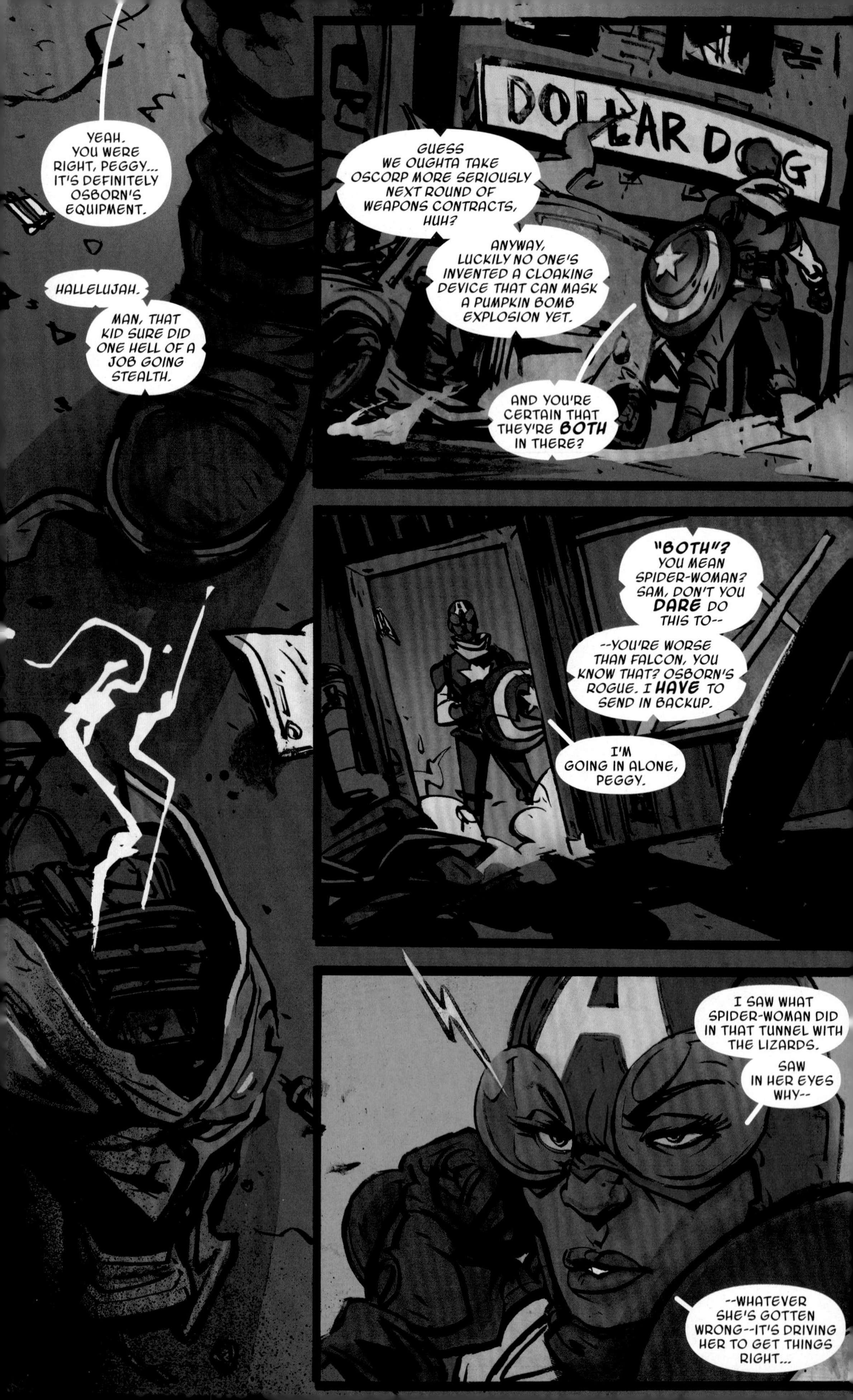
YEAH. YOU WERE RIGHT, PEGGY... IT'S DEFINITELY OSBORN'S EQUIPMENT.
HALLELUJAH.
MAN, THAT KID SURE DID ONE HELL OF A JOB GOING STEALTH.
DOLLAR DOG
GUESS WE OUGHTA TAKE OSCORP MORE SERIOUSLY NEXT ROUND OF WEAPONS CONTRACTS, HUH?
ANYWAY, LUCKILY NO ONE'S INVENTED A CLOAKING DEVICE THAT CAN MASK A PUMPKIN BOMB EXPLOSION YET.
AND YOU'RE CERTAIN THAT THEY'RE BOTH IN THERE?
"BOTH"? YOU MEAN SPIDER-WOMAN? SAM, DON'T YOU DARE DO THIS TO--
--YOU'RE WORSE THAN FALCON, YOU KNOW THAT? OSBORN'S ROGUE. I HAVE TO SEND IN BACKUP.
I'M GOING IN ALONE, PEGGY.
I SAW WHAT SPIDER-WOMAN DID IN THAT TUNNEL WITH THE LIZARDS.
SAW IN HER EYES WHY--
--WHATEVER SHE'S GOTTEN WRONG--IT'S DRIVING HER TO GET THINGS RIGHT...

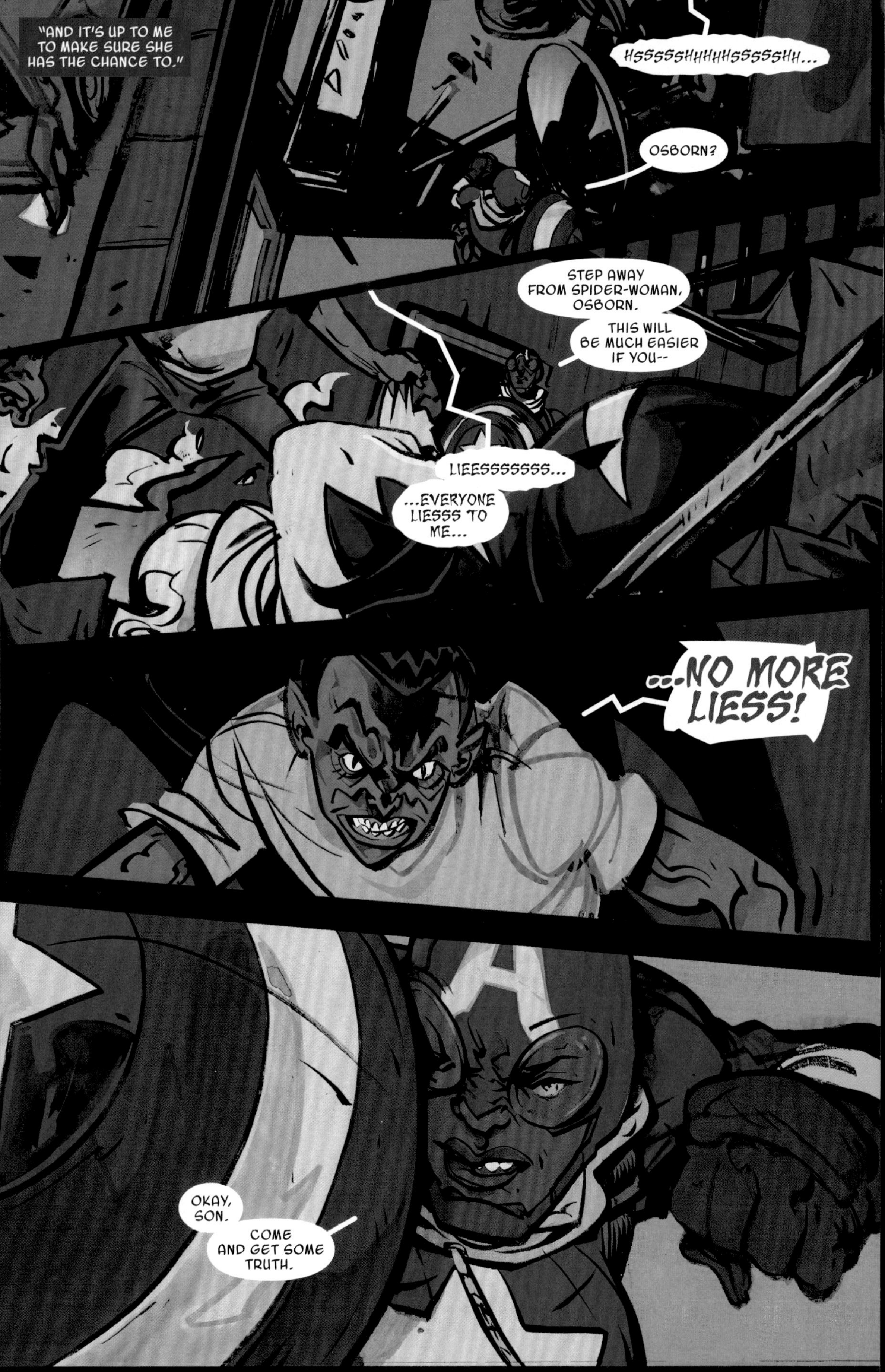
"AND IT'S UP TO ME TO MAKE SURE SHE HAS THE CHANCE TO."
HSSSSSHHHHSSSSSHH...
OSBORN?
STEP AWAY FROM SPIDER-WOMAN, OSBORN.
THIS WILL BE MUCH EASIER IF YOU--
LIEESSSSSSS...
...EVERYONE LIESSS TO ME...
...NO MORE LIESS!
OKAY, SON.
COME AND GET SOME TRUTH.

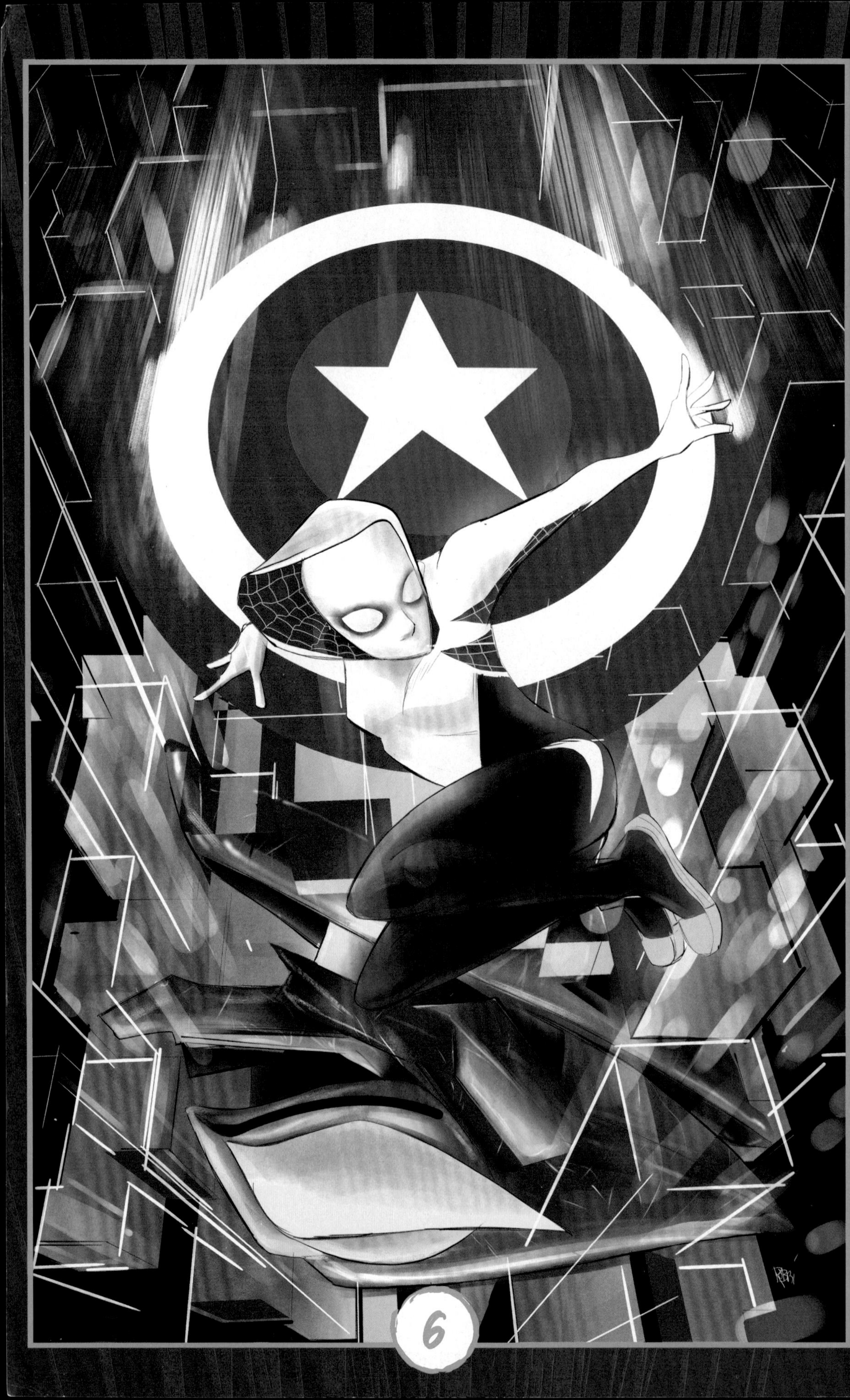
6

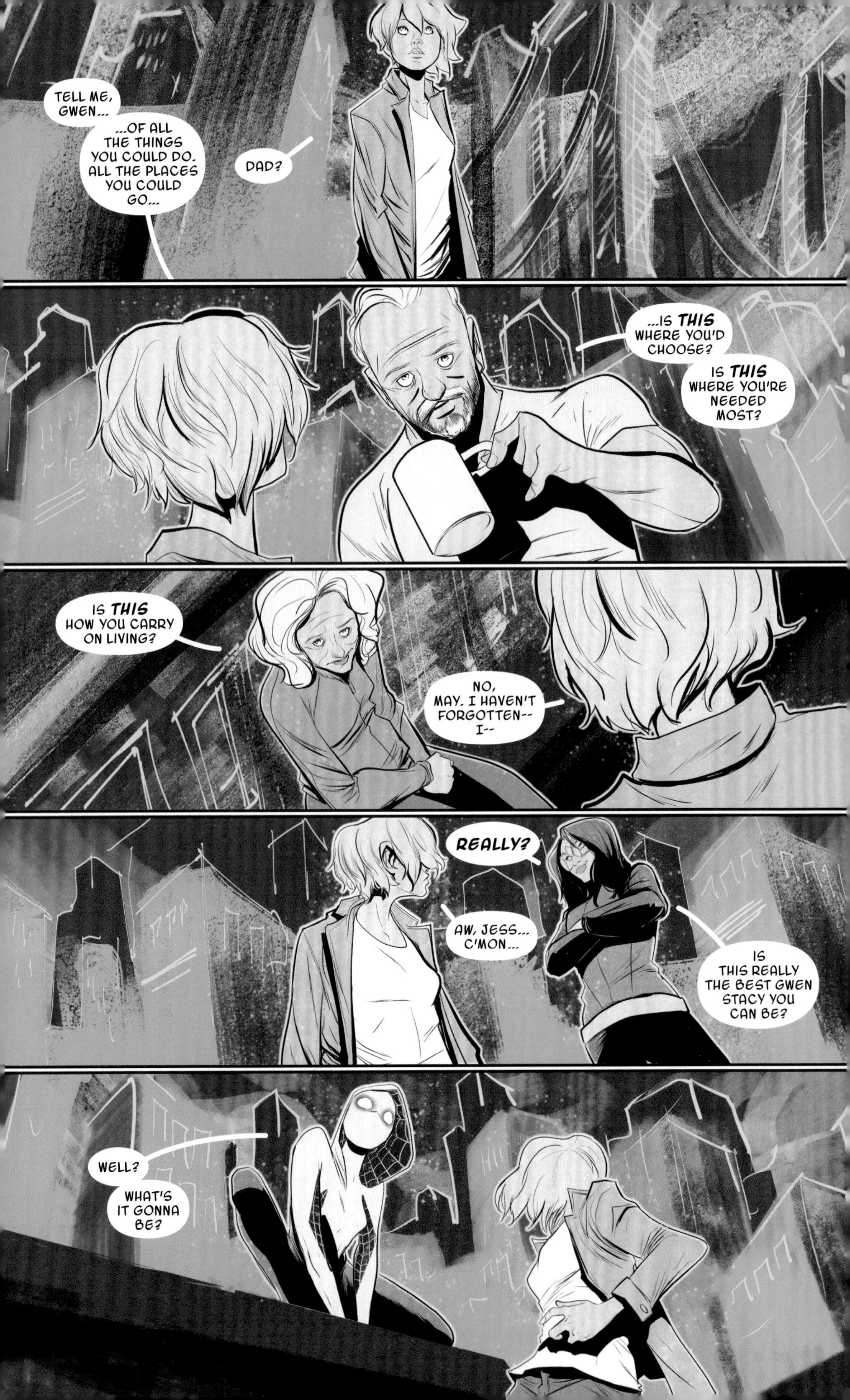
TELL ME, GWEN...
...OF ALL THE THINGS YOU COULD DO. ALL THE PLACES YOU COULD GO...
DAD?
...IS THIS WHERE YOU'D CHOOSE?
IS THIS WHERE YOU'RE NEEDED MOST?
IS THIS HOW YOU CARRY ON LIVING?
NO, MAY. I HAVEN'T FORGOTTEN-- I--
REALLY?
AW, JESS... C'MON...
IS THIS REALLY THE BEST GWEN STACY YOU CAN BE?
WELL?
WHAT'S IT GONNA BE?

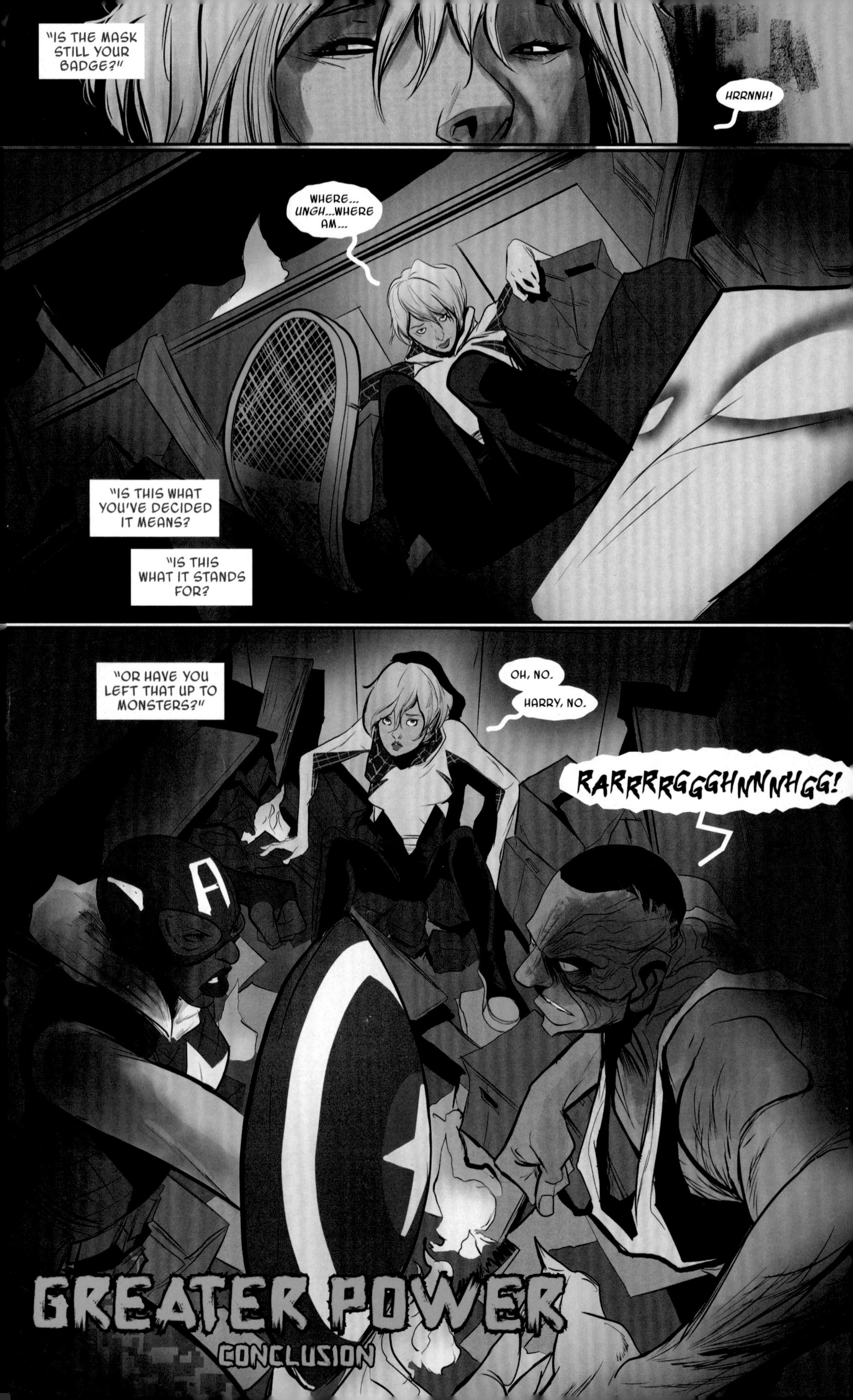

"IS THE MASK STILL YOUR BADGE?"
HRRNNH!
WHERE... UNGH...WHERE AM...
"IS THIS WHAT YOU'VE DECIDED IT MEANS?
"IS THIS WHAT IT STANDS FOR?
"OR HAVE YOU LEFT THAT UP TO MONSTERS?"
OH, NO.
HARRY, NO.
RARRRRGGGHNNNHGG!
GREATER POWER
CONCLUSION

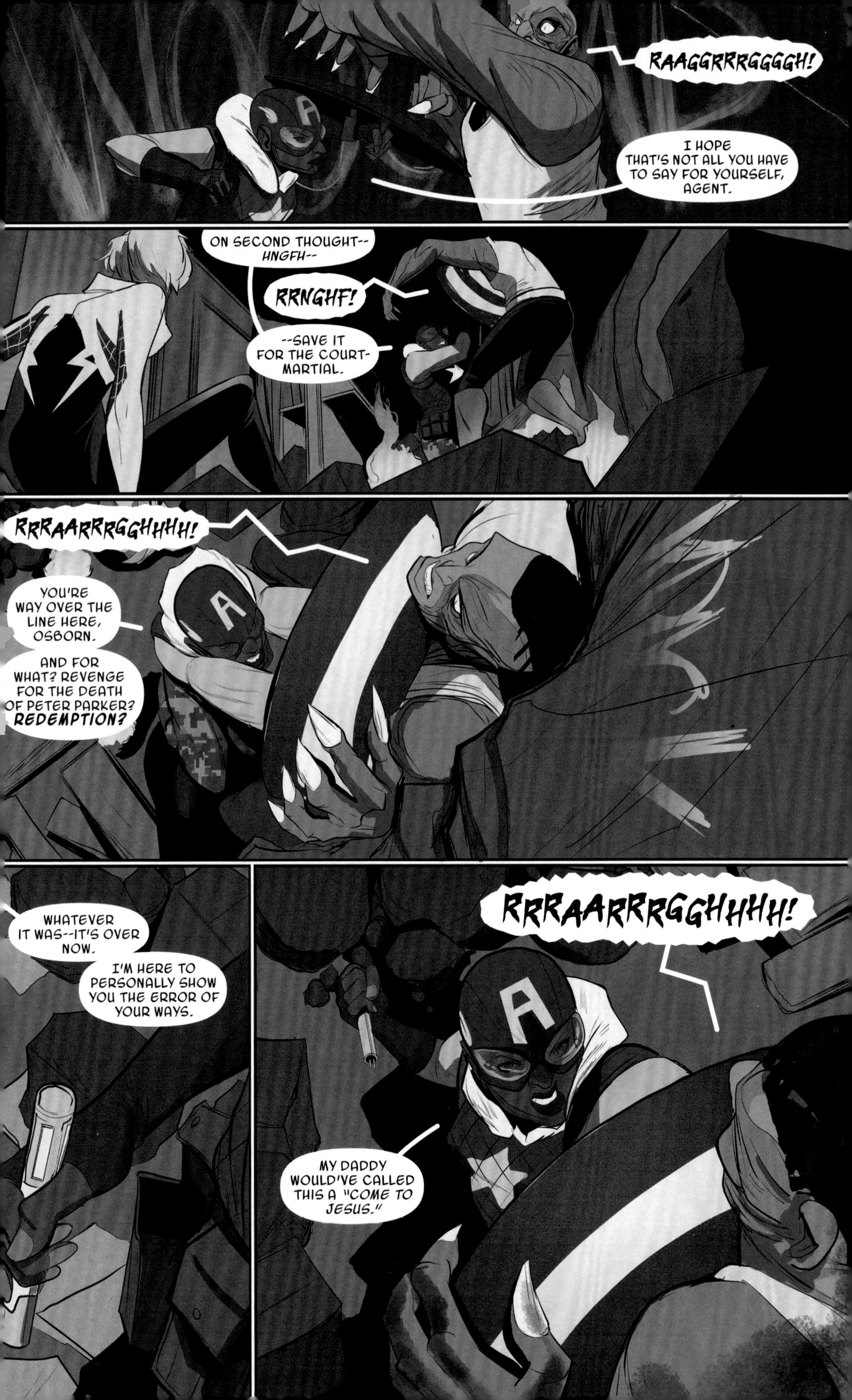

RAAGGRRRGGGGH!
I HOPE THAT'S NOT ALL YOU HAVE TO SAY FOR YOURSELF, AGENT.
ON SECOND THOUGHT-- HNGFH--
RRNGHF!
--SAVE IT FOR THE COURT-MARTIAL.
RRRAARRRGGHHHH!
YOU'RE WAY OVER THE LINE HERE, OSBORN.
AND FOR WHAT? REVENGE FOR THE DEATH OF PETER PARKER? **REDEMPTION?**
WHATEVER IT WAS--IT'S OVER NOW.
I'M HERE TO PERSONALLY SHOW YOU THE ERROR OF YOUR WAYS.
RRRAARRRGGHHHH!
MY DADDY WOULD'VE CALLED THIS A "COME TO JESUS."

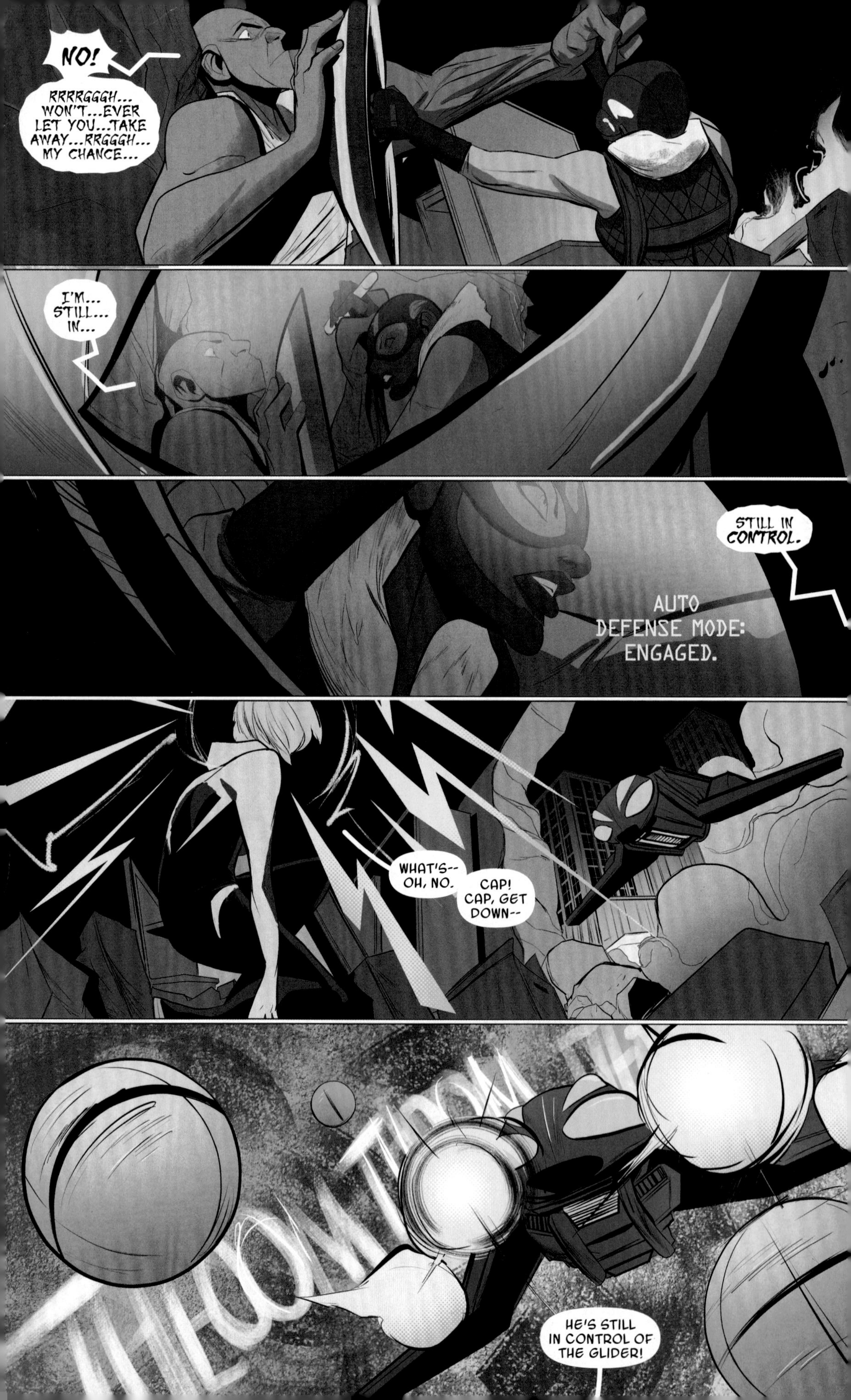
NO!
RRRRGGGH... WON'T...EVER LET YOU...TAKE AWAY...RRGGGH... MY CHANCE...
I'M... STILL... IN...
STILL IN CONTROL.
AUTO DEFENSE MODE: ENGAGED.
WHAT'S-- OH, NO.
CAP! CAP, GET DOWN--
THOOM THOOM
HE'S STILL IN CONTROL OF THE GLIDER!

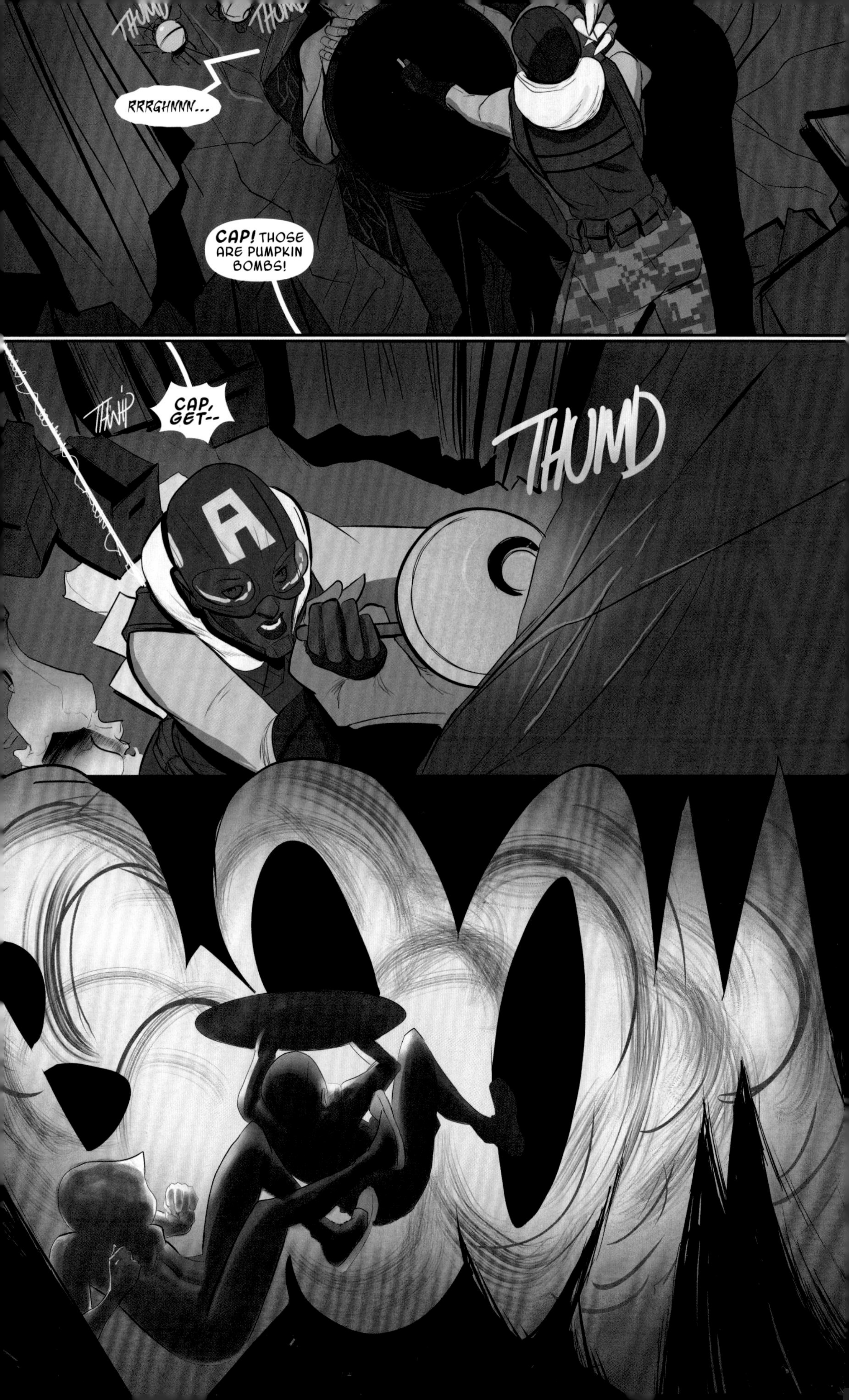
THUMD
THUMD
RRRGHNNN...
CAP! THOSE ARE PUMPKIN BOMBS!
THWIP
CAP, GET--
THUMD

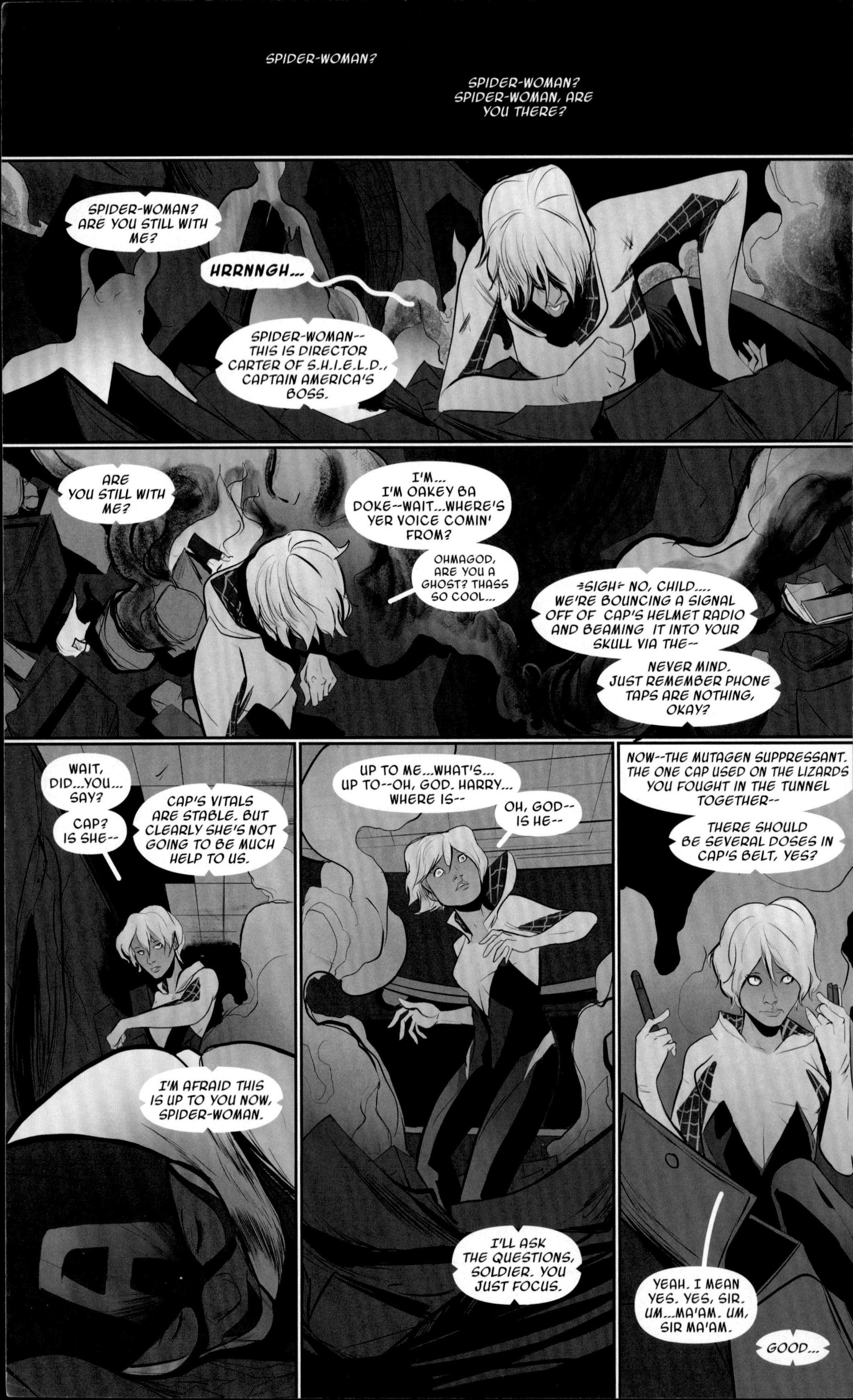
SPIDER-WOMAN?
SPIDER-WOMAN? SPIDER-WOMAN, ARE YOU THERE?
SPIDER-WOMAN? ARE YOU STILL WITH ME?
HRRNNGH...
SPIDER-WOMAN-- THIS IS DIRECTOR CARTER OF S.H.I.E.L.D., CAPTAIN AMERICA'S BOSS.
ARE YOU STILL WITH ME?
I'M... I'M OAKEY BA DOKE--WAIT...WHERE'S YER VOICE COMIN' FROM?
OHMAGOD, ARE YOU A GHOST? THASS SO COOL...
=SIGH= NO, CHILD.... WE'RE BOUNCING A SIGNAL OFF OF CAP'S HELMET RADIO AND BEAMING IT INTO YOUR SKULL VIA THE--
NEVER MIND. JUST REMEMBER PHONE TAPS ARE NOTHING, OKAY?
WAIT, DID...YOU... SAY?
CAP? IS SHE--
CAP'S VITALS ARE STABLE. BUT CLEARLY SHE'S NOT GOING TO BE MUCH HELP TO US.
I'M AFRAID THIS IS UP TO YOU NOW, SPIDER-WOMAN.
UP TO ME...WHAT'S... UP TO--OH, GOD. HARRY... WHERE IS--
OH, GOD-- IS HE--
I'LL ASK THE QUESTIONS, SOLDIER. YOU JUST FOCUS.
NOW--THE MUTAGEN SUPPRESSANT. THE ONE CAP USED ON THE LIZARDS YOU FOUGHT IN THE TUNNEL TOGETHER--
THERE SHOULD BE SEVERAL DOSES IN CAP'S BELT, YES?
YEAH. I MEAN YES. YES, SIR. UM...MA'AM. UM, SIR MA'AM.
GOOD...

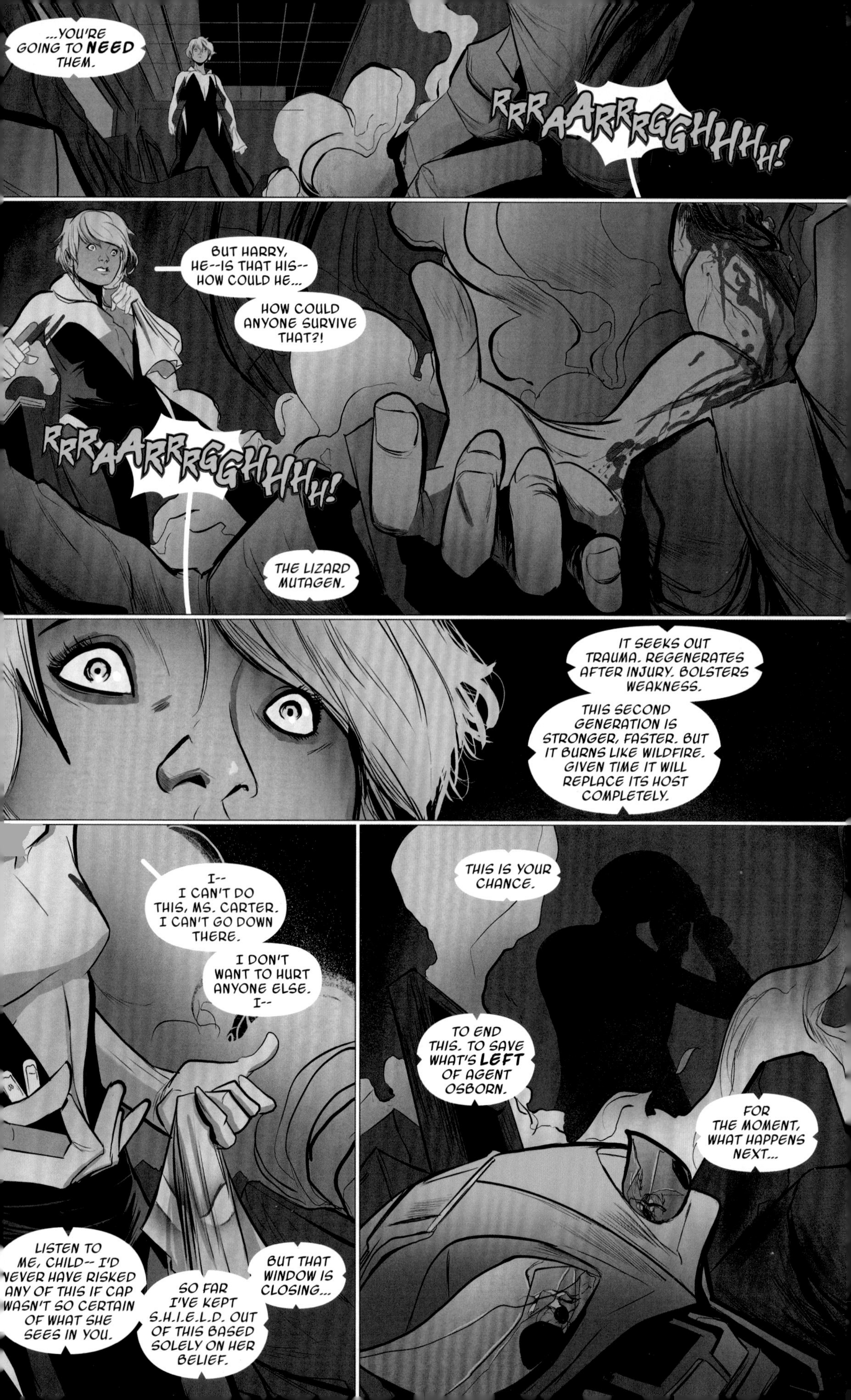
...YOU'RE GOING TO NEED THEM.
RRRAARRRGGHHHH!
BUT HARRY, HE--IS THAT HIS-- HOW COULD HE...
HOW COULD ANYONE SURVIVE THAT?!
RRRAARRRGGHHHH!
THE LIZARD MUTAGEN.
IT SEEKS OUT TRAUMA. REGENERATES AFTER INJURY. BOLSTERS WEAKNESS.
THIS SECOND GENERATION IS STRONGER, FASTER. BUT IT BURNS LIKE WILDFIRE. GIVEN TIME IT WILL REPLACE ITS HOST COMPLETELY.
I-- I CAN'T DO THIS, MS. CARTER. I CAN'T GO DOWN THERE.
I DON'T WANT TO HURT ANYONE ELSE. I--
LISTEN TO ME, CHILD-- I'D NEVER HAVE RISKED ANY OF THIS IF CAP WASN'T SO CERTAIN OF WHAT SHE SEES IN YOU.
SO FAR I'VE KEPT S.H.I.E.L.D. OUT OF THIS BASED SOLELY ON HER BELIEF.
BUT THAT WINDOW IS CLOSING...
THIS IS YOUR CHANCE.
TO END THIS. TO SAVE WHAT'S LEFT OF AGENT OSBORN.
FOR THE MOMENT, WHAT HAPPENS NEXT...

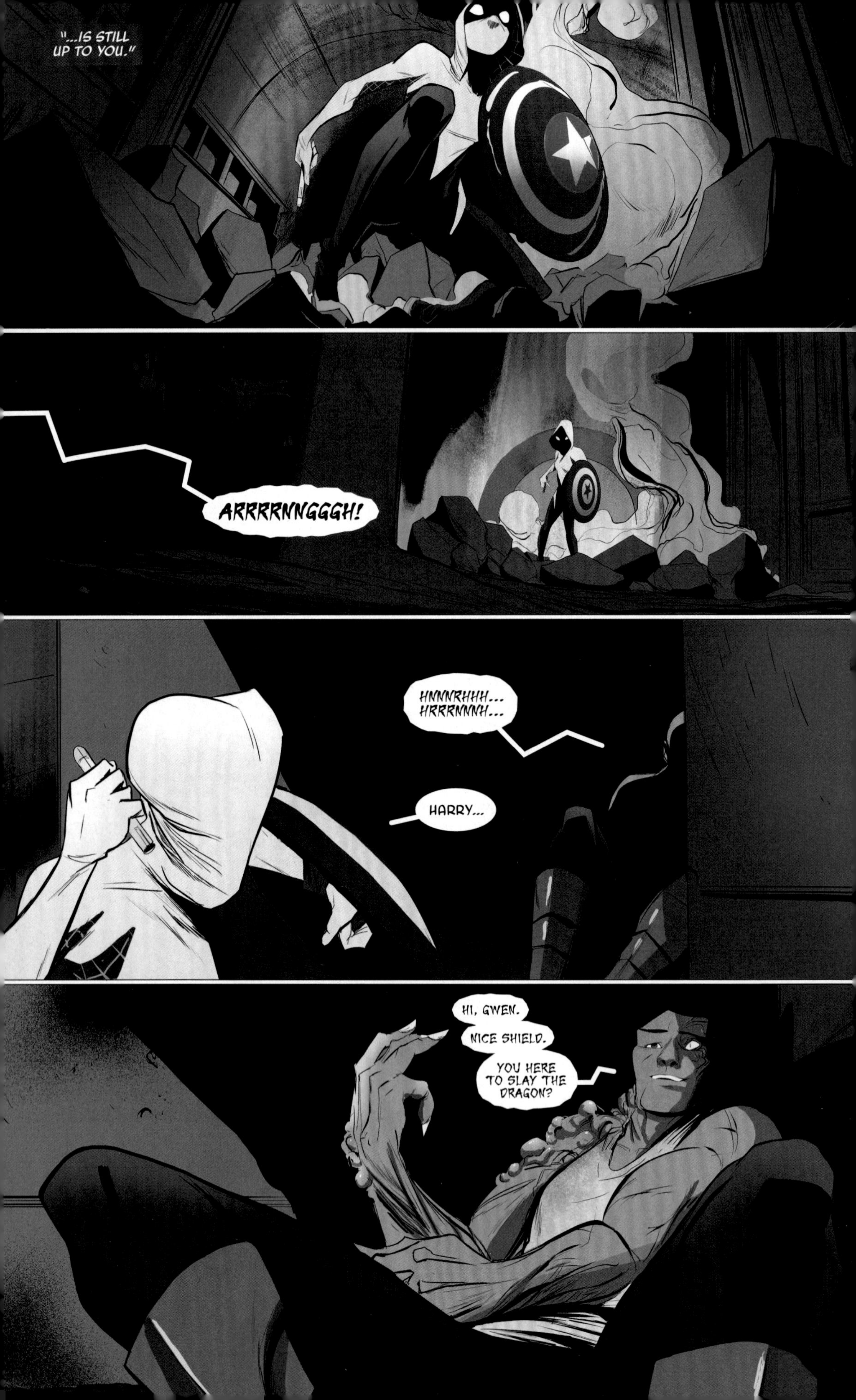
"...IS STILL UP TO YOU."
ARRRRNNGGGH!
HNNNRHHH... HRRRNNNH...
HARRY...
HI, GWEN.
NICE SHIELD.
YOU HERE TO SLAY THE DRAGON?

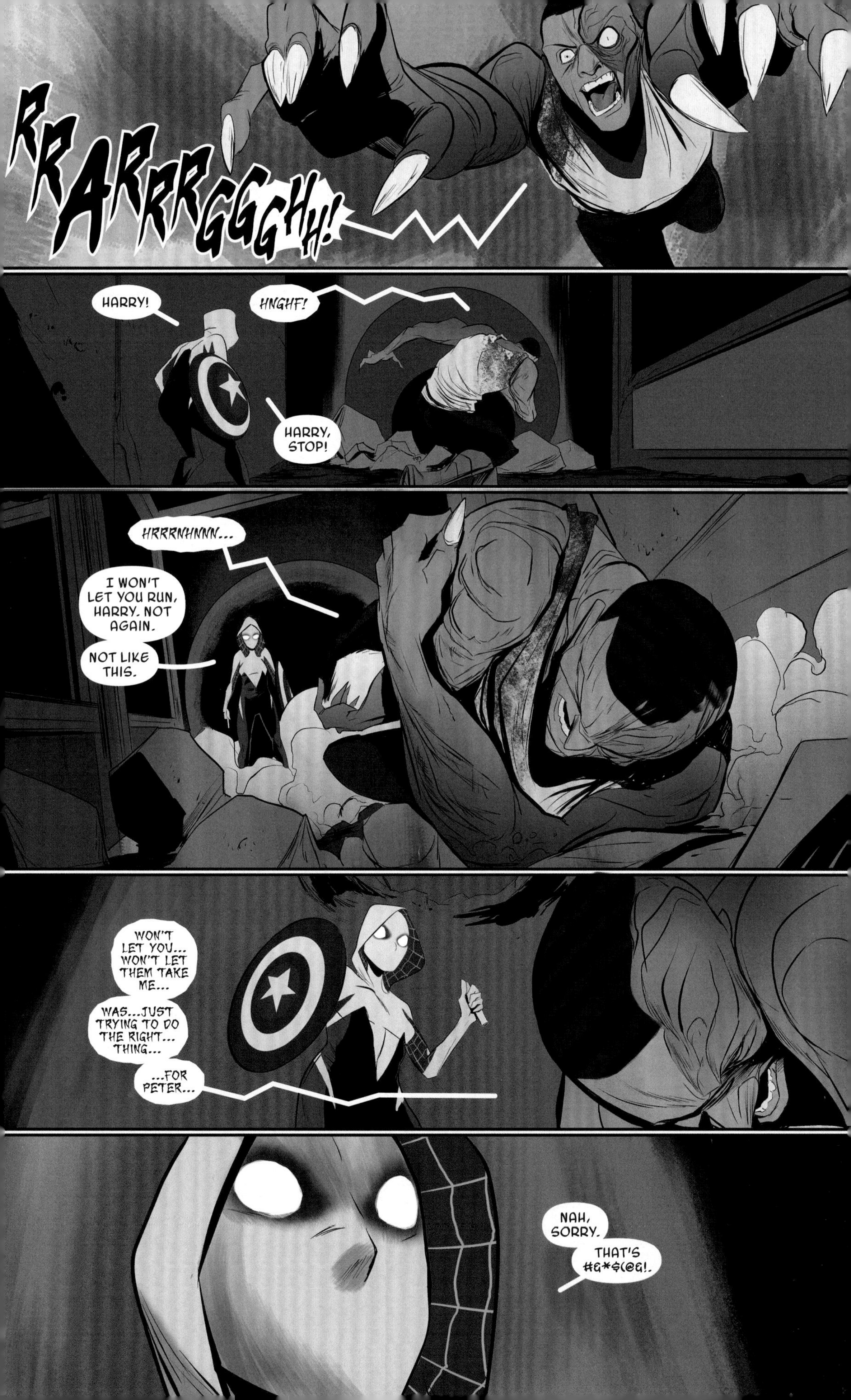
RRARRRGGGHH!
HARRY!
HNGHF!
HARRY, STOP!
HRRRNHNNN...
I WON'T LET YOU RUN, HARRY. NOT AGAIN.
NOT LIKE THIS.
WON'T LET YOU... WON'T LET THEM TAKE ME...
WAS...JUST TRYING TO DO THE RIGHT... THING...
...FOR PETER...
NAH, SORRY.
THAT'S #&*$(@&!.

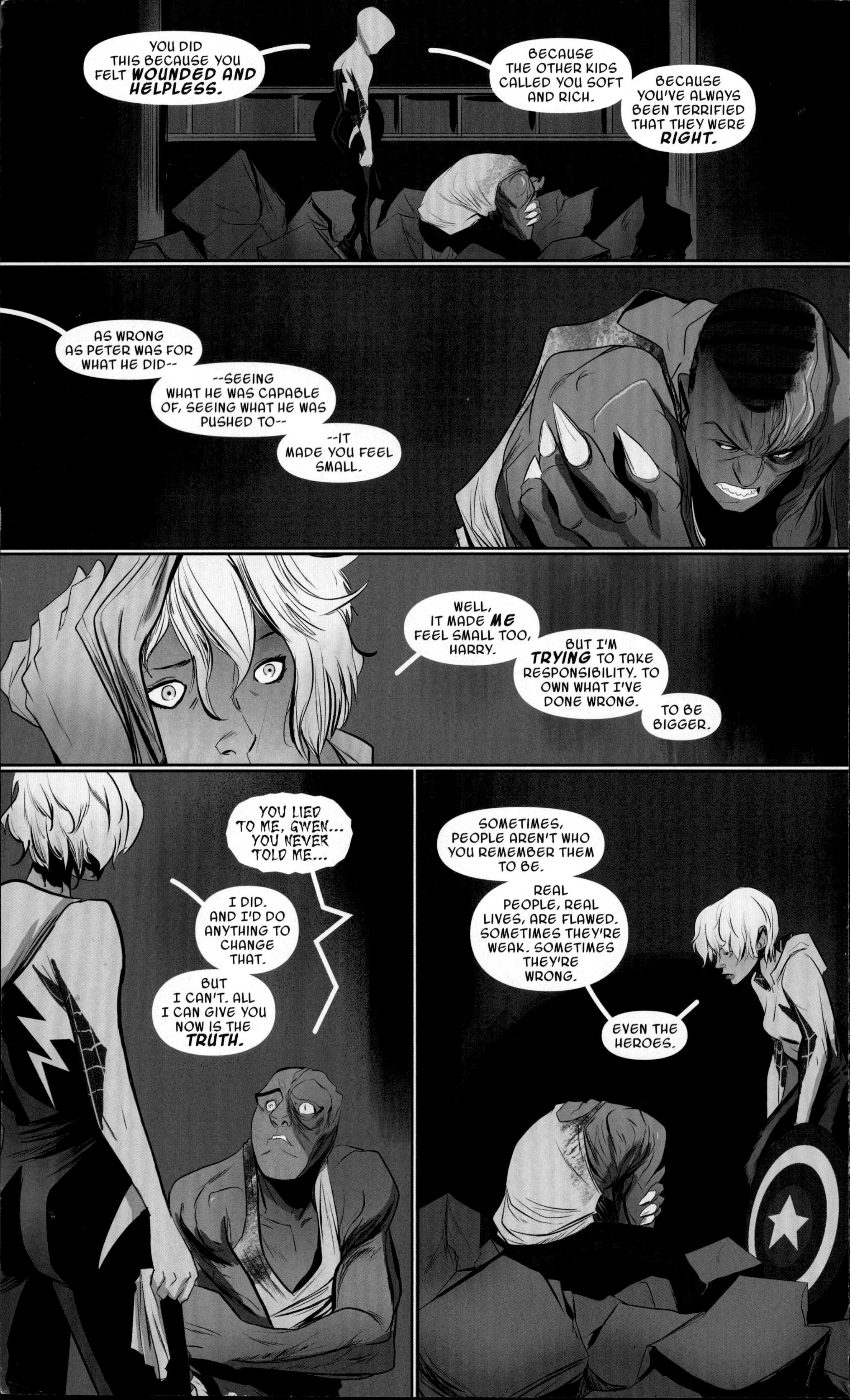

YOU DID THIS BECAUSE YOU FELT **WOUNDED AND HELPLESS.**
BECAUSE THE OTHER KIDS CALLED YOU SOFT AND RICH.
BECAUSE YOU'VE ALWAYS BEEN TERRIFIED THAT THEY WERE **RIGHT.**
AS WRONG AS PETER WAS FOR WHAT HE DID--
--SEEING WHAT HE WAS CAPABLE OF, SEEING WHAT HE WAS PUSHED TO--
--IT MADE YOU FEEL SMALL.
WELL, IT MADE **ME** FEEL SMALL TOO, HARRY.
BUT I'M **TRYING** TO TAKE RESPONSIBILITY. TO OWN WHAT I'VE DONE WRONG.
TO BE BIGGER.
YOU LIED TO ME, GWEN... YOU NEVER TOLD ME...
I DID. AND I'D DO ANYTHING TO CHANGE THAT.
BUT I CAN'T. ALL I CAN GIVE YOU NOW IS THE **TRUTH.**
SOMETIMES, PEOPLE AREN'T WHO YOU REMEMBER THEM TO BE.
REAL PEOPLE, REAL LIVES, ARE FLAWED. SOMETIMES THEY'RE WEAK. SOMETIMES THEY'RE WRONG.
EVEN THE HEROES.

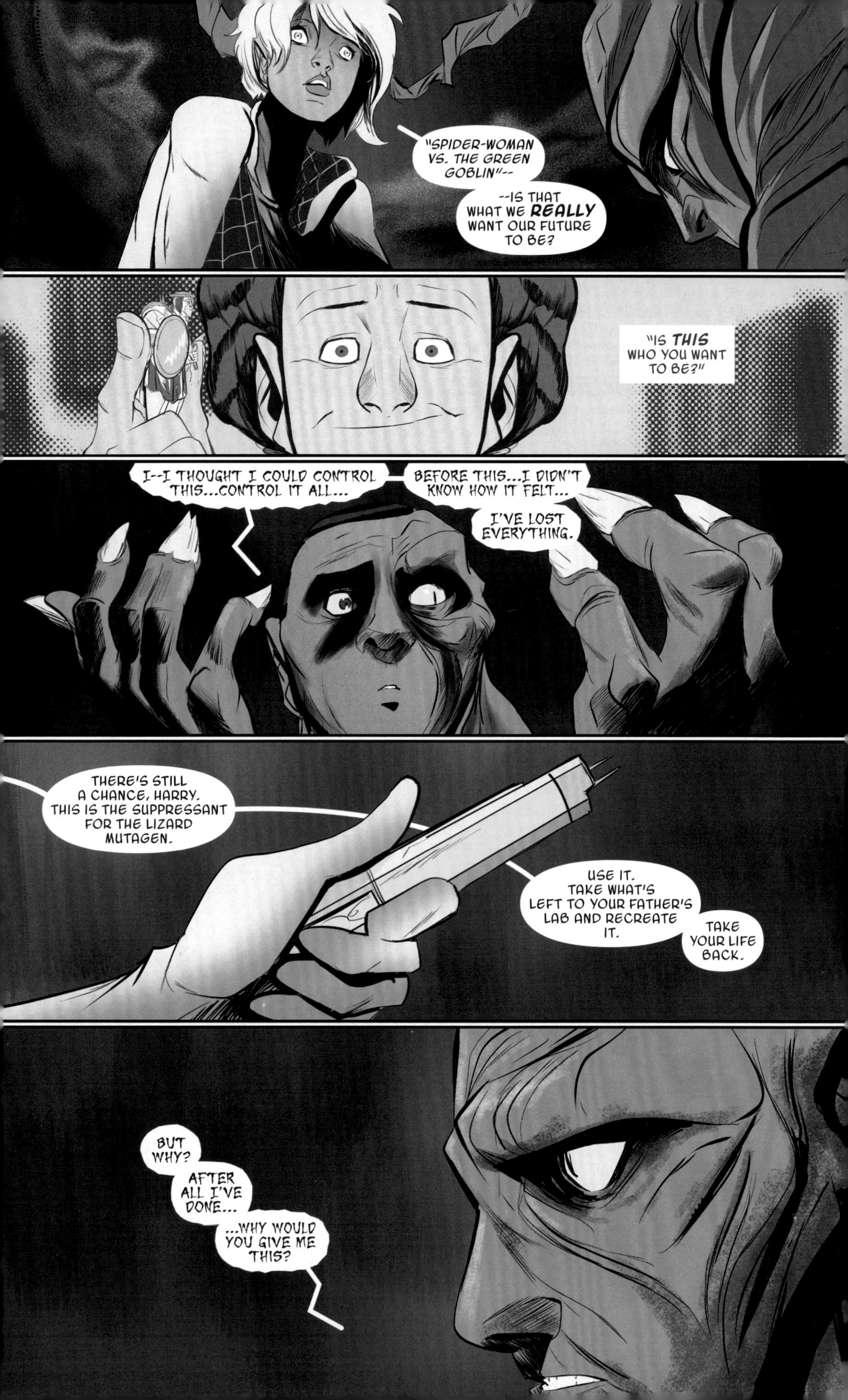
"SPIDER-WOMAN VS. THE GREEN GOBLIN"--
--IS THAT WHAT WE REALLY WANT OUR FUTURE TO BE?
"IS THIS WHO YOU WANT TO BE?"
I--I THOUGHT I COULD CONTROL THIS...CONTROL IT ALL...
BEFORE THIS...I DIDN'T KNOW HOW IT FELT...
I'VE LOST EVERYTHING.
THERE'S STILL A CHANCE, HARRY. THIS IS THE SUPPRESSANT FOR THE LIZARD MUTAGEN.
USE IT. TAKE WHAT'S LEFT TO YOUR FATHER'S LAB AND RECREATE IT.
TAKE YOUR LIFE BACK.
BUT WHY?
AFTER ALL I'VE DONE...
...WHY WOULD YOU GIVE ME THIS?

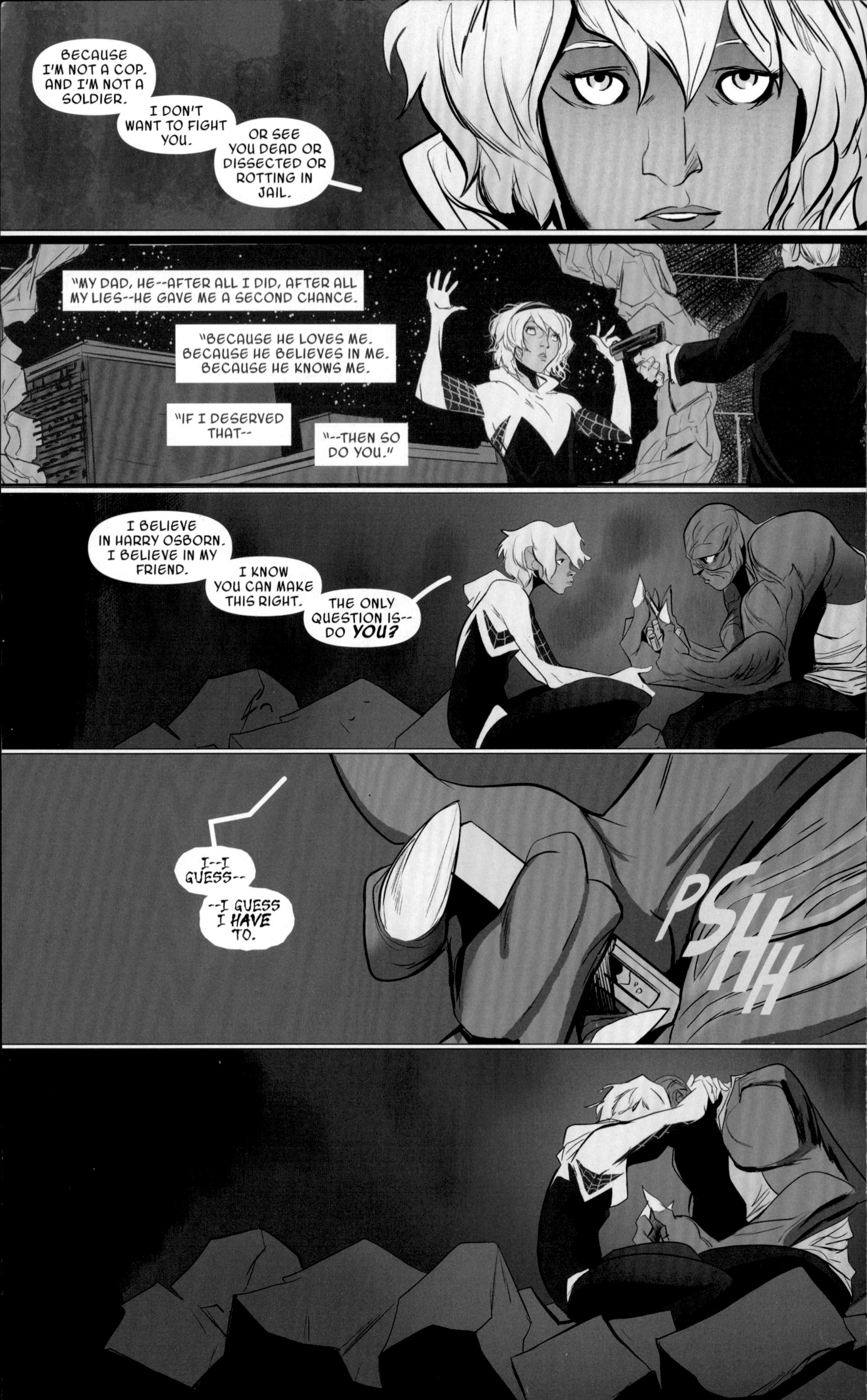
BECAUSE I'M NOT A COP. AND I'M NOT A SOLDIER.
I DON'T WANT TO FIGHT YOU.
OR SEE YOU DEAD OR DISSECTED OR ROTTING IN JAIL.
"MY DAD, HE--AFTER ALL I DID, AFTER ALL MY LIES--HE GAVE ME A SECOND CHANCE.
"BECAUSE HE LOVES ME. BECAUSE HE BELIEVES IN ME. BECAUSE HE KNOWS ME.
"IF I DESERVED THAT--
"--THEN SO DO YOU."
I BELIEVE IN HARRY OSBORN. I BELIEVE IN MY FRIEND.
I KNOW YOU CAN MAKE THIS RIGHT.
THE ONLY QUESTION IS--DO YOU?
I--I GUESS--
--I GUESS I HAVE TO.
PSHH

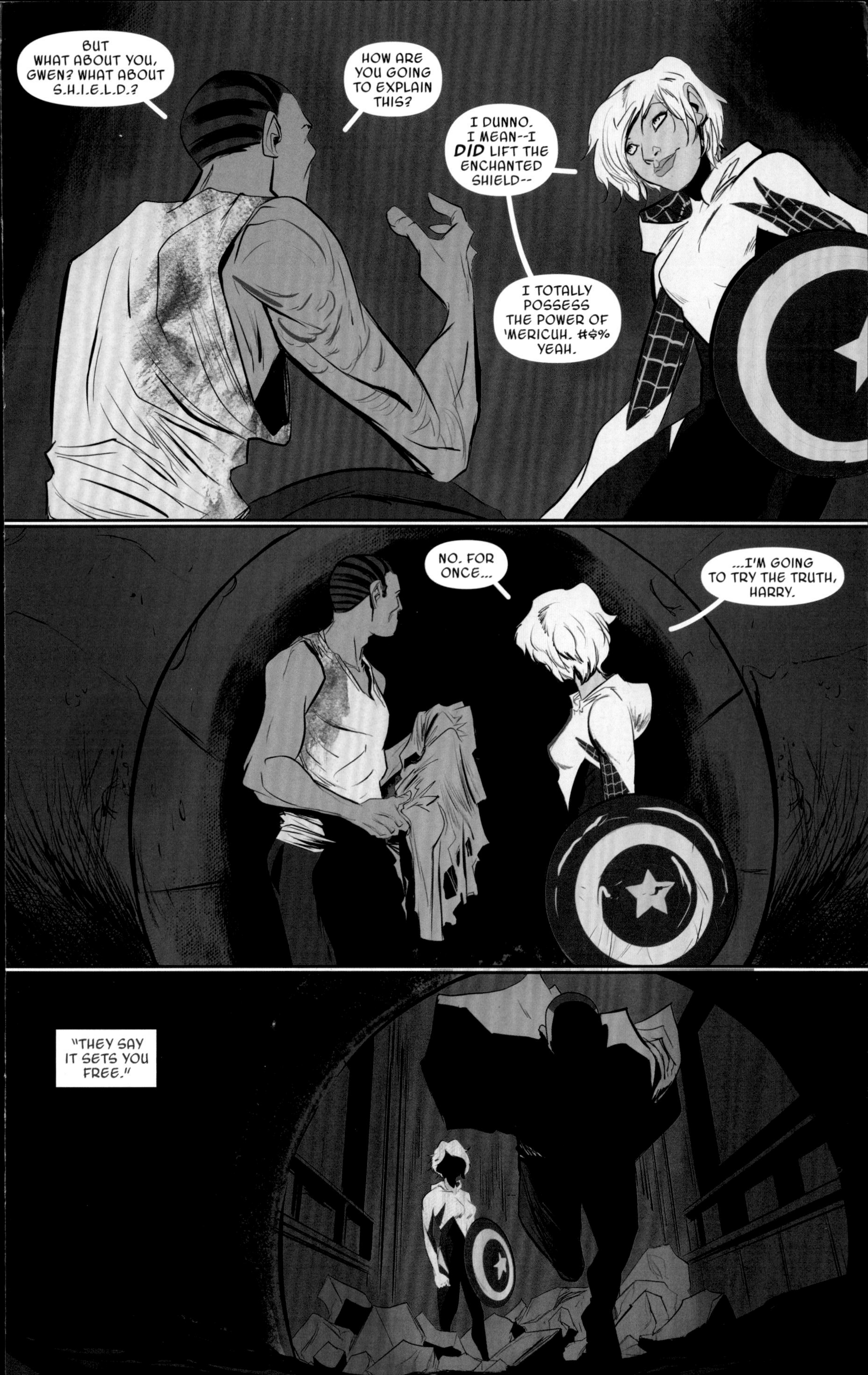
BUT WHAT ABOUT YOU, GWEN? WHAT ABOUT S.H.I.E.L.D.?
HOW ARE YOU GOING TO EXPLAIN THIS?
I DUNNO. I MEAN--I DID LIFT THE ENCHANTED SHIELD--
I TOTALLY POSSESS THE POWER OF 'MERICUH. #$% YEAH.
NO. FOR ONCE...
...I'M GOING TO TRY THE TRUTH, HARRY.
"THEY SAY IT SETS YOU FREE."

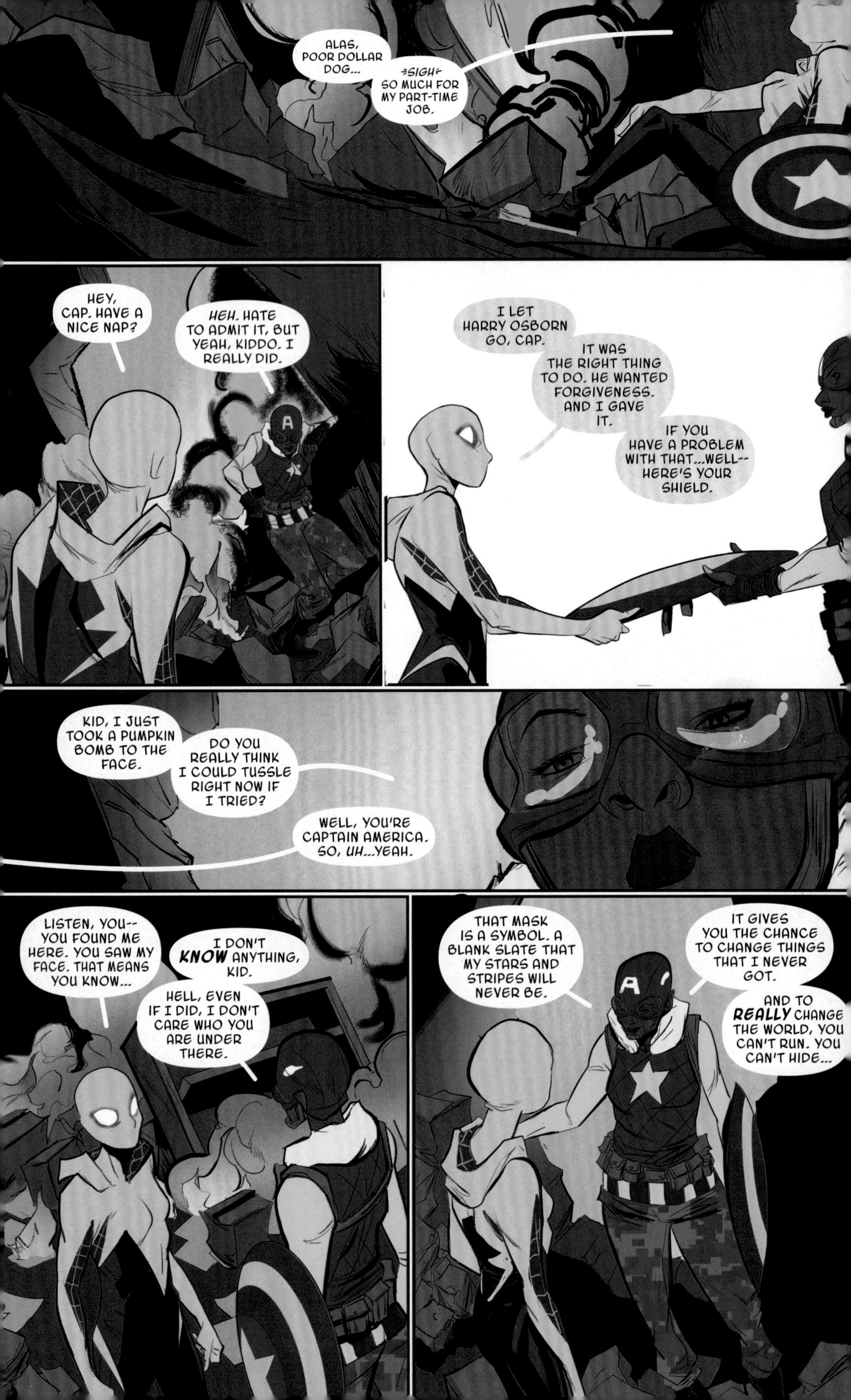
ALAS, POOR DOLLAR DOG...
=SIGH= SO MUCH FOR MY PART-TIME JOB.
HEY, CAP. HAVE A NICE NAP?
HEH. HATE TO ADMIT IT, BUT YEAH, KIDDO. I REALLY DID.
I LET HARRY OSBORN GO, CAP.
IT WAS THE RIGHT THING TO DO. HE WANTED FORGIVENESS. AND I GAVE IT.
IF YOU HAVE A PROBLEM WITH THAT...WELL-- HERE'S YOUR SHIELD.
KID, I JUST TOOK A PUMPKIN BOMB TO THE FACE.
DO YOU REALLY THINK I COULD TUSSLE RIGHT NOW IF I TRIED?
WELL, YOU'RE CAPTAIN AMERICA. SO, UH...YEAH.
LISTEN, YOU-- YOU FOUND ME HERE. YOU SAW MY FACE. THAT MEANS YOU KNOW...
I DON'T KNOW ANYTHING, KID.
HELL, EVEN IF I DID, I DON'T CARE WHO YOU ARE UNDER THERE.
THAT MASK IS A SYMBOL. A BLANK SLATE THAT MY STARS AND STRIPES WILL NEVER BE.
IT GIVES YOU THE CHANCE TO CHANGE THINGS THAT I NEVER GOT.
AND TO REALLY CHANGE THE WORLD, YOU CAN'T RUN. YOU CAN'T HIDE...

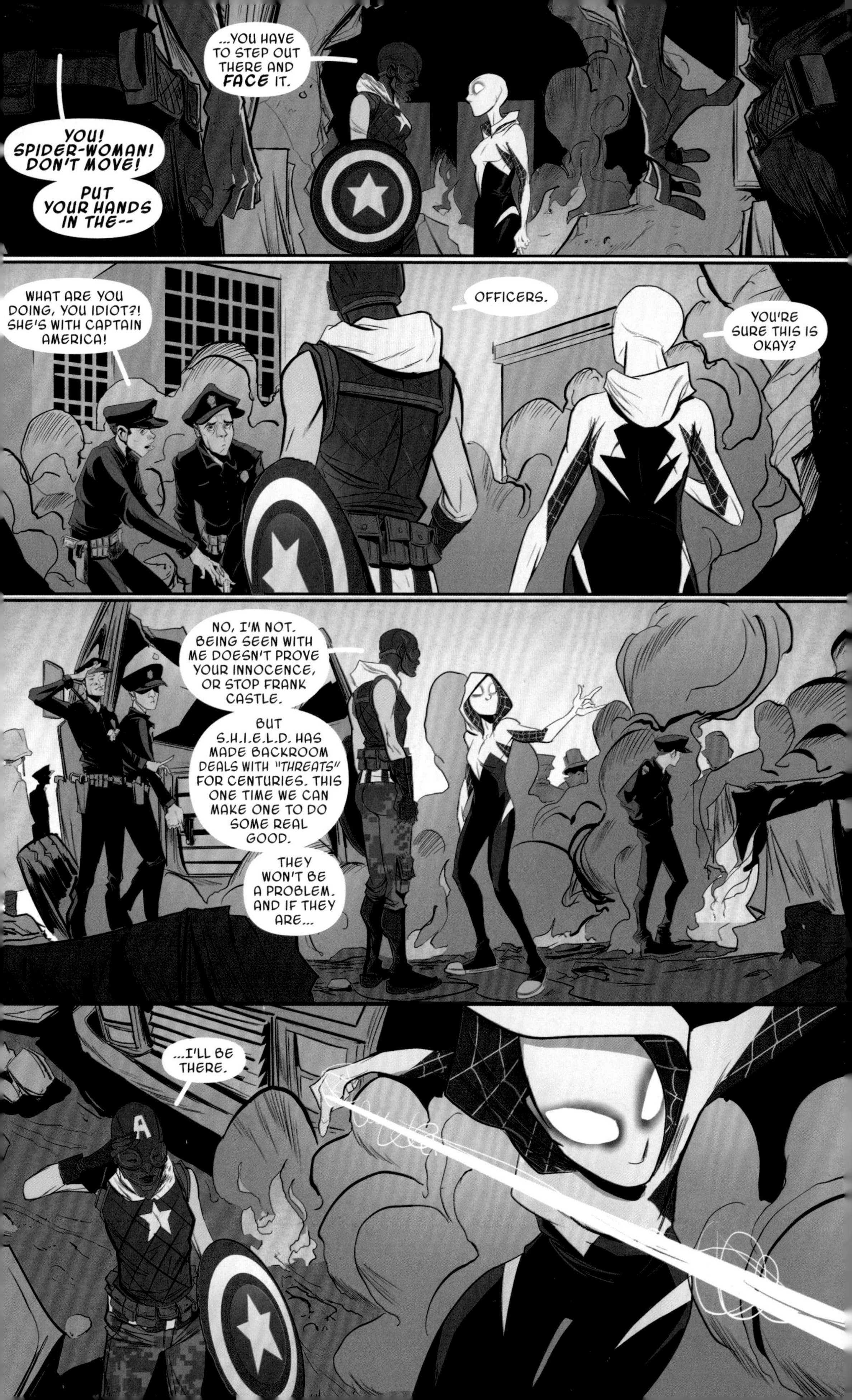

...YOU HAVE TO STEP OUT THERE AND FACE IT.
YOU! SPIDER-WOMAN! DON'T MOVE!
PUT YOUR HANDS IN THE--
WHAT ARE YOU DOING, YOU IDIOT?! SHE'S WITH CAPTAIN AMERICA!
OFFICERS.
YOU'RE SURE THIS IS OKAY?
NO, I'M NOT. BEING SEEN WITH ME DOESN'T PROVE YOUR INNOCENCE, OR STOP FRANK CASTLE.
BUT S.H.I.E.L.D. HAS MADE BACKROOM DEALS WITH "THREATS" FOR CENTURIES. THIS ONE TIME WE CAN MAKE ONE TO DO SOME REAL GOOD.
THEY WON'T BE A PROBLEM. AND IF THEY ARE...
...I'LL BE THERE.

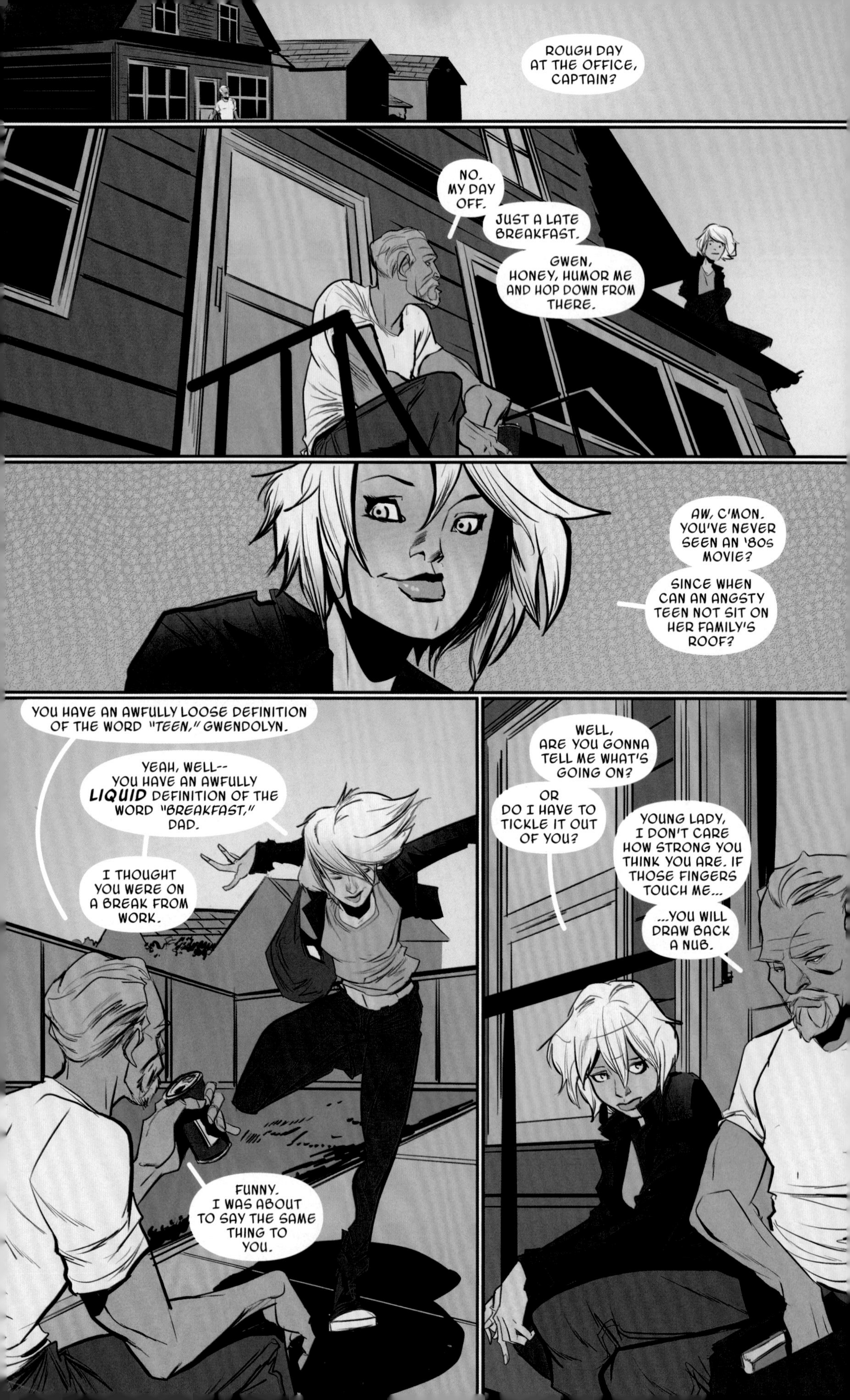
ROUGH DAY AT THE OFFICE, CAPTAIN?
NO. MY DAY OFF.
JUST A LATE BREAKFAST.
GWEN, HONEY, HUMOR ME AND HOP DOWN FROM THERE.
AW, C'MON. YOU'VE NEVER SEEN AN '80s MOVIE?
SINCE WHEN CAN AN ANGSTY TEEN NOT SIT ON HER FAMILY'S ROOF?
YOU HAVE AN AWFULLY LOOSE DEFINITION OF THE WORD *"TEEN,"* GWENDOLYN.
YEAH, WELL-- YOU HAVE AN AWFULLY **LIQUID** DEFINITION OF THE WORD *"BREAKFAST,"* DAD.
I THOUGHT YOU WERE ON A BREAK FROM WORK.
FUNNY. I WAS ABOUT TO SAY THE SAME THING TO YOU.
WELL, ARE YOU GONNA TELL ME WHAT'S GOING ON?
OR DO I HAVE TO TICKLE IT OUT OF YOU?
YOUNG LADY, I DON'T CARE HOW STRONG YOU THINK YOU ARE. IF THOSE FINGERS TOUCH ME...
...YOU WILL DRAW BACK A NUB.

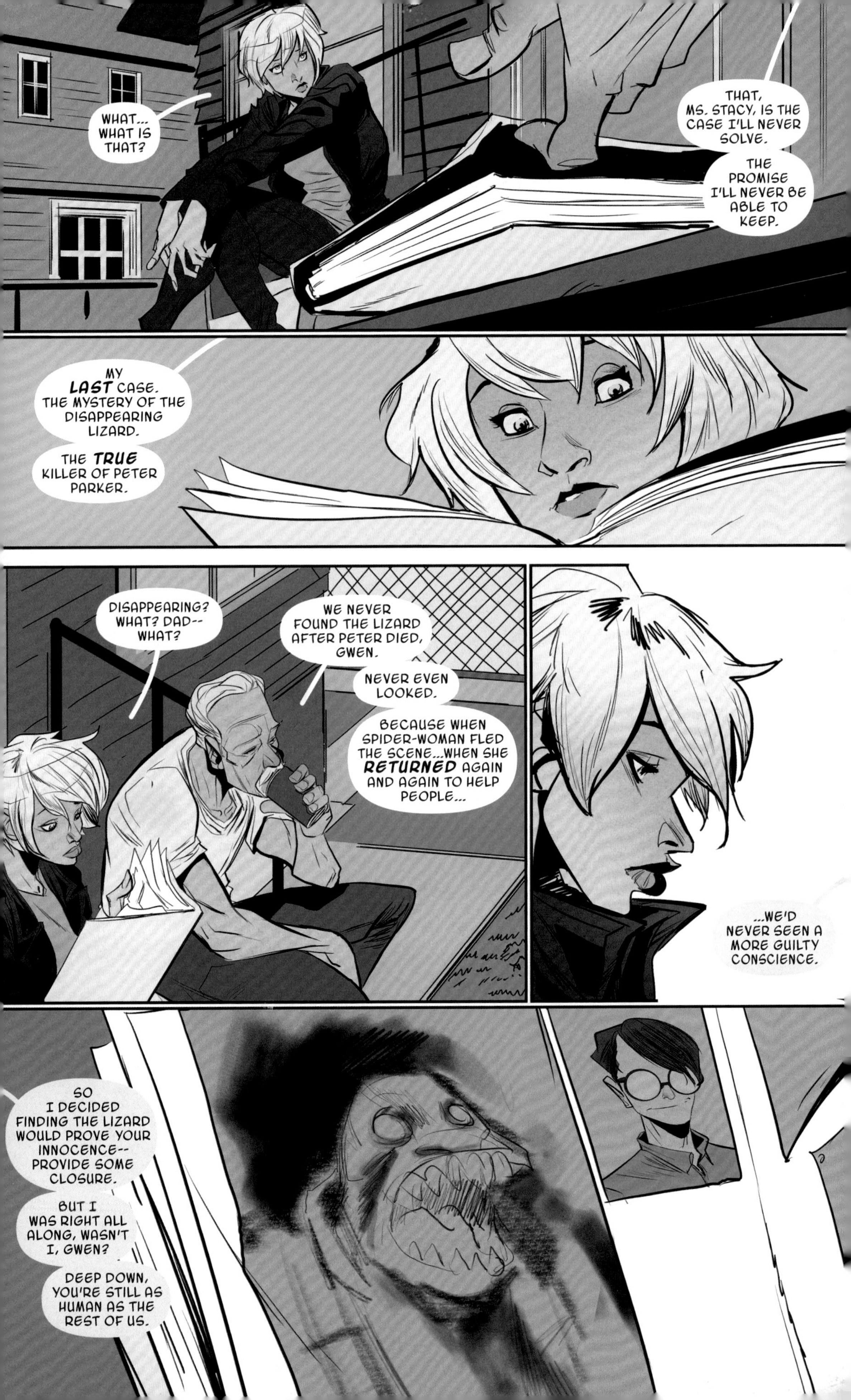
WHAT... WHAT IS THAT?
THAT, MS. STACY, IS THE CASE I'LL NEVER SOLVE.
THE PROMISE I'LL NEVER BE ABLE TO KEEP.
MY LAST CASE. THE MYSTERY OF THE DISAPPEARING LIZARD.
THE TRUE KILLER OF PETER PARKER.
DISAPPEARING? WHAT? DAD-- WHAT?
WE NEVER FOUND THE LIZARD AFTER PETER DIED, GWEN.
NEVER EVEN LOOKED.
BECAUSE WHEN SPIDER-WOMAN FLED THE SCENE...WHEN SHE RETURNED AGAIN AND AGAIN TO HELP PEOPLE...
...WE'D NEVER SEEN A MORE GUILTY CONSCIENCE.
SO I DECIDED FINDING THE LIZARD WOULD PROVE YOUR INNOCENCE-- PROVIDE SOME CLOSURE.
BUT I WAS RIGHT ALL ALONG, WASN'T I, GWEN?
DEEP DOWN, YOU'RE STILL AS HUMAN AS THE REST OF US.

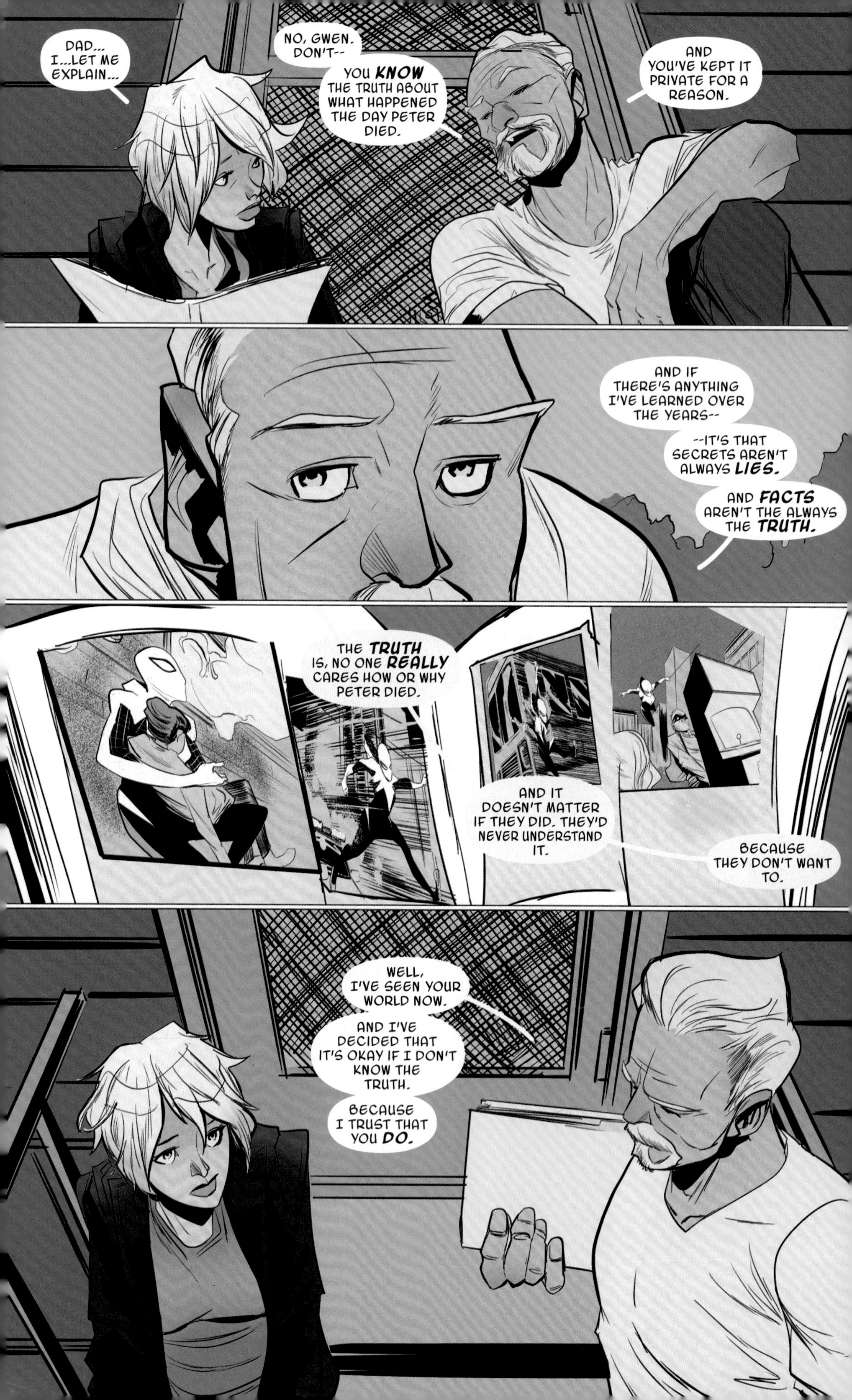
DAD... I...LET ME EXPLAIN...
NO, GWEN. DON'T--
YOU KNOW THE TRUTH ABOUT WHAT HAPPENED THE DAY PETER DIED.
AND YOU'VE KEPT IT PRIVATE FOR A REASON.
AND IF THERE'S ANYTHING I'VE LEARNED OVER THE YEARS--
--IT'S THAT SECRETS AREN'T ALWAYS LIES.
AND FACTS AREN'T THE ALWAYS THE TRUTH.
THE TRUTH IS, NO ONE REALLY CARES HOW OR WHY PETER DIED.
AND IT DOESN'T MATTER IF THEY DID. THEY'D NEVER UNDERSTAND IT.
BECAUSE THEY DON'T WANT TO.
WELL, I'VE SEEN YOUR WORLD NOW.
AND I'VE DECIDED THAT IT'S OKAY IF I DON'T KNOW THE TRUTH.
BECAUSE I TRUST THAT YOU DO.

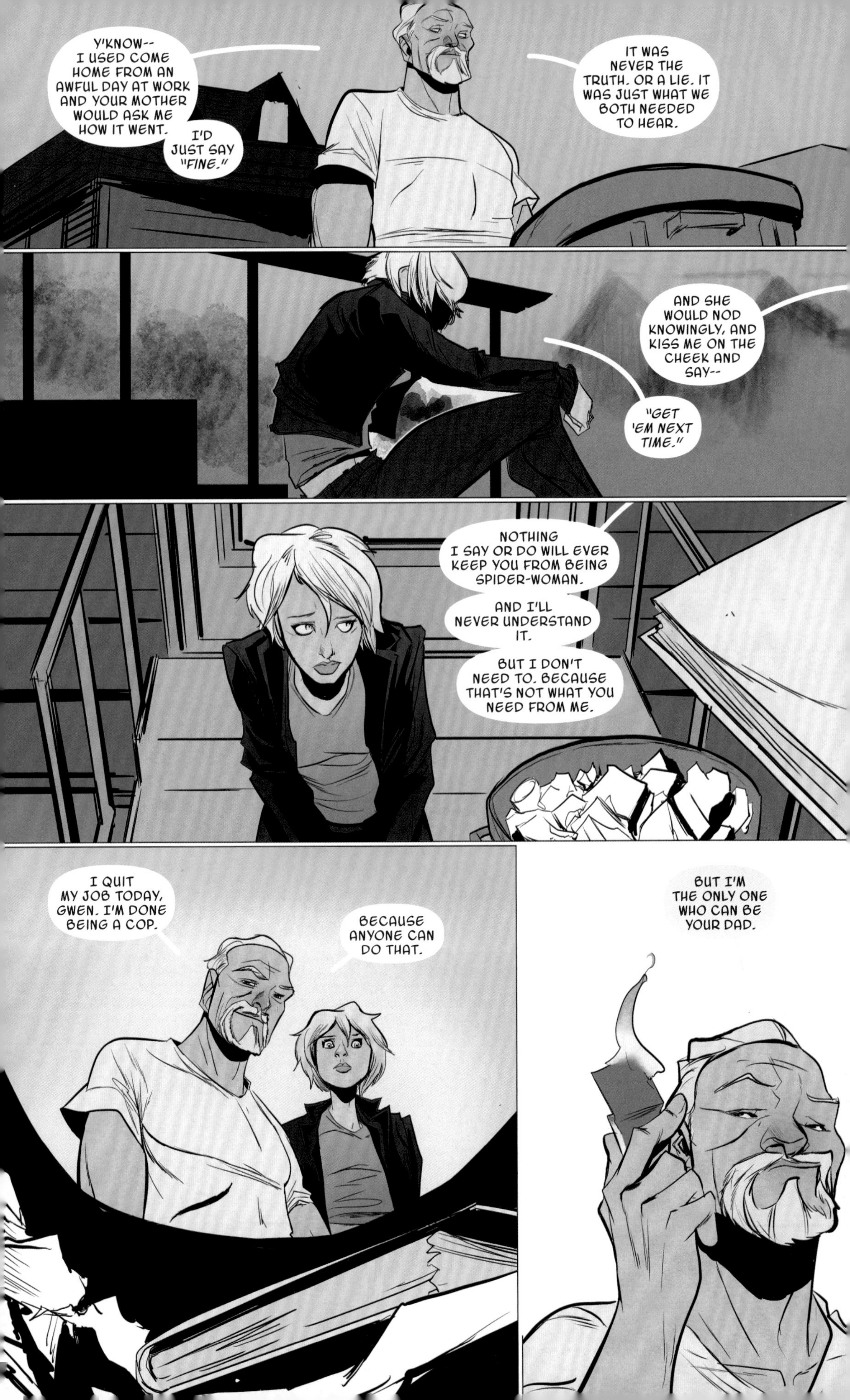
Y'KNOW-- I USED COME HOME FROM AN AWFUL DAY AT WORK AND YOUR MOTHER WOULD ASK ME HOW IT WENT.
I'D JUST SAY "FINE."
IT WAS NEVER THE TRUTH. OR A LIE. IT WAS JUST WHAT WE BOTH NEEDED TO HEAR.
AND SHE WOULD NOD KNOWINGLY, AND KISS ME ON THE CHEEK AND SAY--
"GET 'EM NEXT TIME."
NOTHING I SAY OR DO WILL EVER KEEP YOU FROM BEING SPIDER-WOMAN.
AND I'LL NEVER UNDERSTAND IT.
BUT I DON'T NEED TO. BECAUSE THAT'S NOT WHAT YOU NEED FROM ME.
I QUIT MY JOB TODAY, GWEN. I'M DONE BEING A COP.
BECAUSE ANYONE CAN DO THAT.
BUT I'M THE ONLY ONE WHO CAN BE YOUR DAD.

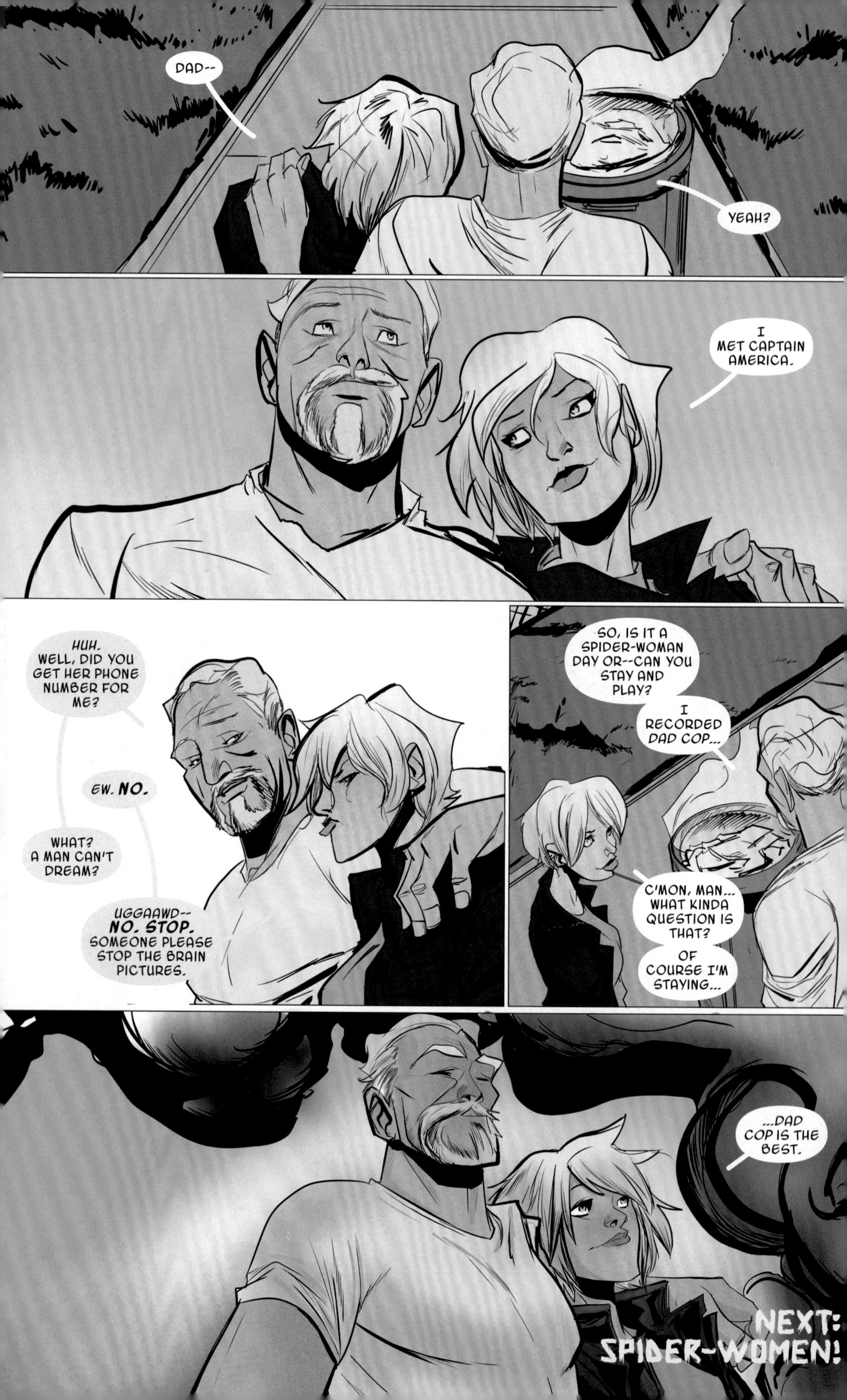
DAD--
YEAH?
I MET CAPTAIN AMERICA.
HUH. WELL, DID YOU GET HER PHONE NUMBER FOR ME?
EW. NO.
WHAT? A MAN CAN'T DREAM?
UGGAAWD-- NO. STOP. SOMEONE PLEASE STOP THE BRAIN PICTURES.
SO, IS IT A SPIDER-WOMAN DAY OR--CAN YOU STAY AND PLAY?
I RECORDED DAD COP...
C'MON, MAN... WHAT KINDA QUESTION IS THAT?
OF COURSE I'M STAYING...
...DAD COP IS THE BEST.
NEXT: SPIDER-WOMEN!

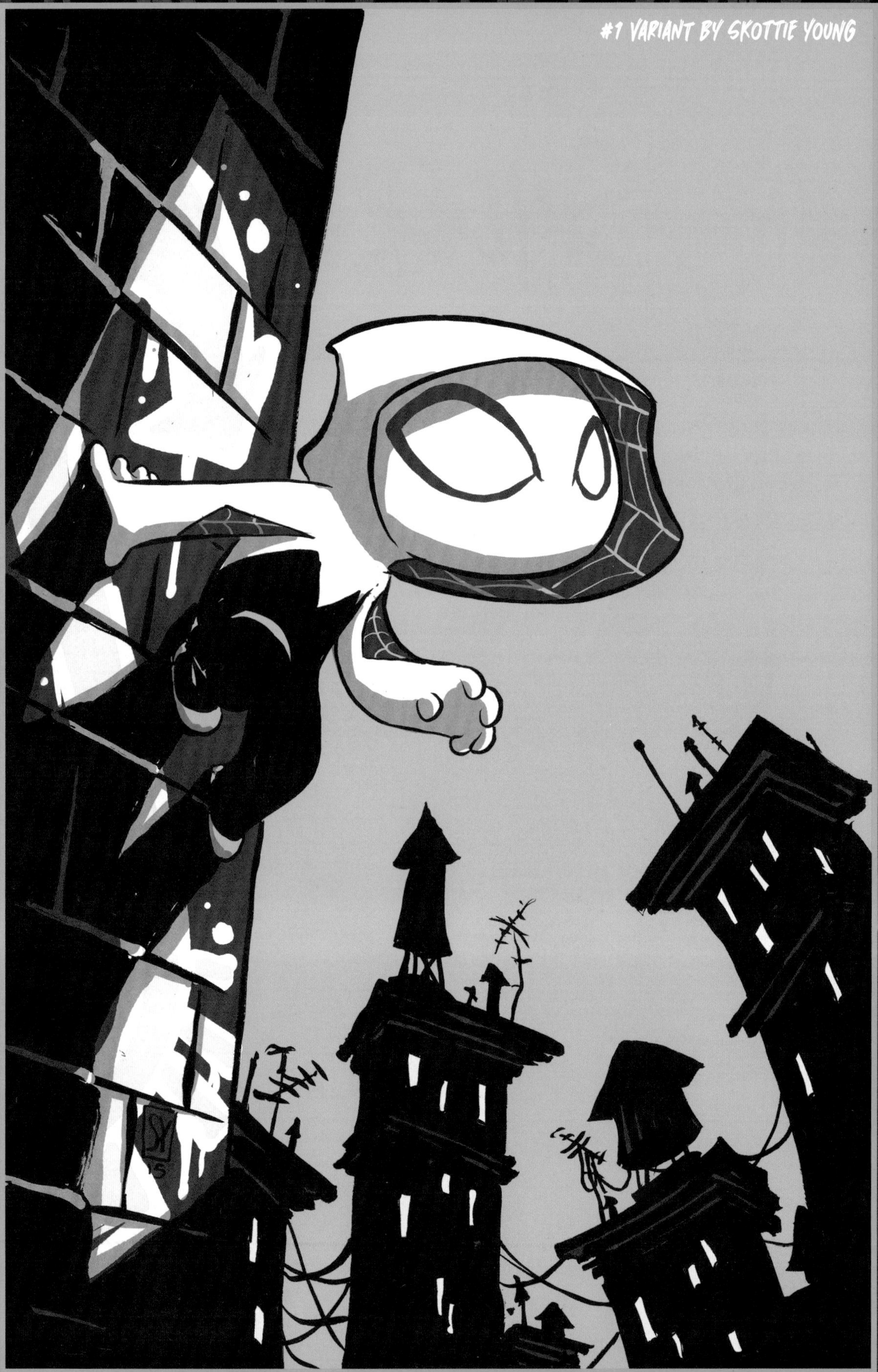
#1 VARIANT BY SKOTTIE YOUNG

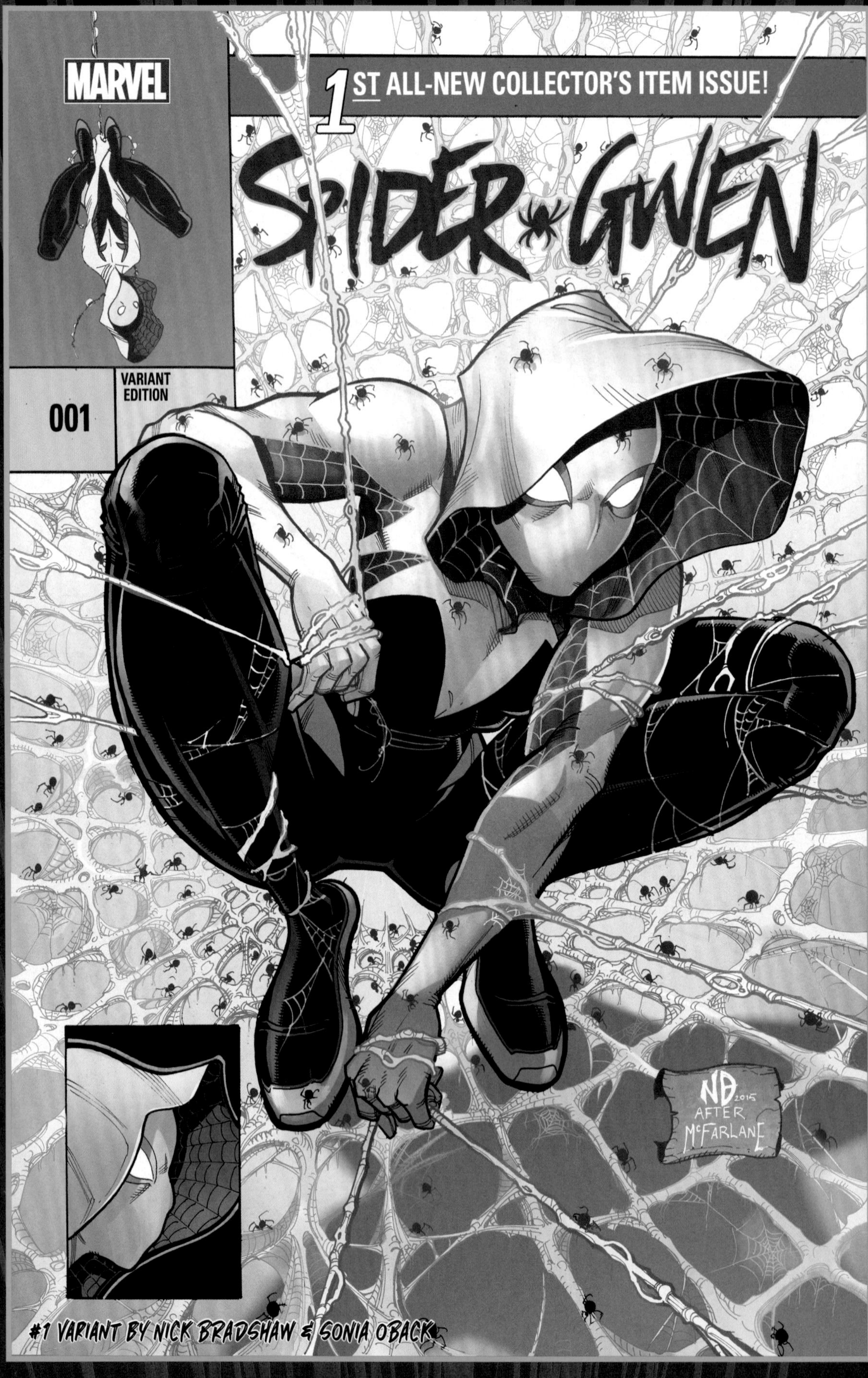
MARVEL
1 ST ALL-NEW COLLECTOR'S ITEM ISSUE!
SPIDER-GWEN
VARIANT EDITION
001
NB 2015
AFTER McFARLANE
#1 VARIANT BY NICK BRADSHAW & SONIA OBACK

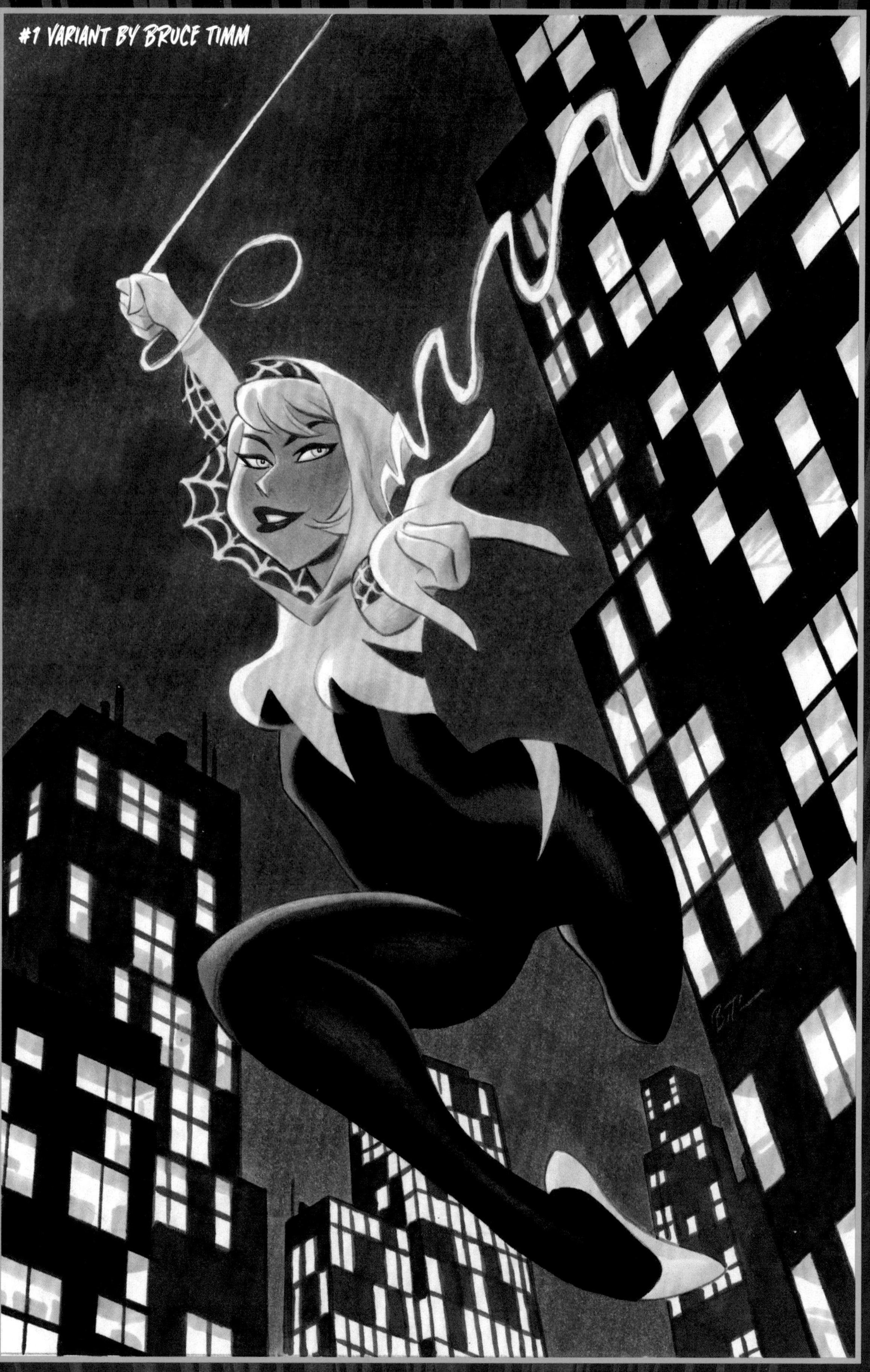

#1 VARIANT BY BRUCE TIMM

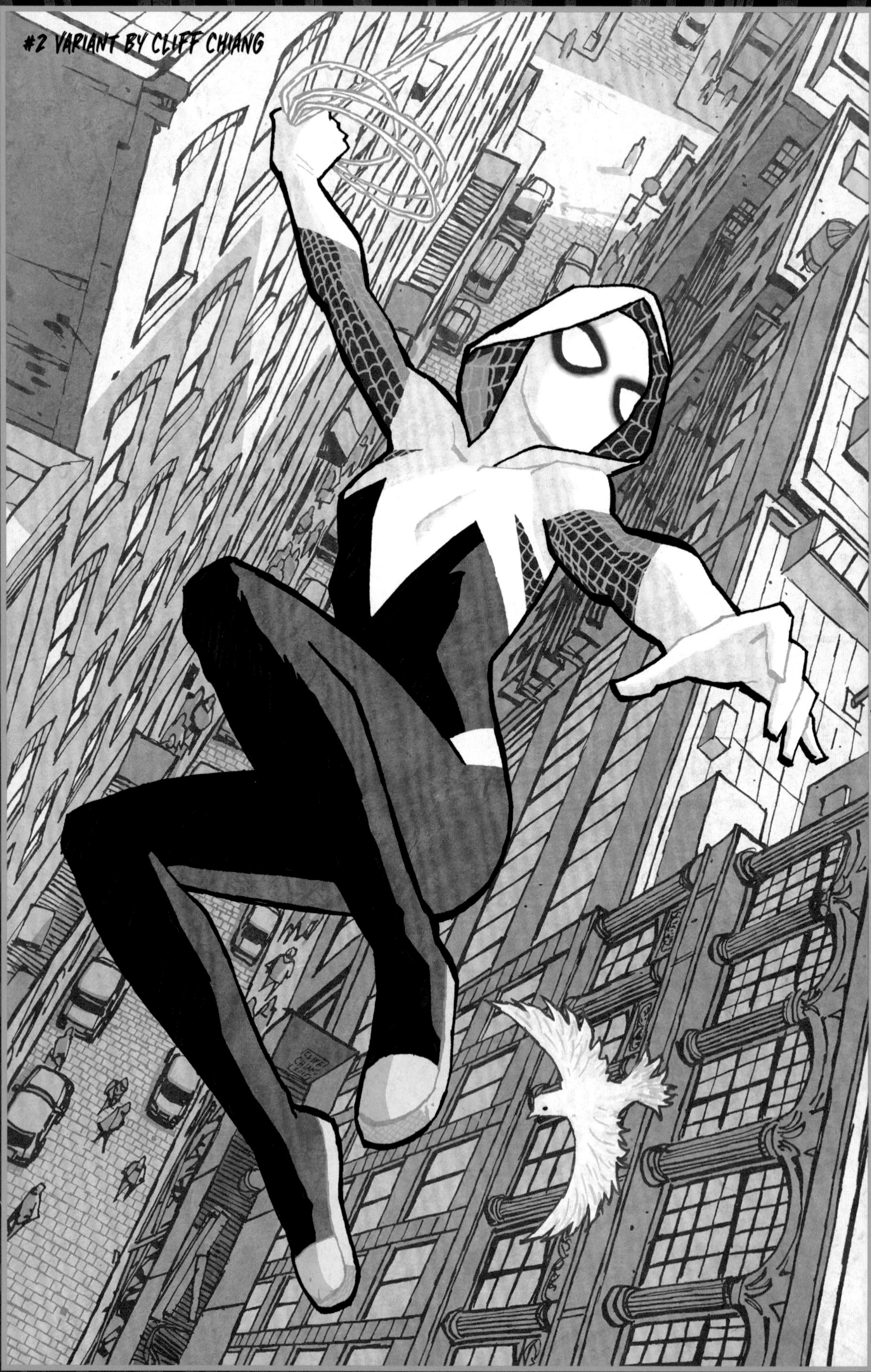

#2 VARIANT BY CLIFF CHIANG

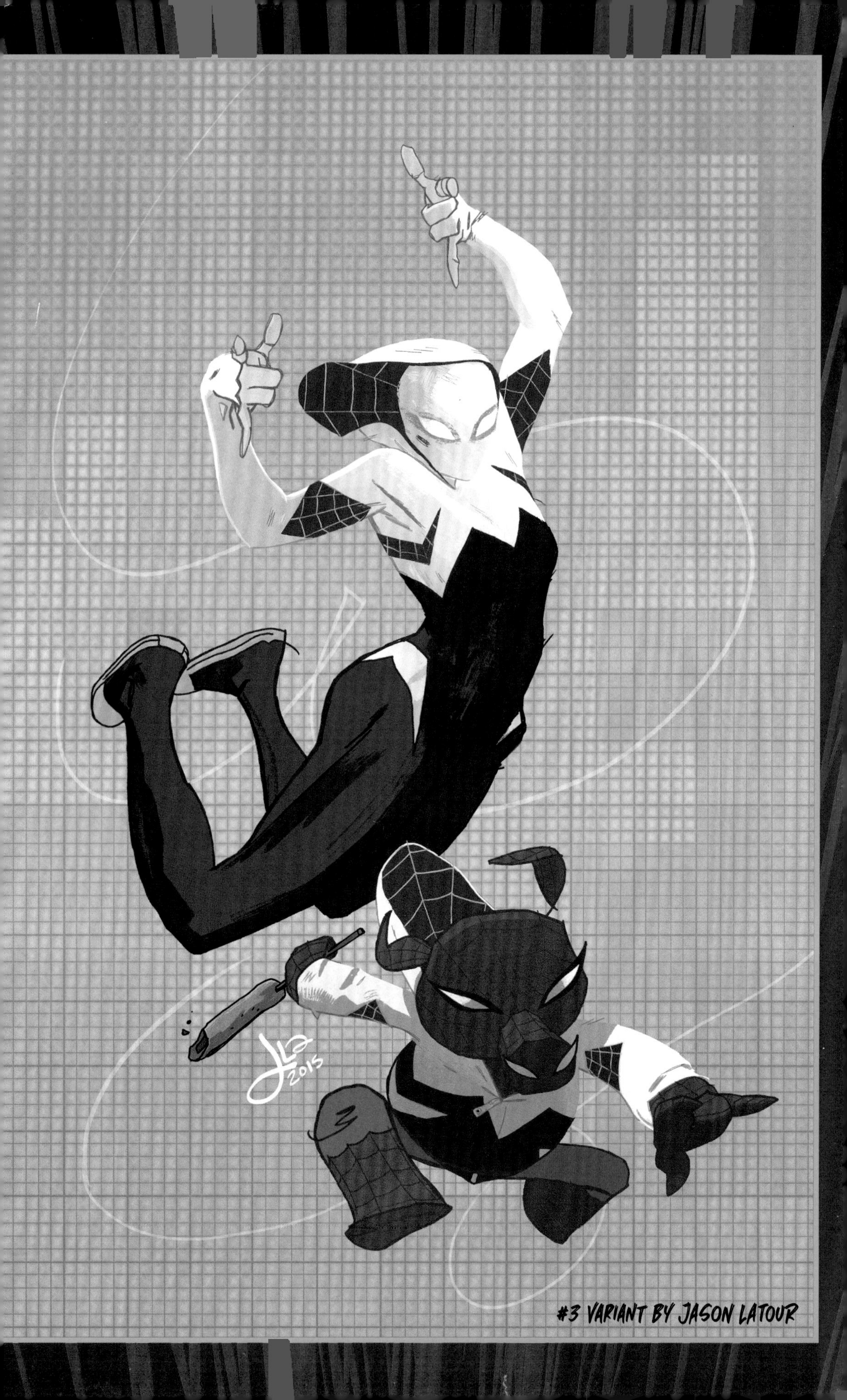

#3 VARIANT BY JASON LATOUR

#1 HIP-HOP VARIANT
BY HUMBERTO RAMOS & EDGAR DEGADO

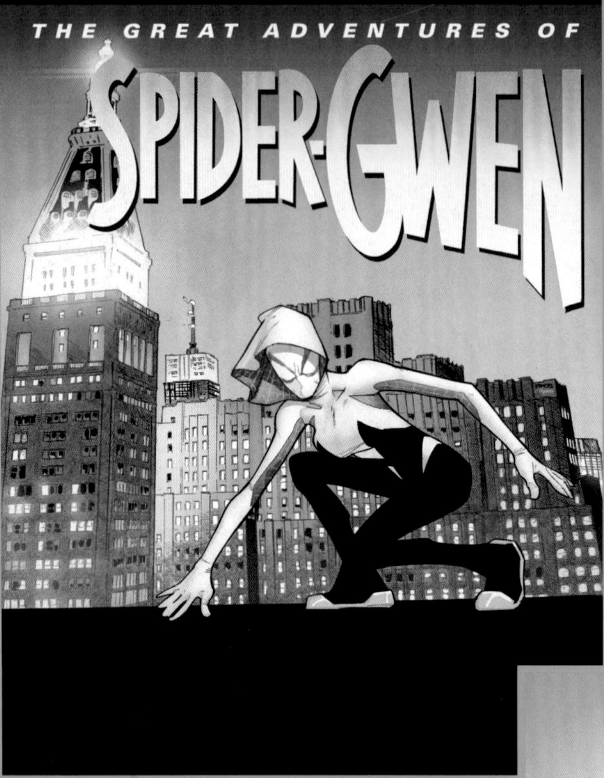
THE GREAT ADVENTURES OF
SPIDER-GWEN

#4 DEADPOOL VARIANT
BY TODD NAUCK & RACHELLE ROSENBERG

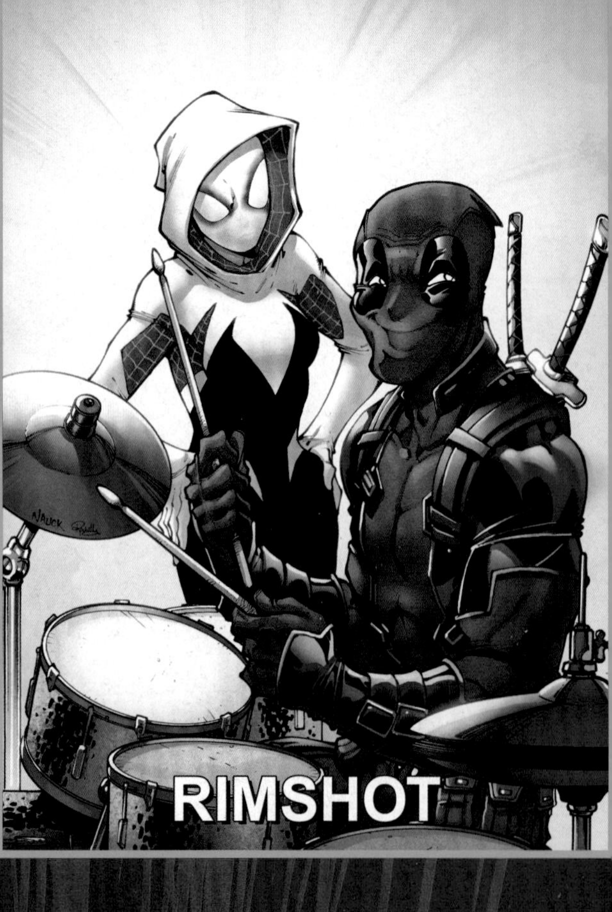
RIMSHOT

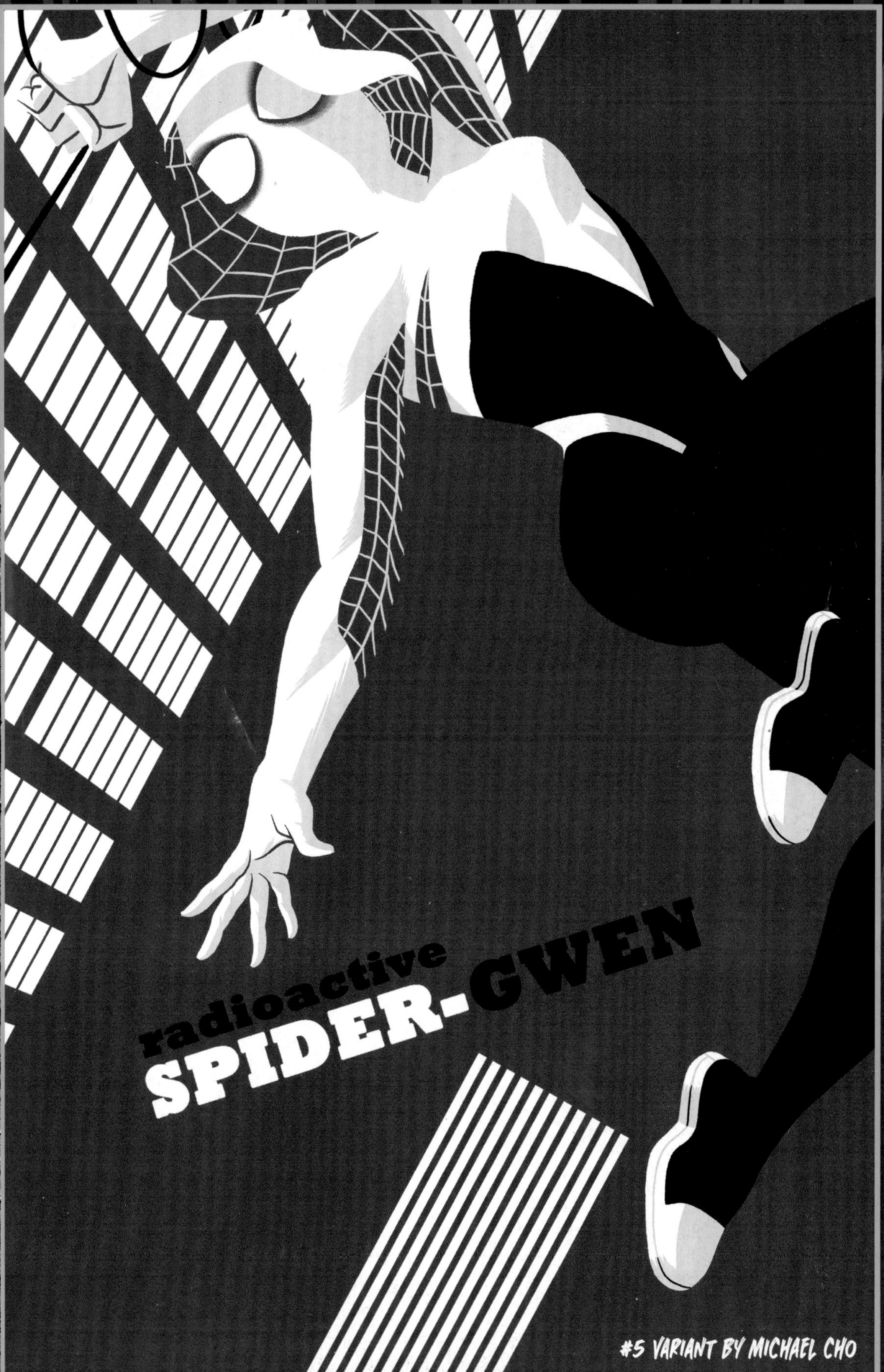
radioactive
SPIDER-GWEN
#5 VARIANT BY MICHAEL CHO

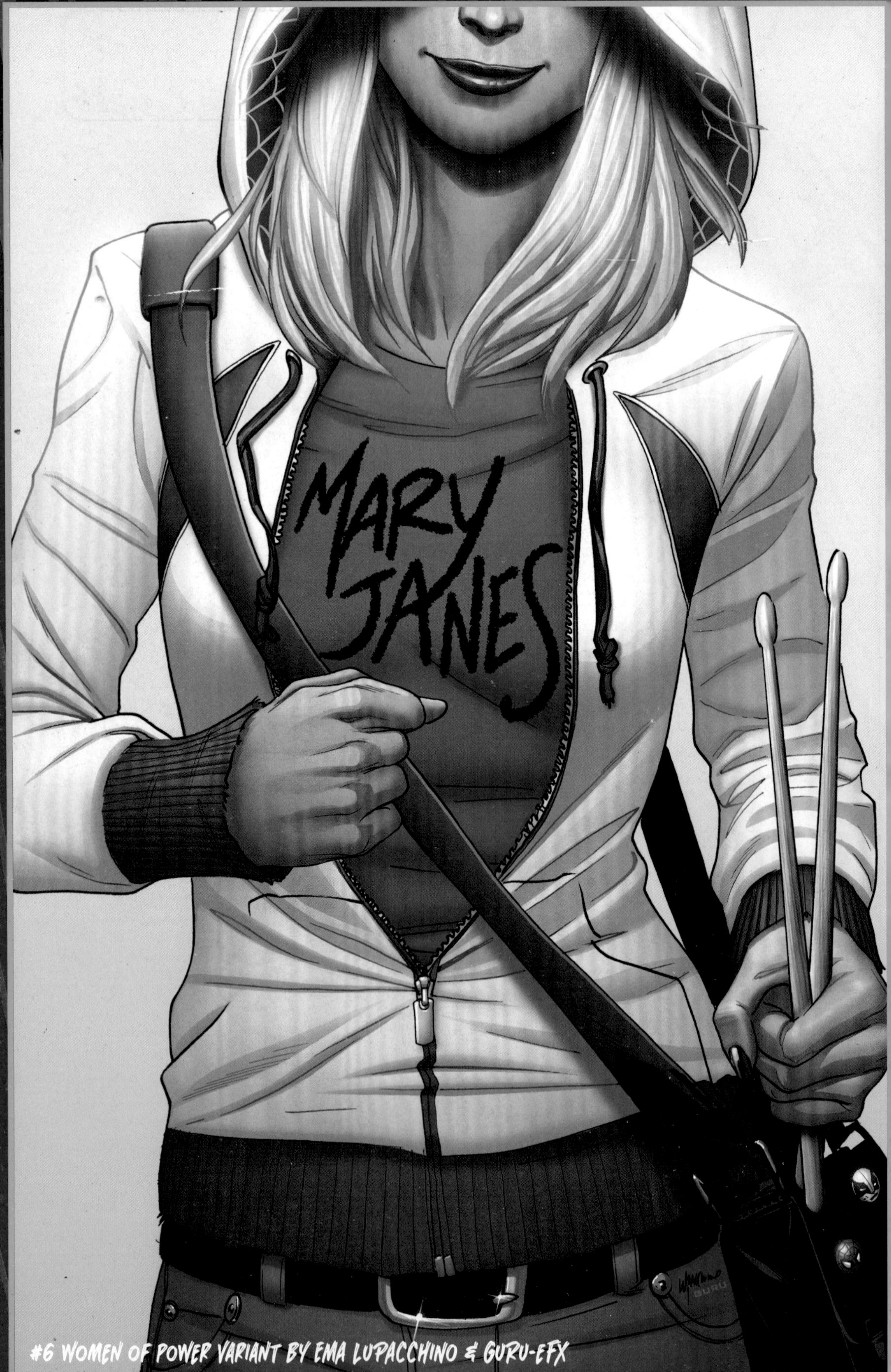
MARY JANES

#6 WOMEN OF POWER VARIANT BY EMA LUPACCHINO & GURU-EFX